This Book Given To The Givler Family June 24, 2004
From The Hearitge Building Group Inc.

# HISTORIC HOUSES *of* PHILADELPHIA

Andalusia. An eagle's-eye view of Andalusia and its park shows its relationship to the Delaware River and Philadelphia in the distance. See page 154.

# HISTORIC HOUSES
## *of* PHILADELPHIA

## A TOUR OF THE REGION'S MUSEUM HOMES

### ROGER W. MOSS

### *photographs by* TOM CRANE

A BARRA FOUNDATION BOOK

UNIVERSITY OF PENNSYLVANIA PRESS

PHILADELPHIA

*10 9 8 7 6 5 4 3 2*

*Published by*
*University of Pennsylvania Press*
*Philadelphia, Pennsylvania 19104-4011*

*Library of Congress Cataloging in Publication Data*
*Moss, Roger W., 1940–*
*Historic houses of Philadelphia : a tour of the region's museum*
*homes / Roger W. Moss ; photographs by Tom Crane.*
*p.     cm.*
*"A Barra Foundation book."*
*Includes bibliographical references and index.*
*ISBN 0-8122-3438-3 (cloth: alk. paper).—ISBN 0-8122-1647-4 (pbk. : alk. paper)*
*1. Dwellings—Pennsylvania—Philadelphia Region.    2. Historical museums—Pennsylvania—*
*Philadelphia Region.    3. Architecture, Domestic—Pennsylvania—Philadelphia Region.*
*4. Philadelphia Region (Pa.)—Buildings, structures, etc.    I. Crane, Tom.    II. Title.*
*F158.7.M67 1998*
*974.8'11—dc21*                                                                 *98-10934*
                                                                                    *CIP*

*Designed by Adrianne Onderdonk Dudden*

❧   Powel House. The front door opens onto the passage with its elaborate mahogany stair, which contains the original woodwork: wainscoting to the height of the chair-rail, pediments over the doors, a denticulated cornice, and fluted pilasters supporting an arch at the point just before the passage widens to accommodate the stair. The painted floor cloth and the blue and white color scheme reflect recent studies of the historical finishes. The portrait to the right is of Anne Shippen Willing (1710–90), Mrs. Powel's mother; the portrait to the left is of Samuel Powel. See page 34.

For Roger W. Moss, Sr.

(1910–1994)

# CONTENTS

❦   Mount Pleasant. The relationship of Mount Pleasant to the Schuylkill River below can now be appreciated only from the air. In the eighteenth century the west front of the house and its terraced gardens had an unobstructed view. See page 94.

No one knows for certain how many historic site museums are open to the public in the greater Philadelphia area; the number certainly runs into the hundreds if all types are included. The diversity of these is great, ranging from the obvious landmarks—Independence Hall, Carpenters' Hall, Christ Church, and the Second Bank of the United States, for example—to less well-publicized sites such as the Athenaeum, Fort Mifflin, and Burholme. But if we remove from the list the political, religious, literary, scientific, archaeological, and military sites, the largest and most popular group remains—historic houses open to the public. Local preservationists estimate the number of these at 177. All are *structures originally erected as private residences* that have subsequently been converted to museums for a wide variety of reasons. They may be associated with persons or events that have made significant contributions to our national, regional, or local history; be outstanding examples of a type, period, or method of construction; or represent the work of a master architect or builder.[1] Finally, there are those former residences that are not in themselves particularly distinguished but are used to display collections of fine and decorative arts.

There were several criteria for selecting the historic house museums that appear in this book. Once it was decided to allow 500 to 1000 words and an average of three photographs for each site, the available space made it necessary to restrict the number of houses to approximately fifty. In selecting fifty sites from a list of 177, the most important determinations were these:

1   The structure had to have been originally constructed as a residence in Philadelphia or its contiguous counties and be close enough that a visitor might see it during an easy trip from Center City.
2   The site must now be operated and interpreted for public education and enjoyment on a regular schedule without prior appointment. (Nonetheless, it is a good idea to call in advance to confirm opening days and hours, which, because they change, are not given in the descriptions.)
3   Finally, I favored houses where there are attempts to interpret a particular period in history with collections of fine and decorative arts that visitors may find interesting in themselves.

To encourage visits to multiple sites, the book is divided geographically with maps of each region. Unfortunately I could only consider a few of the nearby New Jersey historic house museums, and it was reluctantly decided not to cross the line into New Castle County, Delaware, although Rockwood near Wilmington, the Read House in New Castle, and the Corbit-Sharp House in Odessa—to name but three—should be on everyone's life list of houses to visit in the region. It is therefore inevitable that supporters of some historic site museums from the tri-state area that are not included in this book will be disappointed at the omissions.

Philadelphia historic-site administrators have often remarked that this type of museum has never had a book of its own, a single source to which students and visitors alike could turn for information on accessible houses, especially those furnished with

❧   Andalusia. The Doric columns of the Andalusia piazza overlook the Delaware River. The wooden floor is painted to simulate blocks of marble. See page 154.

appropriate decorative arts. Previous historians of Philadelphia architecture and the authors of popular guidebooks to sites open to the public often have had other agendas. Architectural historians are inclined to focus on the seminal buildings of stylistic epochs—whether or not they are furnished and open to the public, or even still exist. Authors of regional guidebooks are compelled to cover the widest range of sites, especially those landmark destinations that consume most of the available space and illustrations in their books—a small house museum cannot hope to compete for space with Independence Hall.

Even though I teach courses on historic site administration at the University of Pennsylvania, I had not seriously thought of undertaking such a book. That is, until one afternoon when there appeared at my Athenaeum office two ladies with a mission. Mrs. Harry C. Bishop and Mrs. James A. O'Neill had put their heads together and decided that Philadelphia needed a book devoted to house museums. They wanted to know if I would be the author. While flattered to be asked, I wasn't encouraging. It would be an expensive and time-consuming book to write. All the houses would need to be researched—few had historic structure reports—and it would require at least 150 new photographs. Even with text and photographs in hand, the final design and production of a color-plate book would put the retail cost beyond the reach of too many potential readers.

Following that initial meeting I gave the project little thought; it just was not practical. I'd just finished *The American Country House* and had not considered beginning another book so soon. But I had underestimated the determination of Deborah Bishop and Susan O'Neill. Many months later I was contacted by Robert L. McNeil, Jr., President of The Barra Foundation, Inc. Would I undertake to write a book on the historic houses of Philadelphia if a photographer, research assistant, designer, and publisher agreeable to me could be found?

Who could resist such temptation? You hold my answer in your hands.

I mention the above because it gives me the opportunity to thank Mesdames Bishop and O'Neill for broaching the idea and then taking it to the Barra Foundation. I also want to thank master photographer Tom Crane, with whom it has been my privilege to work closely as we photographed fifty houses—sometimes under less than ideal conditions. Tom specializes in architectural subjects; he is also a technical perfectionist. On numerous occasions I have stepped back from the camera, nodding approval at the composition, only to have him continue to fuss for another hour until the camera angle and lighting met his exacting standards. Readers who are familiar with other photographs of the interiors illustrated here will wonder at his skill in capturing such difficult spaces.

For several months at the beginning of the project I had the essential assistance of Sarah Allaback, who first came to my attention as a Charles E. Peterson Fellow at The Athenaeum of Philadelphia following the completion of her doctoral dissertation at MIT. We would review her progress each morning, and she would spend the day contacting the curators and site managers, compiling the basic information on the houses that appears in the head notes for each entry, and assembling the bibliography for each site. If the quality of her work for this project is any indication, Sarah Allaback has a promising career ahead of her. I also want to thank the several hundred volunteers, directors, curators, and maintenance people at the houses to be included in the book; with rare exception they cheerfully opened houses at odd hours, removed objects to improve the photographs, and tolerated our intrusion of their domain. They are the unsung heroes of this project.

Once photographs and text were assembled, both passed into the capable hands of the editorial staff of the University of Pennsylvania Press and to Adrianne Onderdonk Dudden, one of the finest graphic designers working in America today. I had long wanted to do a book with my Penn colleagues at the Press and to have it designed by Adrianne Dudden, whose work I have admired for many years. *Historic Houses of Philadelphia* has made both those desires a reality. I also want to acknowledge Christopher Brest, cartographer, who brought order to my doodling on regional highway maps.

Which brings me to Robert L. McNeil, Jr., President, The Barra Foundation, Inc. Clearly, he made this book possible—orchestrating idea, author, photographer, publisher, and designer. He assembled the team, provided the necessary funding, and encouraged us along the way. All who worked on this volume are grateful to have been a part of the project and to have benefited from his support and wise counsel.

*Roger W. Moss*

# HISTORIC
# PRESERVATION
# *in* PHILADELPHIA

Figure 1. 1823 watercolor of the Pennsylvania State House (Independence Hall) by W. L. Breton after a drawing of 1778 by Charles Willson Peale. The Athenaeum of Philadelphia.

❧  Cliveden. The handsome tabernacle frame and other parlor woodwork was supplied by the Philadelphia carvers Nicholas Bernard and Martin Jugiez in 1765; it is relatively simple in comparison with Middle Georgian, urban *rocaille* carving that survives from the Powel House. The fireplace opening is framed with King of Prussia marble. See page 116.

I t is only a slight stretch to claim an eighteenth-century precursor for the preservation of Philadelphia historic houses. Philadelphians began preservation as early as 1749, when the Swedish naturalist Peter Kalm remarked on "a wretched old wooden building . . . preserved on purpose as a memorial to the poor condition of the place before the town was built." He continued, "its antiquity gives it a kind of superiority over all the other buildings in town, though . . . the house is ready to fall down, and in a few years it will be as difficult to find the place where it stood as it was unlikely at the time of its erection that one of the greatest towns in America should in a short time stand close to it."[1]

Whether or not we count Kalm's "wretched old wooden building," the Philadelphia region has long led the nation in the preservation of historic structures, due mainly to the momentous events that occurred here during the American Revolution and the unusual number of surviving buildings of architectural merit from the hands of our early builders and architects. In modern times, the creation of Independence National Historical Park, the passage of city preservation ordinances, and the founding of the Historic Preservation Program at the University of Pennsylvania have propelled Philadelphia to the forefront in training architects, archaeologists, historians, and planners who have gone on to professional positions across the United States.

EARLY EFFORTS AT PRESERVATION   Successful preservation began in Philadelphia with the group of structures that constitute America's most significant historic site (Figure 1). In 1813 the Commonwealth of Pennsylvania—having moved its capital westward—proposed selling the old Pennsylvania State House, the building now known as Independence Hall. Several public-spirited Philadelphians protested the certain demolition of the hall and its related structures—which occupied an entire city block of rapidly appreciating real estate—calling it the birthplace of "the only free Republic the world has seen." This outcry provided only a temporary reprieve. Three years later the state divided the square into building lots to be sold at auction to fund construction of a new capitol in Harrisburg. Objections again rang out, and the City of Philadelphia—which needed more office space anyway—responded by purchasing the property for $70,000. Temporarily, Independence Hall was safe. But Philadelphia's city fathers had unwittingly taken their first tentative steps out onto the slippery slope of historic-site proprietorship.[2]

The City of Philadelphia officially took possession of Independence Hall on June 28, 1818. A few months later an editor of the magazine *The Port Folio* commented on the rapid erosion of colonial and revolutionary-era architecture from "the appropriation of ground to the purposes of business, or for the accommodation of opulence and ease." The immediate cause of this alarm was the demolition of the long-time home of Quaker educator and humanitarian Anthony Benezet (1713–1784) (Figure 2), which had stood on the north side of Chestnut Street between Third and Fourth Streets opposite Carpenters' Hall and near William Strickland's new Bank of the United States. According to *The Port Folio* (which published the engraving by Strickland reproduced in the figure), the justification for preserving the house was not just for its association with Benezet, but rather because it was "one of the oldest, *if not the first brick house* erected in Philadelphia," and the "last specimen in this city" of "the style of architecture adopted by our goodly and adventurous predecessors." Neither claim happens to have been true, but this early appeal to antiquity as justification for preservation would become increasingly popular in the years to come.[3]

There probably wasn't a serious effort to save the Benezet House in 1818, and what effort there was failed. Yet the article in *The Port Folio* suggests a growing awareness of historic sites as the United States approached the fiftieth anniversary of the Revolution and the Declaration of Independence. Daily obituaries reminded Philadelphians that the participants in those stirring events were passing from the scene; now other symbols would be needed to take their place.[4] Thus Independence Hall gradually acquired the veneration as America's most hallowed patriotic shrine that would protect it from demolition—if not from over-zealous restorers. In anticipation of Lafa-

Below left: Figure 2. Anthony Benezet House as drawn by William Strickland for *The Port Folio* (October 1818). The Athenaeum of Philadelphia.

Below right: Figure 3. 1786 engraving of Carpenters' Hall (1770–73), drawn by the master builder of Mount Pleasant, Thomas Nevell (perhaps from the original drawing by Robert Smith, architect of Carpenters' Hall), engraved by John Norman (c. 1748–1817). The Athenaeum of Philadelphia.

yette's triumphal return in 1824 and the fiftieth anniversary of the Declaration of Independence, the city repainted the old State House and redecorated the major ground floor rooms. Advocates for Independence Hall learned an axiom of historic preservation: it is easier to save an historic structure than to restore it authentically.

The first conscious effort to restore Independence Hall began with William Strickland's recreation of the long-lost tower in 1828, followed by John Haviland's 1831 "reinstating" of the "original architectural embellishments" that had been removed from "the Hall of the Declaration of Independence."[5] Strickland's tower—itself now restored—remains one of the most recognizable symbols of the United States. A later effort to return the building to its eighteenth-century appearance prompted the removal of Haviland's paneling, which eventually found new life as a bank lobby in the High Victorian Lits Building on Market Street, a juxtaposition that future generations of visitors may find amusing if not a little puzzling.

Elsewhere in the United States preservationists had also been busy. In 1850 the Hasbrouck House in Newburgh, New York—one of the many buildings occupied by George Washington as he attempted to keep one jump ahead of George III's army—became the property of the State of New York and was opened to the public, thereby establishing what is probably America's first house museum. In Virginia a similar—and ultimately successful—effort to acquire and preserve Washington's Mount Vernon had been launched, and in 1856 the Tennessee legislature authorized the purchase of Andrew Jackson's Hermitage near Nashville.[6] The same year Andrew Jackson's plantation passed into public hands, The Carpenters' Company of the City and County of Philadelphia set about renovating Carpenters' Hall on Chestnut Street near Independence Hall (Figure 3). The Company had been founded as a craft guild in the 1720s. In the 1770s it had been in the process of erecting a meeting hall for its members, which was not yet finished at the time of the First Continental Congress. The carpenters, who favored separation from Great Britain, invited the delegates to meet there—thus giving the modest cruciform structure a permanent association with those defining days of nation forming.[7]

Rented in the post-revolutionary period to a variety of income-producing tenants, the Hall reached its nadir when it was used as an auction house "for the sale of real estate and stocks, fancy goods, horses, vehicles, and harness." The historian Benson J. Lossing discovered it in that guise in 1848. "What a desecration!" he cried: "Covering the facade of the very Temple of Freedom, with placards of groveling mammon!" Perhaps Lossing's expression of "indignant shame" encouraged the Company to declare in 1856 its intention to renovate the building and "preserve, as much as possible, every feature in said Hall as it now exists indicative of its original finish."

Soon after the renovated Hall was opened to the public, the City of Philadelphia approached the Company to determine whether it "would be willing to convey to the City your proud Monument of Revolutionary memory" to be administered jointly with Independence Hall for public edification. In response the Company established a precedent for a similar request from the United States a century later: "We in common with our fellow citizens venerate [the Hall] not only for its associations with the stirring events of the Revolution," but because it represents "a sacred trust committed to us by our predecessors, which nothing shall ever induce us to part with." To this day Carpenters' Hall is Company property, kept open "for the inspection of all who may wish to visit it" without charge and without public funding—one of the earliest American examples of non-governmental preservation and restoration.[8]

Nationally the mid-nineteenth-century movement to preserve structures associated with people and events of the American Revolution gained momentum, spurred on by the success of the Mount Vernon Ladies Association so forcefully supported by Philadelphian Sarah Hale, "editress" of *Godey's Lady's Book*.[9] In stark contrast to these early successes, however, two notorious preservation failures of the 1860s must be mentioned. In Boston and Philadelphia civic leaders attempted to save important historic houses associated with famous colonial and revolutionary period occupants; both houses also happened to be exceptional examples of their architectural type. Unfortunately, the houses occupied rapidly appreciating commercial real estate and the former residents did not have the widespread emotional appeal of George Washington. The John Hancock House in Boston came down in 1863, and the Slate Roof House in Philadelphia, once the residence of William Penn, succumbed to house wreckers in 1867 to make way for an office building to house the Philadelphia Commercial Exchange.

The Slate Roof House on Second Street north of Walnut Street had been erected in the late seventeenth century by Samuel Carpenter, who received the land from William Penn in 1684 (Figure 4). During Penn's second visit to Philadelphia (1699–1701) he used the house as a town residence when not living at his country seat Pennsbury on the Delaware River. (The recreated Pennsbury is now operated by the Commonwealth of Pennsylvania as a house museum.) Following Penn's return to England, the Slate Roof House enjoyed several notable tenants, including James Logan, who would soon build Stenton (now a house museum) and William Trent, founder of Trenton (whose house there is now a museum). The Slate Roof House remained a rental property for 165 years until sold to Charles and Anna Knecht in April 1864 for $20,000.[10]

The Knechts declared their intention to clear the site for development. This alarmed Philadelphia antiquarians, who had long realized the historical and architectural importance of the house. Twenty years earlier, the Historical Society of Pennsylvania, armed with a $10,000 bequest for the purpose, had unsuccessfully attempted to acquire the house to provide for its "perpetual preservation." But the owner at that time refused to sell, and Philadelphia lost its opportunity to acquire what probably would have become the first house museum in the United States.

The Civil War (1861–65) heightened the patriotic appeal of sites and relics associated with early America, and for Philadelphians William Penn remained a potent figure. Just as the acquisition and preservation of the Slate Roof House was again becoming a public issue, the Great Central Fair benefiting the U.S. Sanitary Commission was held in Logan Square (June 1864) to raise funds for "the comfort and relief of

Figure 4. W. L. Breton watercolor, "The Slate House of *PENN* in Second Street previous to its being altered, so called from the Roof and Pavement in front being of Slate." The Athenaeum of Philadelphia.

our suffering soldiers." A group of prominent Philadelphians headed by Eli K. Price furnished a room for the Fair "as nearly as possible after the style of the days of William Penn," with objects lent by the Historical Society and coaxed out of the parlors and attics of old Philadelphia families.[11]

Given the temper of the times it looked as though the Slate Roof House might finally fall into the Historical Society's protective hands. The motivation for acquisition had to be preservation, since the location, size, and condition of the building militated against its being used as a headquarters to replace the Society's rented rooms at the Athenaeum on Washington Square. Unfortunately, opposition began to develop within the Society on the grounds that supporting a house museum would be an inappropriate use of Society funds.

The Historical Society's representatives nonetheless approached the Knechts with an offer of $30,000, and the owners—anticipating a quick $10,000 profit—magnanimously agreed to a stay of execution while a special committee of Society members worked "to take into consideration some means of preserving the Old Slate or Penn House" by special subscription among wealthy Philadelphians. This appeal fell on deaf ears, however, and opponents within the Society forced withdrawal of the offer.[12] Sale and demolition of the building followed, but not before J. M. Read, Jr. spent ten days making measured drawings, one of the earliest attempts systematically to record an endangered structure. Read also gives us a definition of Philadelphia's "reverence for the past," which he calls "preservationism, that spirit of humanity which instinctively defends governments, individuals, and old houses when threatened with destruction." So close to what he would have called "the Great Rebellion," Read probably had a broader issue in mind. "It is folly to think that because we are citizens of a republic, it becomes our duty to demolish the monuments of the past, and to rush eagerly into the uncertainties of the future. . . . The absence of reverence and affection for interesting historical landmarks, is an evidence of defect in the moral organization of a people, not less than of an individual.[13]

FAIRMOUNT PARK   In the meantime, the City of Philadelphia launched a process of acquisition that added substantially to the number of publicly owned buildings dating from the colonial and early Federal eras. Motivated by a desire to supply its citizens with a reliable supply of fresh water, the city constructed America's first urban water system, which went into operation in January 1801. Pumps raised water from the Schuylkill River to holding tanks in the engine house on Center Square—now the site of Philadelphia City Hall. This system quickly proved to be inadequate; a new pumping station was required on the banks of the Schuylkill to raise water to reservoirs excavated on the crest of Fairmount—now the site of the Philadelphia Museum of Art. At first just a few acres around the waterworks were landscaped as a public park, but to keep the water being drawn into the system "free from impurities of City drainage" additional parcels of land were acquired, including two estates on the east bank of the

Schuylkill—Lemon Hill (acquired in 1844) and Sedgeley (acquired in 1857)—on which stood houses by those names. Sedgeley, a villa with Gothic-style details designed by Benjamin Henry Latrobe in 1799, promptly disappeared; Lemon Hill, dating to 1799–1800, survives, and is today open as a house museum (Figure 5).[14]

By the 1860s it had become abundantly obvious that the water being pumped from the river and into reservoirs for distribution in city mains could no longer be relied upon. The city fathers reasoned, "We must possess the ground which surrounds our water supply" to avoid impurities that might be drained from its surface and be drawn into the reservoirs. Consequently, the General Assembly of Pennsylvania empowered Philadelphia to "appropriate and set apart forever the area of land and water comprised with the limits as open public ground and Park for the preservation of Schuylkill water and the health and enjoyment of the people forever."[15]

Thus armed with the broadsword of eminent domain, Philadelphia began to carve out Fairmount Park by purchase and gift. These actions would ultimately bring into city hands several thousand acres of land embracing many country houses and villas, including Mount Pleasant, Laurel Hill, Strawberry Mansion, and Woodford on the east side of the river and Sweetbrier, Belmont, and Solitude on the west bank—all of which would in the future be open to the public as house museums. But it must be

Figure 5. Sedgeley, a picturesque *cottage orné* in the Gothic style built in 1799 from designs by Benjamin Henry Latrobe (1764–1820) for William Cramond's use as a Schuylkill River villa. It was demolished shortly after being acquired by the City of Philadelphia in 1857. This view comes from William Birch, *The Country Seats of the United States of North America* (1808), the first illustrated book on American country houses and villas. The Athenaeum of Philadelphia.

Figure 6. When Philadelphia became the capital of the United States, George Washington occupied 190 High Street (Market Street below Sixth Street), a Middle Georgian four-bay house belonging to Robert Morris. Despite its illustrious history the house came down in 1832; during the Centennial in 1876 its former site was pointed out to tourists. This early nineteenth-century watercolor is by W. L. Breton. The Athenaeum of Philadelphia.

kept in mind that many of these buildings were hardly more than a century old in 1868 and were probably viewed by the Fairmount Park Commission as more nuisance than asset. Consequently, the Commission began systematically to demolish the dozens of barns, stables, and other outbuildings that had supported these residential properties and to rent the surviving houses to Park employees. Some of the older houses—Eaglesfield for example—proved too impractical or expensive to maintain and were also demolished.[16]

Some families who maintained villas along the Schuylkill greeted seizure of their country houses with dismay. For example, the family of Joseph W. Johnson, Jr., owners of Chamounix, a Federal villa erected in 1800–1803, offered to give most of their property to the Park "in consideration of which [we] are allowed to retain the house with six acres of ground surrounding it. . . . A covenant would be made that the place shall be forever occupied only as a private residence and the grounds &c. kept in such good order that it will be no detriment to the beauty of the Park." Johnson then compared his suggestion to Regent's Park, London:

> Unlike other parks [Regent's Park] contains within its boundaries several handsome private residences surrounded by picturesque pleasure grounds. . . In Regent's Park containing I believe about 200 acres there are no less than five private enclosures, in a Park of more than ten times the above area one small reserve neatly enclosed would be scarcely noticeable.[17]

In retrospect it is unfortunate that such an agreement, perhaps using long-term leases, could not have been offered to accommodate the owners of Chamounix and the other Schuylkill riverside villas. The subsequent history of the park would certainly have been different, and many significant eighteenth- and early nineteenth-century houses might have been preserved at private expense.

By the 1870s Civil War wounds had begun to heal. Americans north and south, averting their eyes from the recent past, could at least reflect with shared pride on the events and ideals of the first American revolution.[18] To most historians the Centennial of the Declaration of Independence in 1876 marks the end of Reconstruction, a beginning of recovery from the war, and the emergence of the re-United States as an industrial power. Ten million Americans visited the International Centennial Exposition in Philadelphia, and the press declared it the most successful birthday celebration ever staged. This first American world's fair—like the "sanitary fairs" of the war years—included a log cabin "New England Farmer's Home" intended to illustrate frontier life at the time of the American Revolution. It was complete with candlesticks, spinning and flax wheels, cradles, and guides "dressed in the quaint costumes of their great-grandmothers, and who conduct visitors through the house and explain to them the story and uses of its contents." So popular did this period recreation of "life in olden times" prove to be that it continued as part of the Permanent Exhibition in the Main Building of the International Exhibition after the Centennial closed.[19]

Across the nation historical societies proliferated; often they acquired and (more or less) restored early structures as appropriate housing for their rapidly growing collections. In Philadelphia at the time of the Centennial, no house museums had yet been opened to the public. The villas of Fairmount Park remained leased to concessionaires or rented as private residences, and none were thought worthy of comment in city-wide guidebooks. The Slate Roof House and the former residence of President Washington during Philadelphia's brief tenure as capital of the United States had both been demolished, although *Magee's Centennial Guide of Philadelphia* included their sites on a walking tour (Figure 6). Only the modest Letitia House, described as "the first permanent residence of Penn, and the first brick dwelling erected in the city," made the list of notable structures.

Like the Slate Roof House, the Letitia House had long been of interest to local antiquarians, particularly John Fanning Watson (1779–1860), who deserves the title of Philadelphia's first preservationist. "My desire," he wrote, "is to get the ownership of the 'Letitia House,' for the sake of its perpetual preservation, as a memorable City Relic, worthy to be held in perpetual remembrance." Watson wrongly believed that the house, then occupied as the Rising Sun Inn, had been built for William Penn on land set aside for Penn's daughter, Letitia. "I shall be deeply mortified if the apathy of Philadelphia should allow the house to be pulled down," he wrote. "Such a house with its pictures, & various old furniture, sanded floors, pewter plates & porringers etc, would be a perfect museum, where many of our citizens could be brought to deposit of their old relics."[20]

Watson burned with antiquarian fervor. Writing to Joshua Francis Fisher, Secretary of the Historical Society of Pennsylvania, he breathlessly envisioned how—if the Society acquired the house—it could

> revive the picture of olden time. We could get contributions enough of all old high-backed chairs, settles & Settees, pictures & looking glasses. . . . We might get up quite a museum of old fashioned dresses, house ornaments &c. *The Beau ideal* of the whole, as I can see it, is quite fascinating.

As we have already seen, the Slate Roof House, which Watson correctly identified with William Penn's second visit to Philadelphia, came down in 1867—seven years after the death of its champion. But the house he dubbed the Letitia House survived long enough to be dismantled brick by brick and moved to Fairmount Park in 1883 in commemoration of the Philadelphia bicentennial (Figure 7).[21]

GERMANTOWN    Beginning with the acquisition and opening of Stenton as a house museum in the early years of the twentieth century, Germantown enjoyed greater success and provided more effective leadership for the preservation movement than any other section of Philadelphia. The Germantown Historical Society, founded in 1900, has for a century battled against urban decay and rapacious developers who have taken a ferocious toll on the hundreds of surviving buildings from the seven-

Figure 7. The Letitia Street House, c. 1713, wrongly thought in the nineteenth century to date from the time of William Penn, became the focus of preservation efforts in the 1880s, leading to its being moved to Fairmount Park. The Athenaeum of Philadelphia.

teenth to the nineteenth centuries that once stood along the Germantown Avenue corridor stretching north from the heart of Philadelphia. The Society has directly intervened to preserve more buildings of architectural and historical importance than any other privately-funded group in the region. To its banner have rallied owners of historic homes willing to donate their properties to save them from an uncertain future as well as thousands of individuals willing to give of their time and treasure to support the museum and research library operated by the Society—or to acquire other properties by purchase. Some allied groups within the Society have spun off to form their own non-profit organizations centered on a single property—the Women's Club of Germantown which acquired the Johnson House in 1917, for example—while the Society acquired properties of its own, such as the Concord School House, the Vernon Mansion, and the Conyngham-Hacker House.[22]

In a moment we will meet Miss Frances A. Wister, a woman of indomitable will and impeccable social standing, who founded the Philadelphia Society for the Preservation of Landmarks in 1931. Miss Wister had deep family roots in Germantown and, in 1941, undaunted by financial hard times and the glowering clouds of war, took the lead in acquiring Grumblethorpe (erected in 1744 by immigrant John Wister) as a second property for Landmarks and then helped establish the independent Upsala Foundation in 1944 to acquire and maintain that Federal house, which sits opposite Cliveden. It was also during this period (1939) that Maria Dickinson Logan bequeathed to the city her family's house, Loudoun, together with its contents and an endowment.

The establishment of Germantown house museums continued in the postwar years, beginning with the Deshler-Morris House in 1948. This handsome five-bay Georgian house had been British General William Howe's headquarters during the Battle of Germantown in 1777. During the yellow fever epidemic of 1793, the Deshler-Morris House served as President George Washington's summer residence; it came to the National Park Service in 1948 as a gift from Elliston P. Morris. In 1972 the National Trust for Historic Preservation acquired Cliveden and its six-acre park from the Chew family, thereby opening to the public one of the premier Middle Georgian houses in the United States, and the next year Mrs. Robert B. Haines gave Wyck, one of Philadelphia's most appealing and popular historic houses, to a charitable trust that opened it to the public.

Most of the Germantown house museums date from the eighteenth and early nineteenth centuries, reflecting the typical prejudice of early preservationists against later nineteenth-century buildings. Here again Germantown provided farsighted leadership during the 1960s—even before the Victorian Society in America opened its national headquarters in Philadelphia. Throughout the period when Deshler-Morris, Cliveden, and Wyck were joining the ranks of Germantown house museums, a committee of Germantown Historical Society stalwarts struggled to save the Ebenezer Maxwell Mansion, a streetcar suburb villa that ultimately became Philadelphia's most important mid-nineteenth century house museum.

THE COLONIAL CHAIN   By the early twentieth century, Philadelphia's Fairmount Park villas had also begun to attract powerful and influential advocates, among them the architect and historian Fiske Kimball (1888–1955), who became director of the Philadelphia Museum of Art in 1925. Shortly after his appointment to the Museum—then located in Memorial Hall on the west side of the river—Kimball toured the nearby Park houses with Russell T. Vodges, who like his father had been Chief Engineer of the Park and, having been born in the Park, became virtually a birthright advocate for preserving the surviving historic houses. Kimball did not require much convincing; his training, research, and publications on American architecture—particularly on Jefferson's drawings—had prepared him to see the Schuylkill villas not only as objects of inspiration for their historic association with venerated men of our colonial and revolutionary past, but also as cultural and artistic documents worthy of an art museum's interest. Kimball realized that the villas lining the Schuylkill banks, regardless of losses such as Lansdowne and Sedgeley, constituted a unique survival. Writing in 1926, Kimball contrasted Philadelphia's situation with New York's, where that city "has ruthlessly swept away most of its early landmarks." Having lost the original houses, "the Metropolitan Museum has brought together, in its American wing, a series of single rooms from successive periods, with their appropriate furnishings, which admirably illustrate the history and beauty of American art in the days of the early Republic."[23]

But in Philadelphia such remedial measures proved unnecessary, although the Philadelphia Museum of Art would ultimately gather an important collection of disembodied period rooms used to display decorative arts. Philadelphia, Kimball continues,

has a series of whole houses, mostly in their original setting. Not to mention important houses in other parks, or those in the loving hands of patriotic organizations, it has a dozen in Fairmount park, conveniently located a few hundred yards apart, near its Museum. These by themselves are sufficient to illustrate the evolution of American art from the time of William Penn until the nineteenth century. In several cases these houses are the very finest of their respective periods and types.

Kimball and his wife moved into Mount Pleasant during the renovation and furnishing of Lemon Hill, which they had been offered as the director's residence. Standing in the elegant oval parlor of Lemon Hill, Kimball looked directly onto Fairmount, where the new Philadelphia Museum of Art would soon rise. To his back were the houses he would call Philadelphia's "Colonial Chain."

With the benefit of hindsight it is obvious that Philadelphia civic leaders—like some exotic species of orchid that blooms in fifty year-cycles—periodically awake to the decay of the city's heritage of historic architecture and, having whipped themselves into a frenzy of publicity and repair, then lose interest until the next anniversary. Kimball had the good fortune to arrive on the eve of just such a celebration—the Sesquicentennial. It would generally fail to recapture the excitement of the Centennial Exposition fifty years before. But one feature did prove a popular success: the ladies of the Emergency Aid of Pennsylvania sponsored reduced-scale replicas of famous eighteenth-century Philadelphia buildings—including without irony the long-demolished Slate Roof House—improbably jumbled together along a cobblestone High Street in the manner of a modern shopping mall. These provided a showcase of Philadelphia's historic architecture, each building furnished by interior decorators with replicas of colonial furniture so that the "public may use the knowledge gained by seeing these rooms in a widespread way for future choices" in their own homes.[24]

COLONIAL REVIVAL    The Sesquicentennial helped nurture the popularity of the Colonial Revival style of interior decoration, as would Colonial Williamsburg in later generations. The roots of this style can be traced to the nostalgic fascination with early American decorative arts that emerged in the post-Centennial decades, reaction to Victorian decorative excesses in the 1890s, and a growing clamor among reform-minded design critics for Craftsman simplicity. The American critic Clarence Cook declared, "A change is coming over the spirit of our time, which has its origin partly . . . in the memorial epoch through which we are passing, but which is also a proof that our taste is getting a root in a healthier and more native Soil."[25] Colonial designs, argued the magazine *House Beautiful* in 1899, are among the most restful, graceful, and artistic yet produced, and it is "probable that the liking for them is genuine and lasting."[26] The style that emerged in the early decades of the twentieth century often featured oriental carpets on highly polished soft wood floors, elaborate silk draperies and curtains at windows, bedroom furniture forms in parlors arranged in comfortable "conversation groups," dining rooms with tables permanently ready for use, white or pastel color schemes, and bedstead frames with vestigial textile hangings.

These characteristic traits of the Colonial Revival style would later come under attack from curators trained to academic standards in the post-World War II years. But in the early twentieth century the Colonial Revival decorative approach dramatically influenced how house museums were presented to the public. From those interiors we learn how the first half of the twentieth century idealized the past, not how early Americans actually lived in and used their homes. To this day the debate rages between the comfortable, "pretty" past and the academically correct reinterpretation, which rarely conforms to the *House Beautiful* ideal and is likely to give as much weight to the kitchen, privy, and servants' rooms as to the formal parlors and bed chambers.

In the Philadelphia area visitors can see both unaltered Colonial Revival interiors and academically recreated ones. At Cliveden, Hope Lodge, and Andalusia, for example, the Colonial Revival approach is being preserved and intrepreted. At the National Park Service sites—Bishop White House, Deshler-Morris House, and Dolly Todd House, for example—the recreated interiors reflect the latest scholarship of trained curators, while at Stenton and Bartram the interpretation is constantly being tightened and refined. Some houses—most notably Powel House—are in transition; others seem blissfully unaware of the difference.

In the 1920s, the spirit of historic architecture floated above Philadelphia. Fiske Kimball later recounted the 1926 contribution from Charles H. Ludington to restore Mount Pleasant, the moving of Cedar Grove to Fairmount Park by Miss Lydia T. Morris, and the contribution of Mr. and Mrs. Henry Paul Busch to repair the Letitia House. "Woodford (which had been Park Guard headquarters)," he wrote, "was entrusted to the Estate of Naomi Wood, which restored it architecturally and placed there its collection of antiques. Sweetbriar was restored at the expense of the Junior League. . . . Strawberry mansion was restored by the Women's Committee of 1926. . . . Belmont was restored, to be used as a restaurant . . . [and] the Philadelphia Museum of Art took on the administration of three of the houses: Mount Pleasant, Cedar Grove, and the Letitia Street House (Penn Cottage)."[27] Most of these arrangements have continued in place since the 1920s, and, parenthetically, the houses were more or less restored again during the celebrations surrounding the Bicentennial of 1976.

MISS WISTER AND LANDMARKS     Fiske Kimball's references to museum period rooms would return to haunt Philadelphia a few years later when local preservationists banded together to save the Samuel Powel House. The acquisition of period rooms from historic buildings by leading American museums, including Philadelphia's own, encouraged wealthy private collectors to seek woodwork of the same period as a setting for their fine and decorative arts, which resulted, according to Kimball, in the purchase and demolition of houses "in no way threatened, which might otherwise have been preserved indefinitely."[28] Together the agents of museums and collectors prowled the cities and by-ways of the original colonies in search of appropriate rooms. Unfortunately for the Powel House, both the Philadelphia Museum and the Metropolitan Museum fell on its unappreciated bones and picked them clean.

Powel House—now one of Philadelphia's leading house museums—will be discussed later. Suffice it to say here that in the late 1920s it was one of the finest surviving Middle Georgian town houses in the city. Once home of the last colonial mayor of Philadelphia, the house had fallen on evil days as its Delaware waterfront neighborhood declined. By 1904 it had been purchased by Wolf Klebansky, who described himself as an "Importer, Exporter and Jobber of All Kinds of Russian and Siberian Horse Hair and Bristles," which he supplied to brush manufacturers and hair cloth weavers. Since Georgian woodwork, regardless of quality, cannot be said to contribute to the sale of hog bristles, Klebansky sold one of the principal rooms to the Metropolitan Museum for its American Wing and the other to the Pennsylvania Museum, then the name of the Philadelphia Museum of Art.

Thus stripped, save for its magnificent mahogany staircase and lesser woodwork, Klebansky proposed to sell the house for an "open air garage." This news alarmed the members of the Philadelphia Chapter of the American Institute of Architects, then in the process of conducting a survey of the area now known as Society Hill.[29] At this point entered Miss Frances A. Wister, President of the Civic Club of Philadelphia, who in 1931 mobilized her friends and founded the Philadelphia Society for the Preservation of Landmarks—a long overdue private organization patterned on the Society for the Preservation of New England Antiquities. Through the subsequent decades, Landmarks restored the Powel House and gradually spread its wings to protect three other houses that figure in this book: the nearby Physick House, Grumblethorpe in Germantown, and Anthony Wayne's country house, Waynesborough. For all its ups and downs during the late twentieth century, Landmarks survives as one of the most influential privately-funded preservation organizations in Philadelphia.[30]

GOVERNMENT'S ROLE IN PRESERVATION   From their earliest efforts to save Independence Hall, Philadelphia-area residents tended to favor agencies of government to assume responsibility for historic sites. Consequently, most of the houses included in this book are owned by the United States, Pennsylvania, New Jersey, Philadelphia, or other municipal, county, or township governments. As with the Letitia House, local preservationists assumed that, even when private funds could be raised to acquire, furnish, maintain, and operate a house museum for public education and enjoyment, the appropriate *legal owner* should be an agency of government. In this fashion the City of Philadelphia acquired the house and garden of the botanist and plant explorer John Bartram and his son in 1891, with restoration and operating funds coming from the privately funded John Bartram Association. As with the Bartram house, the City of Philadelphia acquired at Stenton, country estate of James Logan (1674–1751), one of the most important surviving houses of its period to come down to modern times. Today the house is open to the public and furnished with a significant collection of decorative arts reflecting six generations of Logan family taste. Late in the nineteenth century the Logan family transferred title to the family graveyard to the city. In 1908 the city acquired the house itself, for which the National Society of Colonial Dames assumed stewardship. As we shall see, similar co-stewardship agreements with volunteer, not-for-profit groups became the pattern throughout the region as greater numbers of houses were furnished and opened to the public in the twentieth century.

With the return of prosperity after the depression of the 1930s and the war years of the early 1940s, Philadelphia experienced an urban rebirth in which historic preservation provided considerable energy. Central to this effort was the establishment of Independence National Historical Park, which brought to Philadelphia a cadre of trained architects and historians who had learned the latest preservation skills at Colonial Williamsburg, Jamestown, and Yorktown during the depression years. Throughout the 1950s and 1960s these specialists attracted recently graduated historians, architects, and archaeologists to the National Park Service, where they worked with acknowledged leaders in the field such as Charles E. Peterson, founder of the Historic American Building Survey.

As the Park emerged, Philadelphia created a City Planning Commission charged with the rehabilitation of Society Hill, the historic center of the early city, which extended roughly from the Delaware River west to Washington Square and from Walnut Street to South Street. The Park stabilized the northern boundary of this neighborhood, and massive urban renewal removed non-conforming commercial and industrial structures. Gradually the saloons, brothels, flop houses, produce markets, and decaying commercial establishments disappeared as private homes emerged from a century of neglect and well-placed high-rise residential buildings brought needed population density back to the neighborhood. Nearly half a century after the first planning for Independence National Historical Park, the resulting neighborhood has matured into one of the most attractive areas of the city.

Of equal importance to the entire city, the progressive administrations of mayors Joseph S. Clark and Richardson Dilworth made possible the authorization of the Philadelphia Historical Commission in 1955, which began operation the following year. This Commission is nationally celebrated as the first such preservation agency with jurisdiction over an entire major American city. (Previously established agencies in Boston, Charleston, and New Orleans operated within limited areas in their municipalities.) The original ordinance stated boldly that the Advisory Commission on Historic Buildings would "regulate the demolition of historic buildings" by "providing a list and classification of historic buildings; providing for the postponement of the demolition of certain historic buildings; and providing penalties for violations thereof." This ordinance and its successor help protect Philadelphia's historic buildings, and the Commission's research and education functions encourage greater awareness of Philadelphia's architectural heritage. It is this rich heritage that contributes to the urban environment and encourages visitors who increasingly come to Philadelphia to experience what so many other cities have lost.[31]

# CENTER CITY *and* *Nearby* NEW JERSEY

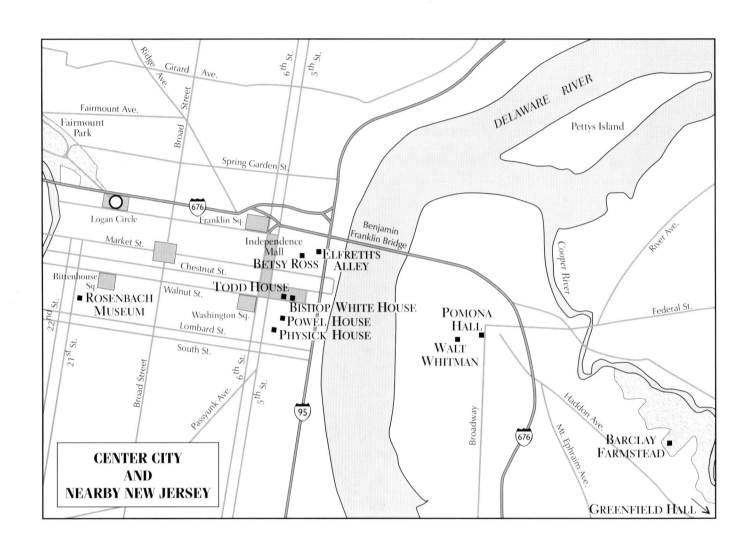

CENTER CITY
AND
NEARBY NEW JERSEY

Physick House. The front passage retains its original marble floor and the over-door fanlight imported from London by Henry Hill in 1787. The wallpaper shown in this photograph is a document reproduction from an original fragment found in the front passage of the artist Thomas Sully's house and now in the collection of The Athenaeum of Philadelphia. Such "ashlar" papers simulating blocks of stone were popular passage and stair wall treatments in the nineteenth century. This paper has been removed since the photograph was taken. Dr. Physick kept his dining table in this area so it could be carried into the front parlor and set up as needed. See page 44.

From its seventeenth-century beginnings, Philadelphia constituted a vast real estate development intended to improve the fortunes of the Penn family while offering refuge to Quakers and other religious sects attracted by the proprietor's liberal guarantee of freedom to worship. "Though I desire to extend religious freedom," Penn wrote in 1681, "yet I want some recompense for my trouble." Shortly after receiving his charter from Charles II, William Penn began selling prepackaged contracts. A purchaser of five thousand inland Pennsylvania acres, for example, would also receive a building lot in the new city and one hundred acres outside the city limits, presumably to erect a country seat.[1]

William Penn's Surveyor-General, Thomas Holme, laid out the city in 1682 on a rigid grid system, "so that the streets hereafter may be uniforme downe to the Water from the Country bounds." The resulting rectangle is two miles long and a mile wide, enclosing approximately 1,280 acres between the mighty Delaware River and the less useful but infinitely more picturesque Schuylkill River. The east-west streets were named for trees, resulting in the jingle,

High, Mulberry, Sassafras, Vine
Chestnut, Walnut, Spruce, and Pine

which unfortunately no longer works because of street name changes in the nineteenth century.

For ease of identification, the north-south streets are numbered. However, early settlers on the river banks counted back from *both* rivers, requiring each street to be additionally identified as "Schuylkill Second," or "Delaware Third," and so on. (Since the mid-nineteenth century the numbering has begun on the Delaware River side, moving westward to the city limits.) According to Frances Trollope (mother of the novelist Anthony Trollope), who visited America in the 1820s, the Philadelphia "mode of distinguishing the streets is commodious to strangers, from the facility it gives of finding out whereabouts you are; if you ask for the United States Bank, you are told it is in Chestnut, between Third and Fourth, and as the streets are all divided from each other by equal distances, of about three hundred feet, you are sure of not missing your mark."[2]

The original Philadelphia plan provided that the city should be bisected with a double width north-south street (modern Broad Street) to intersect a similarly wide east-west one (High Street, later renamed Market). At the juncture of these two wide streets, a ten-acre "center" square marked the heart of the future city. Four additional parks were strategically placed in the seventeenth-century plan, now named for George Washington, David Rittenhouse, Benjamin Franklin, and James Logan. Modern Philadelphians might wish that the original streets had been twelve feet wider, but the rational layout and these regularly spaced parks mean that in center city Philadelphia one never needs to fear getting lost or being required to walk more than a few "blocks" to reach an oasis of grass, trees, and fountains. Both features—as well as impossible rush hour traffic jams—help make modern Philadelphia a walker's city, one filled with uncounted historic buildings, most of which continue to provide homes for her citizens.

The city lots along the Delaware River rapidly filled with houses built by Europeans flooding into the new colony. Antiquarians of the nineteenth century enjoyed romanticizing how the early settlers clawed caves into the river bank for shelter. In fact, the settling of Philadelphia proves on closer examination to be a well-orchestrated invasion that arrived fully equipped with the craftsmen and materiel to build a miniature replica of London.[3] Within months of the first ships' arrival, the saw pits of carpenters and kilns of brick makers were industriously turning out the raw material of a new city.

Throughout the colonial period the building trades of Philadelphia would be her largest and most influential craft group, headed by the master builder/carpenters who would eventually provide the city with architects whose services would be in demand throughout America. The holds of Penn's ships also disgorged boxes of glass and lead for "cames" to fasten it into casement window frames produced by joiners capable from the first of providing credible stools, chairs, and tables. Gradually they—like the carpenters—would specialize as turners, cabinetmakers, and carvers to embellish the paneling and furnish the justly celebrated Middle Georgian furniture of late colonial Philadelphia.

In laying out the city, William Penn was haunted by memories of the great London fire of 1666. He hoped that his agents would encourage purchasers to build in the middle of their lots, so that Philadelphia would be "a greene Country Towne, which will never be burnt and allways be wholesome."[4] Clearly the Delaware River bank formed the center of commerce; everyone crowded onto the river-front lots, which rapidly were subdivided. Good quality bricks made from local clay made Philadelphia a red-brick city virtually from the first.[5] According to Robert Turner, a wealthy merchant who wrote to William Penn in 1685, Philadelphia "goeth on in Planting and Building to admiration" with six hundred houses erected in three years, many of them of brick. Some settlers who "built Wooden Houses, are sorry for it: Brick building is said to be as cheap . . . and now many brave Brick Houses are going up, with good Cellars."[6] Within a few years the distinctive brick row houses with connected common —or "party"—walls became typical. In one sense Penn succeeded. Philadelphia never suffered the devastating fires that forced other early American cities to be regularly rebuilt.

The modern visitor to Philadelphia unfortunately cannot be directed to a single surviving seventeenth-century house, although many house museums in Germantown and the outlying suburbs may incorporate earlier buildings. Most of those erected in the waning days of the seventeenth century were relatively small, and none have come down to us on their original foundations. (In fact, Old Swedes Church is probably the only seventeenth-century structure to survive in a form that the earliest Philadelphians would recognize.) The closest approximation available, and an excellent place to begin visiting Philadelphia house museums, is the narrow **Elfreth's Alley**, which may be—as its residents claim—"the oldest unchanged and continuously inhabited street in Phila-

Rosenbach Museum. Visitors gain entrance by passing through a pair of wrought-iron gates by the Polish-born Philadelphia master craftsman Samuel Yellin (1886–1940). Yellin created these in 1926 for the Rosenbachs' first Delancey Place house (number 2006); they were later moved to 2010. Against the wall of the front hall are a pair of Late Georgian English side tables, over which hang a pair of Middle Georgian English pier glasses. See page 46.

delphia." It certainly is the best surviving example of eighteenth- and early nineteenth-century urban dwellings erected for artisan cabinetmakers, silversmiths, carpenters, and pewterers. Similarly, the modest **Betsy Ross House** illustrates the scale of urban houses occupied by craftspeople in the colonial city.

Land in the area between the Delaware River and the Pennsylvania State House (Independence Hall) commanded a premium price throughout the eighteenth and early nineteenth centuries, with many houses being erected on speculation by entrepreneurial builders. Most people rented their homes which were typically modest affairs. A later and better quality example of this type is the **Todd House**, occupied by Dolly Payne Todd Madison and her first husband in the 1790s, which has been restored and opened as a house museum by the National Park Service.[7]

Too many visitors come to Philadelphia attracted by the shrines of Independence National Historical Park and leave again without realizing that they had been only steps from one of America's most appealing historic residential neighborhoods. Society Hill, named for the Free Society of Traders, a group of merchants granted title by William Penn to a strip of land between Spruce and Pine Streets, is now more informally defined as the area south of Chestnut and north of South Street extending west from the Delaware River to Sixth Street. This area contains three of Philadelphia's most important house museums—**Powel House**, **Physick House**, and the **Bishop White House**—associated respectively with Samuel Powel, colonial grandee and civic leader; Philip Syng Physick, physician and father of American surgery; and William White, prince of the American Episcopal Church. These houses are all within easy walking distance of Independence Hall and fairly reflect the apogee of Philadelphia's Middle Georgian and Federal town houses—all erected by owners of considerable wealth in the preeminent city in English-speaking North America.

Surrounding these three houses and providing their urban context are the several hundred privately restored homes of Society Hill, occupied as they have been for the past three hundred years by Philadelphians from all walks of life. A day spent visiting the historic area house museums should include strolls along Spruce, Delancey, and Pine Streets between Second and Sixth, perhaps with lunch or dinner on nearby South Street.

In the nineteenth century, wealthy Philadelphians began to drift westward, filling out Penn's original city plan and anchoring their neighborhoods with elegant Victorian churches, clubs, and cultural institutions. The focus of this development is Rittenhouse Square, which shares with restored Society Hill the cachet of being among the city's most desirable residential neighborhoods.[8] Unlike Society Hill, however, the Rittenhouse Square area did not decline in the twentieth century; instead it developed the kind of blended urbanism characteristic of the world's great cities. While the major streets continued to be lined with stately town houses of the merchant aristocracy (long ago divided into apartments) the interspersing small streets and mews became, in the early decades of the twentieth century, a congenial haven for artists and architects, small theater groups, art galleries, and the multitude of restaurants that rapidly spring up to serve such a clientele. This appealing mix continues to bubble with vitality; here the American flight to the suburbs ebbs. From census to census, Center City gains in population as Philadelphians rediscover the undeniable charm of urban life. While the cityscape may have suffered successive architectural intrusions of astounding beauty or unmitigated ugliness, a great city manages to retain its historicity, humane scale, and livability. If you would experience this in Philadelphia, walk west from the Delaware River to the Schuylkill River on Spruce Street, dropping down to Delancey Street at Sixteenth and continuing on toward the Schuylkill. On your way you will encounter the **Rosenbach Museum**. It is justification in itself for spending at least part of a day exploring the charms of the Rittenhouse Square neighborhood.

NEARBY NEW JERSEY    Visitors to Philadelphia often overlook the geographically nearby house museums of New Jersey because private transportation is needed to reach most of them. Directly across the Delaware River and not far from the New Jersey Aquarium in Camden is the modest clapboard home of the poet **Walt Whitman**, which he purchased in 1884 and occupied until his death in 1892. It is now a State of New Jersey historic site museum. There are often interpretive exhibitions in the adjoining property as well.

The area that constitutes Camden County had already been settled by English Quakers when the first Philadelphians came up Delaware Bay. Nonetheless, the new city quickly dominated the economic, religious, and cultural life of the entire region, and southern New Jersey has long turned to Philadelphia to market the produce of its fertile fields. This agricultural legacy is represented by two museums that can easily be reached from Philadelphia. The earliest of these, **Pomona Hall**, dates from 1726 with major additions in 1788; it is maintained by the Camden County Historical Society. The Society also operates a nearby museum and library that sponsors interesting local history exhibitions; be sure to ask for a program guide when planning a visit.

Not far away is the **Barclay Farmstead** in Cherry Hill. Erected in the early nineteenth century, this attractive brick farm house is the center of a thirty-two-acre remnant of a much larger farm dating to the seventeenth century. Periodically during the year the Township of Cherry Hill sponsors craft demonstrations and other programs designed to remind local residents and visitors of the rural heritage of southern New Jersey. Finally, there is **Greenfield Hall** in Haddonfield, itself one of the most appealing villages in the Philadelphia suburbs—which one suspects the residents hope will not be "discovered." The house itself dates to 1841 and is the home of the Historical Society of Haddonfield.

These four houses can be reached in the time it takes to drive across Philadelphia. All can be visited in the course of a morning with time for lunch in one of Haddonfield's small restaurants followed by a leisurely stroll down the King's Highway simply to enjoy the local architectural diversity and to consider which house museums to visit tomorrow.

# ELFRETH'S ALLEY

Front and Second Streets between Race and Arch Streets, Philadelphia, PA 19106

Architect/builder unknown, c. 1740–62

National Historic Landmark

Owned and operated by the Elfreth's Alley Association

Telephone for opening days and times, 215.574.0560

❧ The front parlor of number 126, Elfreth's Alley probably doubled as Sarah Melton's place of business as a mantuamaker. The room is furnished simply, as suggested by her estate inventory of 1794: a table, ladder-back and Windsor chairs, no window curtains, and a small Venetian rug on the unvarnished floor.

In the eighteenth century the "middling and lower sort" of society rarely owned their homes. Most artisans and tradesmen such as cabinetmakers, pewterers, hatters, tailors, and house carpenters rented houses that often doubled as workshops or retail stores. Of course the most successful of their brethren did own houses and invested their profits by purchasing or erecting houses to be rented to younger or less prosperous craftsmen and small shopkeepers. Elfreth's Alley is typical of this pattern of residence as it existed in early America.

Narrow of front—usually one room wide and two stories high with a dormered garret—these modest and once ubiquitous houses rarely survive in anything approaching their original context. Elfreth's Alley, often called the oldest residential street in the United States, comes closer than any other in Philadelphia to preserving the sense of colonial scale. It is also a perfect place to begin a tour of Center City house museums.

Elfreth's Alley derives its name from the prosperous blacksmith Jeremiah Elfreth, who acquired land on both sides of the narrow passage from two of his five wives, both of whom were related to John Gilbert, who originally created the alley. Elfreth built number 126 as an investment property between 1739 and 1762, selling it in the latter year to the spinsters Mary Smith and Sarah Melton, both identified as mantuamakers.

As such they ranked at the top of the colonial needleworkers' craft, specializing in fitting and sewing gowns, which required higher skills and more refined taste than that usually possessed by seamstresses. Not surprisingly, mantuamaking is a woman's craft —one that might provide a widow or spinster a degree of financial security in an age when a woman alone had limited opportunities she could pursue with decency.

The Elfreth's Alley Association owns The Mantua Makers' House and operates it as a museum; the furnishing plan is based on Sarah Melton's estate inventory of 1790. All the other houses in Elfreth's Alley are private residences whose owners, while tolerant neighbors, deserve to have their privacy respected.

Narrow Elfreth's Alley is lined with privately owned houses of the colonial and Federal periods. One property, number 126, is open as a house museum. Most of the late eighteenth-century residents pursued trades such as cabinetmaker, dressmaker, and pewterer. The Elfreth's Alley Association is one of the oldest preservation groups in the city, dating to 1934.

# BETSY ROSS HOUSE

239 Arch Street, Philadelphia, PA 19106

Architect/builder unknown, c. 1740;
restoration by R. Brognard Okie, 1937

Owned and operated by the City of
Philadelphia

Telephone for opening days and times,
215.627.5343

Whether or not Elizabeth Griscom Ross Ashburn Claypoole designed the American flag or even lived in this modest Philadelphia row house (rather than in a similar house nearby, as some historians maintain), she has long been a potent symbol of women's contributions during the darkest days of our nation's formation. That she turned her skills as a seamstress to making flags for the Pennsylvania State Navy Board during the Revolution is well documented, and her first two (of three) husbands died in the service of the new nation: the first in an accidental gunpowder explosion, the second in a British prison after his ship was captured at sea.

As a young woman Betsy Griscom, who had been raised a Quaker, eloped to marry the Anglican upholsterer John Ross, for which act the Society of Friends disowned her. The Rosses established an upholstery shop on Arch Street and, like most artisan families, lived on the premises. Two years later Ross died accidentally, leaving his widow to support herself by continuing the upholstery business. She counted among her clients Benjamin Franklin and the revolutionary Pennsylvania government. Throughout the war and British occupation of Philadelphia, Betsy remained on Arch Street while her second husband languished in prison. After his death she married John Claypoole; they left the house in 1786.

Like many of the houses on nearby Elfreth's Alley, the Betsy Ross House once stood in a row of nearly identical two-story-with-dormered-garret structures erected as rental properties. Presumably the front room on the ground floor, which is accessible directly from the street by the front door, would have been used as the upholstery shop. Also typical of Philadelphia row houses, the kitchen was in the basement. The back rooms of the ground floor and the second and garret level chambers would be occupied by the family as parlor and bedrooms. Some objects that belonged to Elizabeth Claypoole are on display; most of the furnishings are representative of objects she might have owned.

The Betsy Ross House is representative of what Philadelphia craftspeople and shop keepers of modest means—who rarely owned their homes—would have rented in the eighteenth and early nineteenth centuries. The architect R. Brognard Okie (1875–1945), who is best remembered for his recreation of William Penn's country house known as Pennsbury, restored the house in 1937.

# TODD HOUSE

343 Walnut Street, Philadelphia, PA
19106

Builder, Jonathan Dilworth, carpenter, c.
1775; restored by National Park Service,
1961–63

National Register of Historic Places

Operated by Independence National
Historical Park

Telephone for opening days and times,
215.597.8974

Speculative builder Jonathan Dilworth erected this "neat and well finished" brick house in 1775 and rented it to a succession of tenants. After his death, his widow sold the property to the young Quaker lawyer John Todd, Jr., who moved in with his bride Dolly Payne Todd (1768–1849); she would one day become the wife of James Madison and among the most celebrated American first ladies.

Dolly's first husband and infant son died during the yellow fever epidemic of 1793 (which tragically killed thousands of Philadelphians without respect for age, sex, or occupation), leaving her and her surviving son alone and virtually destitute. The following year she married the Virginia planter and U.S. Representative James Madison and began a highly successful forty-two-year marriage. The Madisons made Philadelphia their home until 1797, when they moved to his estate, Montpelier, in Virginia.

While built as a rental property, the Dilworth-Todd House is larger than the artisans' houses of Elfreth's Alley or the Betsy Ross House. Three stories with dormered garret covering a footprint roughly 16 feet by 35 feet, with an 11- by 9-foot kitchen wing, the house occupies a corner lot, giving it an additional front along Fourth Street as well as the usual short row house elevation on Walnut Street. This design allows for a main entrance with passageway from the long side, which divides the ground floor into two major rooms without reducing their width—as would happen in the more typical row house plan seen at the Powel House.

Extensively altered in the nineteenth century, the house has been carefully restored

by the National Park Service and refurnished to portray the home of a younger upper-middle-class professional family in the final years of the eighteenth century, when Philadelphia served as the social and political capital of the new United States. Here the Park Service architects and curators benefited from the survival of an estate inventory taken after John Todd's death. Use of this document has resulted in a particularly authentic and believable recreation of an historic house interior.

The inventory and surviving Todd family correspondence indicate that the family possessions were of above average quality—expensive and perhaps including inherited items such as a sideboard, tall-case clock, settee, and fully furnished bed—and that the first-floor front room had been used as Todd's law office. This pattern of room use follows the arrangement described by Peter Stephen DuPonceau: "Almost every house had two apartments below . . . most commonly having separate doors in an entry. The front room was devoted to business. If the master of the house was a lawyer, it was his office. . . . The back room was appropriated to the family; here they took their meals, and drank tea in the evening."

On the second floor, "there was a room, equal in length to the whole front of the house which was called the tea room, and, by fashionable people, the drawing room. . . . Evening visits were in fashion at that time; the most fashionable ladies sat in the tea room to receive them; those who did not pique themselves so much upon elegance, saw their friends in the common [dining] parlor" on the ground floor.

❦ Master carpenter Jonathan Dilworth built the house now known as the Todd House at the corner of Fourth and Walnut Streets, c. 1775. Briefly it housed John Todd, Jr. and his wife Dolly Payne Todd, who after her husband's death married James Madison. The interior has been recreated to the time of the Todds' residence.

❦ John Todd used the ground floor front room as his law office, and the furnishings are relatively simple and functional. Law books fill the shelves—Todd's library contained 350 volumes. According to his estate inventory, he used bow-back Windsor side chairs, owned a mahogany desk and bookcase, and used a practical Franklin stove in the fireplace—all items represented here by objects from the second half of the eighteenth century. Wooden-slat blinds and strips of flat-woven Venetian carpet sewn together to form a rug are typical treatments for the period.

# POWEL HOUSE

244 South Third Street, Philadelphia, PA
19106

Architect/builder unknown, 1765

National Register of Historic Places

Owned and operated by the Philadelphia
Society for the Preservation of
Landmarks, 1931

Telephone for opening days and times,
215.627.0364

By the 1760s Philadelphia had become the largest English-speaking urban center in North America and had matured into a provincial city of considerable sophistication. As her merchants prospered in commerce with the motherland, Philadelphia attracted master builders, brick masons, plasterers, cabinetmakers, and carvers able to satisfy a growing demand for suitably embellished town houses and country seats. The Powel House is the finest Philadelphia town house to survive from that period. It was occupied for many years by the last colonial mayor of Philadelphia, Samuel Powel, and his wife Elizabeth Willing Powel.

Samuel Powel (1738–1793) became independently wealthy at an early age. After graduating from the University of Pennsylvania in 1759, he set off in the fashion of English gentry on a grand tour of European capitals that lasted seven years. This journey put him in London for the coronation of George III. He then traveled to Italy in the party of the Duke of York, had an audience with Pope Clement XIII, had his portrait painted by Angelica Kauffman, and purchased crates of objects "after the antique" to ship home to Philadelphia.

Upon his return, and in anticipation of marrying Elizabeth Willing (1742–1830), Samuel Powel purchased the Third Street house from the failed merchant Charles Stedman, who had commissioned it in 1765. Located on one of the best streets in Philadelphia, next door to Governor John Penn's residence, and not far from that of his wife's parents, it had been advertised as "large and well finished . . . three Stories high, 31 Feet front, and 46 Feet deep, with a large convenient back building." Nonetheless, the Powels launched into a program of improvements, directed by the Scottish-born master builder Robert Smith (1722–1777), which included extensive carving by the London-trained carver and gilder Hercules Courtenay, who had recently arrived in Philadelphia prepared to work "in the newest Taste."

When the storm of revolution swept over Philadelphia, the Powels cast their lot with the rebels. They remained resident in the city during the British occupation in the winter of 1777–78 and were forced into the service wing to accommodate the earl of Carlisle, who impressed the house for his own use. (Incidentally, Carlisle described the house as "one of the best . . . in town . . . a very excellent one, perfectly well furnished.") After the revolution the Powels resumed their role as social and political leaders in the city and he again served as mayor. In 1793, however, he contracted yellow fever and died. Mrs. Powel sold the house a few years later. It passed through several hands until acquired in 1931 by Miss Frances Wister and her friends, who formed the Philadelphia Society for the Preservation of Landmarks (see pages 17–18).

Since an inventory of Samuel Powel's personal property has not been discovered, the house has been furnished by Landmarks with a mix of objects, some with Powel family history, others of the appropriate age and style. The marquis de Chastellux tells us the house had been "furnished in the English manner . . . adorned with fine prints and some very good copies of the best Italian paintings." Because it has been open as a museum for many years, the interpretation was until recently dated, owing more to the Colonial

⚘ The Philadelphia Middle Georgian brick facade of the Powel House is laid in Flemish bond (that is, alternating "headers" and "stretchers"—see illustrated glossary, pages 222–24) and the otherwise symmetrical three-bay plan is interrupted by placing the entrance to one side rather than in the middle. The most important decoration is the doorway with its original "frontispiece."

The room next to the ground floor office is believed to have been the dining room for which Samuel Powel purchased furniture in London. John Adams attended a dinner given by the Powels in September, 1774, and later reported to his wife: "Dined at Mr. Powel's . . . with many dignitaries, a most sinful feast again! Everything which could delight the eye or allure the taste . . . jellies, sweetmeats of various sorts, 20 sorts of tarts . . . punch, wine, beer . . . were served." The display of china shown in this photograph is from a large service that belonged to Mrs. Powel.

The ground floor front room is shown here before and after the recent reinterpretation. In both cases the room is furnished with Middle Georgian objects of Philadelphia and English origin, although only the fire screen and the Neo-Classical urns have a history of Powel ownership. The fine portrait shown in the "before" photograph is by Gilbert Stuart (1755–1828), who worked in Philadelphia at the end of the eighteenth century. The subject is Anne Pennington (1784–1806), an ancestor of Miss Frances Wister. Notice the Middle Eastern carpet, heavy silk window curtains, costly looking glass, and bed chamber dressing table. The "after" photograph shows the room more sparsely furnished as an office where mayor Powel might well have conducted business. The books are all from Samuel Powel's library and carry his armorial bookplate.

Revival than to modern museum scholarship (see pages 16–17). Gradually, however, the house is being reinterpreted by repositioning objects, removing the Middle Eastern carpets and heavy silk textiles at windows so beloved by house museum committees in earlier decades, and introducing more Grand Tour objects reflective of Powel's known "taste for the fine arts." This ongoing effort to refine the interpretation makes periodic return visits worthwhile for anyone interested in Middle Georgian American architecture and decorative arts as enjoyed by the "upper sort" of eighteenth-century Philadelphians.

❧ The largest and finest room in the house is the second floor parlor, often called the ballroom because of Sally Bache's letter to Benjamin Franklin recounting her dance with George Washington at a ball given by the Powels in honor of the Washingtons' twentieth wedding anniversary. During his extensive redecoration Powel embellished the room with mahogany doors, an ornamental plaster ceiling in the Rococo style, floor to ceiling paneling, fluted pilasters, magnificently carved broken pediments surmounting the door frames, and a mantel featuring the "Dog and His Shadow" from Aesop's *Fables*. These decorations are recreated from the originals now at the Philadelphia Museum of Art. The overmantel of the original did not survive. Fiske Kimball designed what is shown here, which features the Powel coat of arms—attractive but unlikely. Following mid-eighteenth-century fashion, chairs and settees are arranged around the wall.

# BISHOP WHITE HOUSE

309 Walnut Street, Philadelphia, PA
19106

Architect/builder unknown, 1786–87;
restored by the National Park Service,
1952–62

National Register of Historic Places

Operated by Independence National
Historical Park

Telephone for opening days and times,
215.597.8974

Bishop William White (1748–1836) is a major historical figure in the Episcopal Church. Prior to the Revolution he served Philadelphia's Christ Church and St. Peter's Church as rector. (White is buried beneath the chancel of Christ Church.) An ardent patriot after the colonies adopted the Declaration of Independence, this sagacious and scholarly cleric served as Chaplain of the Continental Congress and moved with ease among the leaders of the new nation, many of whom counted themselves among his parishioners. Once Great Britain acknowledged American independence, White helped to establish the American Episcopal Church and became the first bishop of the new Diocese of Pennsylvania.

The house White built in 1786 for himself, his wife Mary Harrison, and five children—then ages two to thirteen years—is one of the finest surviving examples of a late eighteenth-century upper-class Philadelphia row house; he lived there in considerable style for nearly fifty years, providing for his needs with a private income. The entire scale of the house is large by Philadelphia standards of the time: twenty-six-foot frontage on Walnut Street, three stories high with dormered attic, finely detailed carved stone window lintels, and a decorative modillion cornice. At a time when window glass over 8″ × 10″ in size sold at a premium, the Reverend Doctor White's window panes measured 12½″ × 22½″, causing the Mutual Assurance Company to refuse to insure them. Nonetheless, the house is conservative; it owes more to Middle Georgian design than does the nearby Late Georgian or Federal style Physick House erected the same year. (This conservatism is heightened by the pedimented frontispiece at the Walnut Street entrance, which was added by the Park Service and may never have existed.)

The interior demonstrates the typical Philadelphia row house plan. There are three major sections. The front extends the full width of the lot, with a passageway on one side giving access to two large parlors of approximately equal size. Behind the passageway is a narrow stair passage that Philadelphians call the "piazza." This passage connects the front building to a back service wing which is wider than the piazza but narrower than the front building, thus allowing a side yard and garden to the rear. The two parlors on the ground floor in the front building are interpreted as the formal drawing room, and the back parlor is shown set up for meal service.

The second floor front room is Dr. White's bed chamber and the connecting back chamber is his library. This must have been his *sanctum sanctorum*; shortly after Dr. White died, his family commissioned a painting of the room which is so detailed that even his partially smoked cigars can be seen perched precariously on the chair rail. This painting, now exhibited in the room, proved to be a primary document for the National Park Service curators and architects who recreated the interior—including cigar butts. Bishop White's estate inventory has never been found, but descendants scattered from South Africa to Hawaii responded to a call for information about the family, the house, and its furnishings, and a large percentage of the objects now on exhibit were there in the eighteenth and nineteenth centuries. These surviving objects

During the nineteenth and early twentieth centuries the main facade of the Bishop White House had been greatly altered to accommodate commercial use. The pedimented frontispiece, the windows, and the decorative console brackets on the dormers are all modern recreations based on surviving evidence, photographs and paintings of the house, and similarity to other Philadelphia buildings of the period.

provided useful clues to the style and quality of missing furniture, just as archaeology on the site suggested the type and pattern of porcelain, glass, and pottery objects used at Dr. White's table. So carefully did the Park Service restore and furnish the house that it is the most historically accurate recreation of all the center city house museums, albeit only for the two floors that are open to the public.

❧ A painting by John Sartain (1808–1897) of Bishop White's study on the second floor had been commissioned by the family shortly after his death. So detailed is this painting that the Park Service curators could follow it for the recreation, including the grass matting on the floor, the types and positions of the chairs, and the "rough and ready" way additional shelving has been added to the book presses around the room.

❧ The back parlor on the ground floor is interpreted as a dining room and furnished with Late Georgian objects of the type White would have owned. Notice the pair of silver-plate Argand-burner lamps on the mantel. Such imported lamps burned whale oil and are only found in the houses of wealthy Americans in the Federal period. For the purposes of this photograph the "recess closets" built into the chimney breast have been opened. These are typical of Philadelphia houses and provided useful storage.

# PHYSICK HOUSE

321 South Fourth Street, Philadelphia,
PA 19106

Commissioned by Henry Hill, 1786–88;
restoration architect George B. Roberts,
1965–66

National Historic Landmark, 1976

Owned and operated by the Philadelphia
Society for the Preservation of
Landmarks

Telephone for opening days and times,
215.925.2251

Philadelphian Philip Syng Physick (1768–1837), who would one day be hailed as the father of American surgery, enjoyed wealth and social position as a birthright. He studied at the University of Pennsylvania and then in London—where he apprenticed with the brilliant surgeon John Hunter—followed by a medical degree from Edinburgh. Thus trained, he returned to Philadelphia, where he launched an extraordinary career of practice and teaching during which he invented several surgical instruments and procedures that became widely adopted. Perhaps most important, he trained an entire generation of young surgeons and thereby raised the standards of that practice in America.

In 1800 Dr. Physick married Elizabeth Emlen, with whom he had seven children. In 1815, however, the Physicks legally separated and Dr. Physick established a new home for himself and his children in the Fourth Street house built in 1786–88 for the wine merchant Henry Hill. From the perspective of two centuries it is difficult to appreciate how remarkable this house must have appeared when new—except when contrasted to Bishop White's nearby house, which dates from the same time. Here there are no window lintels with keystones, no doorway marked by projecting columns or pediment. White's house is conservative—perhaps appropriate for the home of a promising cleric—and owes more to the style of pre-revolutionary Middle Georgian Powel House than to what came later. Henry Hill's brick house is in the new, lighter Late Georgian, or Federal, style based on the latest London fashion introduced there by Robert Adam; it is also unusual in a city of row houses for being free-standing and virtually square—48 feet by 52 feet—three stories plus attic high, with a double front door surmounted by an arch fanlight imported from London. In fact, Hill had eagerly sought the latest fashion, what he called "in the plainest State of elegance" that is "neither Extravagant or economical." Hill's house shares more stylistically—if not in

➶    The front parlor could be converted into a dining room. A highlight of this space and one of the great treasures of the Landmarks collection is this Philadelphia mahogany sideboard attributed to the Irish-born cabinetmaker and carver Joseph B. Berry (1757?–1839), who advertised in 1810 "a variety of the newest and most fashionable Cabinet Furniture, superbly finished in the rich Egyptian and Gothic style." Thomas Sully (1783–1872) painted the posthumous portrait of Dr. Physick's estranged wife, Elizabeth Emlen Physick, from a miniature. The wallpaper shown here has been replaced.

costly grandeur—with its nearby contemporary, the town house of William Bingham, designed by the London architect John Plaw and now unfortunately demolished.

For many years historians believed that the present house reflected extensive post-1815 alterations by Dr. Physick, an attribution since disproved by more thorough research. Compounding that error is the unfortunate loss of much original interior fabric during the long ownership of Mrs. Charles Penrose Keith, whose phobia against dust compelled her to strip out most of the original Federal woodwork, including interior shutters, baseboards, door surrounds, mahogany doors, and stair balusters. Fortunately the extraordinary "American marble," mirror-inlaid chimney piece supplied to Hill in 1796 by marble worker William Payne survived this sweep. Once the house had been acquired by the Philadelphia Society for the Preservation of Landmarks, the interior trim had to be replaced. In this the supervising architect—having convinced himself of the later date—erroneously detailed the work in the bolder Grecian style that would have been appropriate for a house of Physick's period, but not for one of Hill's. The house has also been furnished in the high French Empire Revival Style made fashionable in the 1960s by the redecoration of the White House during the Kennedy administration. The resulting interiors are handsome but do not follow the detailed Physick inventory that could result in a fine recreation. Gradually, however, the Landmarks staff and a committee of dedicated volunteers are reinterpreting this important house as an appropriate memorial to the selfless career and surgical genius of Dr. Philip Syng Physick.

✾ The townhouse built in 1786–88 for wine merchant Henry Hill in the "plainest State of elegance" is one of the earliest Philadelphia examples of the new Federal style that began to appear after the American revolution. It is also unusual for being free-standing in a neighborhood of row houses. Dr. Philip Syng Physick, the "Father of American Surgery," lived here from 1815 to 1837. The commodious walled garden is planted according to a 1960s design by George B. Tatum.

# THE ROSENBACH MUSEUM & LIBRARY

2010 Delancey Place, Philadelphia, PA 19102

Built by Charles, Joseph, and John McCrea, c.1865; alterations by Clarence S. Thalheimer and David D. Weitz, 1940

National Register of Historic Places

Telephone for opening days and times, 215.732.1600

Dr. A. S. W. Rosenbach, the leading American antiquarian book and manuscripts dealer in the first half of the twentieth century, combined scholarship, business savvy, and a shameless flair for showmanship. He bought and sold with brio. The greatest bibliographic treasures became his daily stock and trade: Shakespeare first folios, Gutenberg Bibles, and Bay Psalm books—the latter being the first book published in the English colonies. In addition he acquired the original manuscripts of such literary

⟐ The last home of the antiquarian book and furniture dealers Philip H. and A. S. W. Rosenbach dates from c. 1865, with alterations in 1940 that include the Georgian window to the left of the front door. The 2000 block of Delancey Place is considered by many to be the most attractive and elegant in Philadelphia. Most of the houses remain single-family residences. The museum has acquired the house next door, into which it is planning to expand.

⟐ Most of the house is furnished as left by the Rosenbach brothers. Philip, who specialized in art and antiques for the family company, favored British decorative arts. The furnishings for their house came from company stock and reflect the mix of styles, periods, and cultures that became popular in the first decades of the twentieth century. Most of the furniture in the dining room is showy Georgian revival, but the painting over the mantel is an excellent Thomas Sully (1783–1872) dating from 1828. To the left of the fireplace is a view of the Venetian quay from the school of Giovanni Antonio Canaletto, c. 1725–1750.

works as Lewis Carroll's *Alice's Adventures in Wonderland* and James Joyce's *Ulysses*, not all of which he sold.

Dr. R.'s brother and partner, Philip, specialized in art and antiques, particularly British decorative arts. In 1926 they acquired a house at 2006 Delancey Place and later moved to number 2010, where they resided until their deaths in 1952 and 1953. The decorative environment they created reflects the sophisticated mix of styles, periods, and cultures that was popular with wealthy urban collectors in the first decades of the twentieth century. If the Rosenbach Museum can be said to be a house museum, the period is the 1950s—and the style is eclectic. Certainly it is the only such institution in Philadelphia, and the staff works to preserve the sense that you are visiting a private home. There are no scholarly labels here to break the spell.

The Rosenbach Museum is located in a block of largely unchanged row houses erected by the speculative builders Charles, Joseph, and James McCrea at the end of the Civil War. Despite their Victorian date, these center-hall, double-wide, red-brick, white marble trimmed houses exhibit the Federal detailing of an earlier period: plain-brick arched openings containing recessed marble arches with keystones and semicircular fanlights. Originally the four-bay facades provided two windows in the front parlor to the right of the entrance and an identical single window to the left in the reception room. In 1940, however, the then owner of number 2010 embellished the facade with a Georgian revival window and leaded glass fanlight in place of the single window. The house greatly contributes to one of the most elegant and attractive streets in the Rittenhouse Square neighborhood.

After the Rosenbach brothers died, the house and its contents became the property of a non-profit corporation, which operates the museum and regularly mounts exhibitions based on its 30,000 rare books and 300,000 manuscripts devoted to the topics of British and American literature from Chaucer to the present; book illustration from medieval illumination to Maurice Sendak; and Americana from the earliest explorers to World War II. These exhibits—set against the background of the Rosenbach house —make this museum a not-to-miss experience for visitors to Philadelphia.

A 1931 portrait of Abraham Simon Wolf Rosenbach by Nikol Schattenstein (1879–1954) surveys the library at the heart of the house. Most of the bookcases were transferred to Delancey Place when the Rosenbach store at 1320 Walnut Street closed. Shelved here and in the adjoining reading room are some of the Rosenbach Museum's greatest bibliographic treasures, available for use by qualified scholars who have made advance appointments.

# WALT WHITMAN HOUSE

330 Mickle Street, Camden, NJ 08103

Architect/builder unknown, c. 1848

National Historic Landmark, 1963

Owned by the State of New Jersey, 1947; operated by New Jersey State Park Service

Telephone for opening days and times, 609.964.5383

Walt Whitman (1819–1892), world renowned for *Leaves of Grass* and arguably "the most passionate and best" nineteenth-century American poet, came to the Delaware Valley in consequence of a paralytic stoke he suffered in 1873. For the previous ten years Whitman had lived in Washington, D.C., variously engaged as newspaper correspondent, government clerk, and, during the Civil War, hospital nurse. The latter activity, he would later claim, brought on the ill health that plagued the second half of his life. His brother, George W. Whitman, lived on Stevens Street in Camden, New Jersey, where Walt took up residence for the next eleven years, paying room and board. Despite his illnesses, this was a creative period; five new editions of *Leaves of Grass*, three collections of new poems, and much of his best prose appeared, including *Memoranda During the War* (1875) and *Specimen Days and Collect* (1882–83).

With modest income from his publications and cash gifts from friends and admirers both at home and abroad, Whitman purchased a simple two-story free-standing frame house on Mickle Street in Camden that later would be boxed in by taller brick row houses. Throughout the early nineteenth century the land on which the Whitman house stands had been subdivided into ever smaller lots. In 1847 a clerk named Adam Hare paid $350 for a single lot on which he probably erected the house that Rebecca Jane Hare sold to Whitman in 1884 for $1,750.

Lacking furniture for his new house and needing someone to care for him, Whitman offered the widow of a Camden sea captain the opportunity to move in with her furniture and live rent free in exchange for services as nurse and housekeeper. He paid a small stipend and all her living expenses; this suited both parties and she remained until Whitman's death. The house is unprepossessing, and the neighborhood even then "was the last place one would expect a poet to select for a home." One friend called it "a coop at best, and a much better located and more comfortable house could have been bought in Camden for less money." None of his friends could understand the choice, since "it contained no furnace, and his bedroom ceiling could be easily touched with the hand." Probably Whitman had been influenced by "the fact that there was a tree in front of it, that it was convenient to the ferries, and the lilacs grew in the back yard." Modest and obscure as his home might be, a steady stream of admirers crossed from Philadelphia to sit with the "good gray poet."

330 Mickle Boulevard is the only house Walt Whitman ever purchased for himself, and after he died in 1892 most of the contents remained in the house. His heirs sold it to the City of Camden in 1921; it was opened to the public as a shrine to Whitman's memory in 1926; and in 1947 the property was transferred to the State of New Jersey, which operates the site with the support of the Walt Whitman Association.

Late in life Whitman remarked, "Camden was originally an accident—but I shall never be sorry. I was left over in Camden. It has brought me blessed returns."

Walt Whitman's bedroom on the second floor front of his Camden, New Jersey home is furnished with the modest, late nineteenth-century furniture found throughout the house. This is the bed in which he died on March 26, 1892; the rocking chair appears in several famous photographs of the poet. Bathrooms had been installed; the tin bathing tub was used after Whitman's second stroke in 1888 confined him to this room.

# POMONA HALL

Park Boulevard and Euclid Avenue,
Camden, NJ 08103

Architect/builder unknown, 1726; major
additions, 1788

National Register of Historic Places

Owned by the City of Camden, 1915;
operated by the Camden County
Historical Society

Telephone for opening days and times,
609.964.3333

❧  The original stair of the 1726 section of
Pomona Hall is one of the finest surviving
examples from the Early Georgian period in
the Delaware Valley. The wide arch that
allows the stair to be seen from this angle is
a late modification of the wall that
separates the 1726 and 1788 sections of
the present house.

When William Penn's first settlers arrived in Philadelphia there were already British Quakers well established on the West Jersey side of the Delaware. By 1690 the upstart city had rapidly grown to dominate the economics, religion, and culture of the entire region. The Cooper family found themselves drawn into this vortex; they had already settled on a point of land opposite the future site of Philadelphia, where a creek that now bears their name flows into the Delaware. In 1713 the grandson of the first West Jersey Cooper, Joseph Cooper, Jr. (1691–1749), married Mary Hudson of Philadelphia and set up housekeeping on a four-hundred-acre tract in a modest one-and-one-half-story wood-frame structure.

A decade later Joseph and Mary Cooper erected a new gambrel-roofed brick structure next to the frame house, which then became a kitchen. Following already well established Philadelphia building practice, they used Flemish bond with glazed headers on the main facade and English bond on the other exposed walls. Taking advantage of the decorative possibilities of the glazed headers, the date of construction (1726) and the owners' initials appear traced in the gable—a common practice in the Middle Atlantic colonies. A small pent eave ran across the main facade to shelter the window and door.

The interior of the Coopers' new house consists of two rooms on each floor and a stair hall. The ground floor includes an elaborately paneled parlor that architectural historians have long declared to be among the finest in southern New Jersey. Bolection moldings are used to create the mantel shelf and define the fireplace, which is flanked by grilled closets with paneled doors. More important, the closed stringer stair with its

⊛ Pomona Hall in Camden, New Jersey reflects two major building campaigns of the Cooper family. The north end of the present house dates to 1726, the south end to 1788, as indicated in the patterned brick initials and dates that can still be seen on the gables. The pedimented frontispiece is a later replacement.

bold and elaborately turned balusters, massive square newels, and molded caps ranks among the most significant surviving examples in the Delaware Valley—a small group that includes the stairs at the Trent House, Bellair, and Harriton.

The expanded house proved adequate for the family until 1788, by which time it must have seemed small and out of fashion. Marmaduke Cooper (1748–1797), nephew of the builder, pulled down the oldest frame section and erected a three-bay brick addition that created a five-bay, center-hall, two-and-one-half-story vernacular Georgian house. A new roof line joined the old and new sections, the pent eave disappeared, and the entrance acquired a pedimented frontispiece. Fortunately the Coopers retained the 1726 stair, which might easily have been replaced in such an extensive remodeling. Through the subsequent century the house passed from generation to generation of the extended Cooper family, often being rented to tenants, until it was sold in 1901 and later passed to the City of Camden as a park. The house has been administered and restored by the Camden County Historical Society since 1924, and it is being refurnished to the Cooper period of occupancy.

The name by which the house has been known at least since the early nineteenth century probably dates from the time of Marmaduke Cooper. Pomona, a Roman nymph of classical mythology, presided over gardens and fruit trees. She disdained working in the fields and the fatigues of hunting, favoring instead the gentle, celibate, and solitary arts of pruning and grafting.

# BARCLAY FARMSTEAD

209 Barclay Lane, Cherry Hill, NJ 08034

Architect/builder unknown, early nineteenth century; restored by John M. Dickey, FAIA, 1975–76

National Register of Historic Places

Owned and operated by the Township of Cherry Hill, acquired 1974

Telephone for opening days and times, 609.795.6225

⚜ The rear parlor wall color and stencil pattern were copied from another nineteenth-century South Jersey farm house. The Venetian carpet strips and the simple window curtains looped over pins are appropriate treatments for the period.

Rural communities within commuting distance of American cities share unregulated urban sprawl, which permits subdivision of farms and conversion of country roads to multi-lane highways lined with strip malls and choked by automobiles. Occasionally, however, communities strike back and preserve a reminder of what is rapidly disappearing. One such example is the thirty-two-acre Barclay Farmstead purchased in 1974 by the Township of Cherry Hill in Camden County.

Chestnut Grove Farm, the name of the property until it was acquired from its last private owner, Helen Barclay, has been farmed since the seventeenth century, but the present house dates to sometime after Quaker yeoman Joseph Thorne (1767–1856) acquired the land in 1816. Thorne purchased 168 acres with borrowed funds when real estate prices were at their peak after the War of 1812. By 1819, however, an agricultural depression had settled over the country and land prices fell by half, leaving Thorne unable to meet his obligations. After years of legal maneuvering, the sheriff seized the farm in 1826 and sold it at public auction to Joseph W. Cooper. His daughter, Ellen C. Cooper, married Charles Barclay; their daughter sold most of the farm for development between 1954 and 1962, retaining 32 acres surrounding the house and associated farm structures.

Shortly after acquiring Chestnut Grove Farm, Thorne had erected the handsome, sturdy Federal-style five-bay, two-and-one-half-story brick house. The main facade is laid in Flemish bond and the other walls in common bond; there are also molded brick cornices. End-wall chimneys define the gable roof with dormers, all windows have exterior shutters, and the simple front door has a semicircular fanlight. The rear facade is asymmetrical with a large, unusual arched opening to a small piazza off the kitchen. The interior consists of a center hall with double parlor to one side and kitchen to the other. The house has been furnished with a donated collection to reflect the period of the Thorne and early Cooper occupancy.

Joseph Thorne's Federal house was once the center of a 168-acre farm in what is now Cherry Hill Township, Camden County, New Jersey. This 32-acre oasis amid suburban sprawl is only a short drive from center city Philadelphia.

# GREENFIELD HALL

343 King's Highway East, Haddonfield, NJ
08033

Architect/builder, George Dilks, master
carpenter, 1841

National Register of Historic Places, 1971

Owned and operated by the Historical
Society of Haddonfield, 1960

Telephone for opening days and hours,
609.429.7375

Founded in the seventeenth century where the King's Highway crosses the Cooper River, modern Haddonfield, New Jersey must be one of the most appreciated suburban communities within easy reach of Philadelphia. In the colonial period it benefited from navigable access to the Delaware River, in the nineteenth century railroads linked it to the city and the Jersey shore, and today its residents who must commute do so on the High Speed Line unfettered by an automobile. Haddonfield's village center could illustrate a gazetteer of American architecture, and the secondary streets are lined with nineteenth-century suburban villas, many designed by outstanding Philadelphia architects. The better to protect their architectural heritage from demolition and inappropriate alterations, the residents passed a Historic District Ordinance in 1971 that helps preserve this fragile and unusual survival.

In the middle of Haddonfield is Greenfield Hall, now occupied by the local historical society founded in 1914 "to study the history of our area, to collect and preserve articles of historic value, to establish an historical library and to publish, from time to time, historical information." The substantial brick house is the third on the site since 1725, when the tract was leased to John Gill. The first is said to have been "a small hipped-roof frame building," which was replaced c. 1747. By the time Gill's great-grandson inherited in 1838, it was again time for something new.

Banker and sometime politician John Gill IV (1795–1884) eschewed the Philadelphia architects who might have provided a design in the latest Greek Revival or Italianate fashion. Instead, he elected to use local builders to run up in a single year a conservative Delaware Valley design that differs only in its details from a house that might have been erected twenty years earlier. According to Gill's account book, he paid

James Dobbs for brick ("to be taken from my kiln any time previous to the 1st day of April") in January 1841, and by May he had master carpenter George Dilks on the job supervising the lesser trades. The masonry appears to have been laid by Collins & Lippincot, and by late July the plasterers were being paid on account. On October 14, 1841 Dilks received $470 from Gill "being a ballance in full for building his new House in Haddonfield," although an additional payment appears on December 31, 1841, which suggests some work for which accounts have not survived may have continued into 1842.

Gill's new free-standing five-bay, center-hall, two-and-one-half-story brick house sits squarely on the street without setback. The bricks are finely made, allowing for thin mortar beds and tight joints. The millwork and wide frontispiece are Classical Revival details that appear in Philadelphia row houses of the 1830s, as do the round-head dormers. The interiors follow the traditional double-pile plan, and the mantels, doors, and other interior millwork are typical for the time and place—simple, handsome, and practical. Only a few rooms are furnished with an assembled collection of objects spanning the mid-eighteenth to the mid-nineteenth centuries, several of which have Haddonfield or South Jersey provenance.

❧ The estate inventory made when Elizabeth French Gill died in 1854 provides a "snapshot" of Greenfield Hall furnishings. The carpeted parlor followed late Neo-Classical Grecian taste that would have been popular a decade earlier: two pier tables and pier glasses, two sofas, ten mahogany chairs, two ottomans, a center table, a rocking chair, a lounge chair, three foot stools, two "Old chairs," a fruit stand and four vases, four candle sticks, an "Astra" (Astral) lamp, a lard lamp, and a candle snuffer with tray. While the furnishings shown in this photograph make no attempt to follow the inventory, the window interpretation (no curtains, wooden Venetian blinds with decorative cornices) is certainly correct for the period.

# SCHUYLKILL RIVER *and* FAIRMOUNT PARK

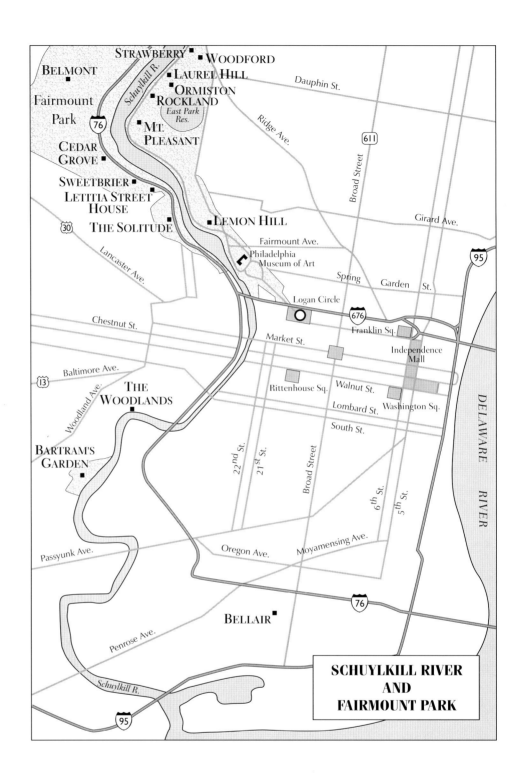

**SCHUYLKILL RIVER
AND
FAIRMOUNT PARK**

Lemon Hill. The steep winding stair rises from the marble-floored front passage to the second floor, passing a niche holding a copy of Apollo from the Belvedere Courtyard at the Vatican Museum, believed in the nineteenth century to be among the greatest works of art in the world. See page 90.

It would be useful—at least in your mind's eye—to approach Philadelphia by her rivers, as if you were an early settler. First of all, they are of entirely different characters. The wide, alluvial Delaware has contributed to the city the coursing blood of industry and commerce; the barely navigable, steep-banked Schuylkill has long given its citizens life-sustaining water to drink. Both have greatly influenced settlement patterns.

As you pass from the Atlantic Ocean into Delaware Bay, with the marshes of southern New Jersey to starboard and the featureless lowlands of Delaware to port, the waterway gradually narrows, forcing your ship to begin a wide reach to the northeast past New Castle, Wilmington, Chester, and the Philadelphia International Airport. At the point where the course swings almost due east, a smaller river flows into the Delaware from the north. Today the Schuylkill must find its way through oil refineries, dockyards, and a sewage treatment plant; in the seventeenth century the navigable channel beckoned settlers through the marshes to higher, solid ground that could be easily cleared and planted. Those who continue a short distance on the Delaware as it turns northward again arrive at the site of William Penn's great town.

Later we'll return to the Delaware; for the present let's follow the Schuylkill.

The earliest settlers along the Schuylkill, including the Swedes who established plantations on the lower reaches of the river a generation before the arrival of William Penn's agents, generally built rather modest structures only gradually joined by those of more architectural pretension. Humble or grand, farm house, villa, or gentleman's estate, virtually all the private houses erected along both sides of the Schuylkill River below the site of the waterworks at Fairmount ultimately fell victim to later nineteenth-century factories, refineries, and railroads. Their absence forcefully reminds us what would have happened above Fairmount were it not for Philadelphia's effort to protect the source of its drinking water.[1]

An accessible example of the seventeenth-century farm house type that might once have lined the river is the gambrel-roofed, stone **Caleb Pusey House** at Upland, Delaware County, which is discussed in the western suburbs section (page 220–21). The only house museums from the pre-Revolutionary period on the lower reaches of the Schuylkill also happen to be two of the earliest surviving Philadelphia structures. Both suffer from being off the usual tourist track; both deserve to be better known, particularly the idiosyncratic stone **John Bartram House** (c. 1730), once the home of the internationally renowned American botanist and his son William, which probably incorporates elements of an even earlier seventeenth-century Swedish structure. Across the river on the east side is the steep-roofed **Bellair Manor** (c. 1714–20), sole surviving example of the country seats located south of Philadelphia on the east bank of the Schuylkill.

Northward, the river banks grow steeper as we approach Fairmount—present site of the Philadelphia Museum of Art. Here the merchant aristocracy of the mid-eigh-

Figure 1. The Federal villa Lemon Hill (1800), here surrounded by early fall foliage of Fairmount Park, looks out across "boat house row" to the Schuylkill River below.

teenth century built Georgian country seats commissioned from the same master builders, carvers, and plasterers who were creating houses like Samuel Powel's city house. (Figures 1, 2). One of the earliest and grandest of these to survive—albeit greatly altered—is William Peters's Belmont (c. 1742–45) which at this writing is not open to the public but hopefully will soon be restored to a semblance of its earlier glory. Contemporary references to the house, the extensive gardens, and its site over-looking Philadelphia and New Jersey beyond give us some sense of its impact on visitors in the eighteenth century (Figure 3). For instance, Hannah Callender records her impressions in the summer of 1762 when the house and gardens had matured:

> . . . went to William Peters's house having some acquaintance with his wife. She was at home and with her daughter Polly received us kindly in one wing of the house. After a while [we] passed through a covered passage to the large hall [which is] well furnished, the top [ceiling] adorned with instruments of music, coats of arms, crests and other ornaments in stucco, its sides by paintings and statues in bronze.

From the front of this hall you have a prospect bounded by the Jerseys like a blue ridge. A broad walk of English Cherry trees leads down to the river. The doors of the house opening opposite admit a prospect of the length of the garden over a broad gravel walk to a large handsome summer house on a green. From the windows a vista is terminated by an obelisk. On the right you enter a labyrinth of hedge of low cedar and spruce. In the middle stands a statue of Apollo. In the garden are statues of Diana, Fame and Mercury with urns. We left the garden for a wood cut into

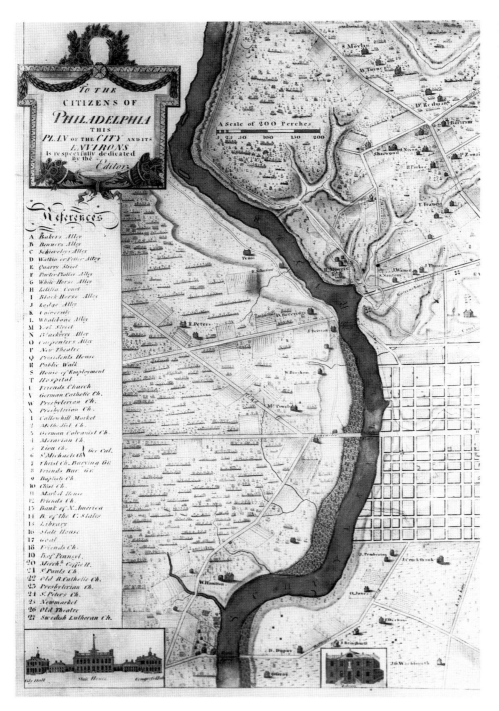

Figure 2. Villas along the Schuylkill had already begun to appear in the 1790s when Peter C. Varlé published this map of the area. Historical Society of Pennsylvania.

vistas. In the midst is a Chinese temple for a summer house. One avenue gives a fine prospect of the City. With a spy glass you discern the houses and hospital distinctly. Another avenue looks to the obelisk.[2]

Sadly, Belmont's even grander west bank rival is totally lost. Governor John Penn's Lansdowne (1773) was the largest and one of the most elegant pre-Revolutionary Middle Georgian houses in America, boasting a Palladian, two-story, pedimented portico and decked hip roof that looked out over the Schuylkill from a high bluff. John Adams, then vice-president, wrote to his wife in 1795, "went to Lansdowne on Sunday, about a half mile on this side of Judge Peters [Belmont], where you once dined. The place is very retired, but very beautiful—a splendid house, gravel walks, shrubberies, and clumps of trees in the English style—on the banks of the Schuylkill." Another visitor, confined at Lansdowne by an outbreak of yellow fever in Philadelphia, characterized the house as "superb. It commands a noble view of the Schuylkill and the seats in the neighborhood, and at a distance the steeples of some of the churches in Philadelphia." After the Revolution Joseph Bonaparte, former king of Spain and elder

Figure 3. Belmont (c. 1742–45) occupies one of the most spectacular sites on the west bank of the Schuylkill. A visitor on the eve of the American Revolution remarked, "The country round [Philadelphia] is very pleasant and agreeable, finely interspersed with genteel country seats, fields and orchards, for several miles around, and along both the rivers for a good many miles."

brother of Napoleon I, and William Bingham, one of the richest men in America, successively occupied the house as a summer retreat. Lansdowne fell victim to boys playing with fireworks on July 4, 1854; the City of Philadelphia demolished the shell after purchasing the estate for Fairmount Park in 1868 (Figure 4).[3]

On the east bank of the Schuylkill three Middle Georgian houses erected before the Revolution are now open as museums. All three have hipped roofs, central axial entrances, and Palladian details such as projecting pavilions and pedimented doorways. The most famous of these is **Mount Pleasant** (1763), which John Adams called "the most elegant seat in Pennsylvania."[4] If a visitor had to select a single house to visit in Fairmount Park it would be Mount Pleasant, especially as now furnished by the Philadelphia Museum of Art with the finest quality eighteenth-century Philadelphia furniture. The other two houses of approximately the same age, albeit more modest in scale, are **Woodford** (c. 1756), which is handsomely furnished with the Naomi Wood collection, and **Laurel Hill** (c. 1762), sited advantageously close to the bluff where visitors can easily grasp the summer appeal of these riverside houses before the age of air conditioning.

Figure 4. Erected by Pennsylvania Governor John Penn on the eve of the American Revolution (1773), Lansdowne was destroyed by fire in 1854, its loss one of the great tragedies of American architecture. This view comes from William Birch, *The Country Seats of the United States of North America* (1808), the first illustrated book on American country houses and villas. The Athenaeum of Philadelphia.

One mid-eighteenth-century house remains to be mentioned. **Cedar Grove** (c. 1748), ancestral home of the Morris family, came late to the banks of the Schuylkill as a preservation effort—first dismantled and then moved to the Park from Frankfort in 1926 as part of the Sesquicentennial celebration. Now supervised by the Philadelphia Museum of Art, Cedar Grove is open to the public and well worth visiting, especially for those interested in early Delaware Valley decorative arts.

Immediately after the Revolution, the banks of the Schuylkill bloomed with a new crop of houses. The most important of these to survive is William Hamilton's **Woodlands** (1780s), which is sited down river from the waterworks near Bartram's Garden. The Woodlands survived not by inclusion in Fairmount Park but rather by the fortunate circumstance of being acquired as the site of a Victorian rural cemetery. Thereafter (in terms of date) come **Strawberry** (1788–89), **Sweetbrier** (1797), and **Lemon Hill** (1799–1800)—the latter with oval rooms and Adamesque grace. In addition to many other houses that are rarely accessible to the public, there are three closely related structures that have from time to time been furnished and open; in the hope that they again will be, they are discussed together here for their architectural importance: **The Solitude** (1784–85), now surrounded by the Philadelphia Zoo; **Ormiston** (1798); and **Rockland** (1810).

On the whole, these houses are best described as villas—a term used by the ancient Roman Pliny the Younger who described his villa near Ostia on the Tyrrhenian Sea as being "seventeen miles from Rome, so it is possible to spend the night there after necessary business is done." This is the essential characteristic of a villa: that it be erected in the country, near enough to a city to reach easily, yet far enough away to escape the crowds and disease of the city. By the late seventeenth century the term had appeared in England, where Roger North, in his *Treatise on Building* (London, c. 1695), defined a villa as "a lodge for the sake of a garden, to retire to enjoy and sleep, without pretense of entertainment of many persons." In eighteenth-century England the word had come into common currency, according to Johnson's *Dictionary*, as a seasonal dwelling in the country, generally of smallish, symmetrical, and classical character. In Philadelphia the term appears at least by the late eighteenth century; in 1795 American financier Robert Morris remarked in a letter written from The Hills— his property on the Schuylkill where Lemon Hill now stands—"I have just parted with my little visitor, he is gone to the neighboring villa."[5]

Several reasons motivated owners to erect villas, but matters of health and comfort seem paramount. Pliny described one of his as being "at the very foot of the Apennines, which are considered the healthiest of mountains. . . . The summer is wonderfully temperate, for there is always some movement of the air." To eighteenth- and nineteenth-century Philadelphians, healthful air concerned everyone. In 1793, to cite but one of several possible examples, the city suffered a severe outbreak of yellow fever that effectively shut down the United States government. Dr. Benjamin Rush, Philadelphia's most prominent physician, advised those with the means to leave the city. Thomas Jefferson, residing for the summer in a rented villa on the Schuylkill known as

Rhoads' Place, reported to James Madison in Virginia that "everybody who can, is flying from the city, and the panic of the country people is likely to add famine to the disease" because they fear to bring their produce into city markets.[6]

Physicians were at a loss to deal with the yellow fever and cholera epidemics that regularly descended on the city. Little wonder. Neither germ theory nor the role of insects and rodents in spreading disease was understood, and treatment for the victims—bleeding and purging—often turned out to be worse than the disease. Dr. Rush and his European-trained colleagues believed that the 1793 fever derived from noxious air that had been infected by "some damaged coffee, which putrefied on a wharf," while others thought it had been passed by contact with refugees from Santo Domingo. In fact, that summer had been unusually wet, leaving many stagnant pools in

Figure 5. We know more about The Solitude and its grounds than about most eighteenth-century American properties. The layout of the garden has come down to us in the form of the surveyor's plan, as have Penn's own sketches for the house, which are based on a design from Robert Morris's *Select Architecture* (London, 1757), a copy of which he owned. An inventory survives of all the contents from shortly after Penn furnished and occupied the house.

Figure 6. The east wall of The Solitude parlor, with its French doors leading out to the portico, is shown here as refurnished during the Bicentennial by the Philadelphia Museum of Art. The inventory of John Penn's furniture lists three "elegant large settees having [horse] hair bottoms, with satin stripe, a double row of gilt nails and fluted legs," all in the "modern fashion." There were two armchairs and twenty-four matching side chairs similarly upholstered, four "cotton and worsted [wool] striped parlour curtains, with cord," and "an elegant Wilton carpet, 20 by 12." Photograph by Eric Mitchell, 1985; Philadelphia Museum of Art.

Figure 7. Typical of late eighteenth-century practice, the parlor at The Solitude doubled as a dining room. Penn's inventory included a "large semicircular side board table, in which are three drawers, the middle drawer divided into eleven partitions, leaded for liquors; 1 large dining table and 2 semicircular tables to fix at each end, which 2 being put together form a round table of themselves." Photograph by Eric Mitchell, 1985; Philadelphia Museum of Art.

Figure 8. The entrance hall at The Solitude is long and narrow, its most dramatic feature being the wrought-iron balustrade of the stair, probably of Philadelphia fabrication. The circular ends of the dining table may have been kept here, together with many of the chairs, which could be brought in when the parlor was set for dining. Photograph by Eric Mitchell, 1985; Philadelphia Museum of Art.

which the *Aëdes aegypti* mosquito could breed, sallying forth to bite infected refugees and spread the contagion. Whatever the cause, prudence dictated that those who could afford to flee Philadelphia's nearly tropical summers should do so. In 1793 alone 10 percent of the Philadelphia population died.[7] Like the American Revolution, yellow fever looms large in the history of Philadelphia-area house museums.

In providing its owners with escape from the stressful and often life-threatening city on which their wealth depended, the villa also offered opportunity for display. By the early nineteenth century few of the Schuylkill villas were out of sight of one another. Designed to provide pleasurable gardens and distant views, these houses opened to healthful, cooling country breezes and could be seen and appreciated as features in their landscape. Artful design of house, site, and garden delighted owner and passerby alike.

The design and siting of villas was intended to take full advantage of distant vistas, as the Italian architect Andrea Palladio had suggested in the sixteenth century, so that "the mind, fatigued by the agitations of the city, will be greatly restored and comforted, and be able quietly to attend the studies of letters, and contemplation." Consequently, windows needed to be large. As owners in the late eighteenth and early nineteenth centuries demanded easier access to gardens, "which are the sole and chief recreation of a villa"—large windows and "French" doors began to appear at ground level. Likewise, the orientation of a villa took into account the prevailing winds to allow for cross ventilation. These points are fundamental to Palladio's designs for the Italian Veneto, which profoundly influenced English and, ultimately, American villa design.

By definition, a villa is within easy reach of the city, and this feature that made them popular also put them at risk as eighteenth-century cities expanded. Consequently, country houses of the villa type have largely been lost in America. (Even the term, once commonly used, is rarely understood today except by architectural historians.) Isolated examples survive in or near modern Baltimore, New York, and Boston, but the finest group of surviving villas in America is found in Philadelphia. Of those from the Federal period, The Solitude (1784–85), built for John Penn, Jr. and now incorporated into the grounds of the Philadelphia Zoo, is one of the most significant and probably served as the prototype for several four-square seasonal structures erected in the following decades (Figure 5).

As the grandson of Pennsylvania's founder—and younger cousin of Governor Penn of Lansdowne—John Penn, Jr. rushed to Philadelphia after the Revolution in a futile effort to salvage his inheritance. While here he purchased fifteen acres on the west bank of the Schuylkill for £600 and built a two-and-one-half-story classical cube (29′ × 29′ × 29′) a with parlor and hall on the ground floor and a library and two small bedrooms on the floor above. The younger Penn had access to nearby Lansdowne, so he built his "villa near Philadelphia" patterned on what the English architect Robert Morris called "a little building intended for Retirement or for Study, to be placed in some agreeable Part of a Park or Garden" (Figures 6, 7, 8).

Across the Schuylkill are two other houses erected as summer retreats which, like

Figure 9. Ormiston Villa (1798), the property of Edward Burd near Woodford, is typical of the modest three-bay Philadelphia area houses of The Solitude type.

The Solitude, are presently not furnished and cannot be toured except by special arrangement: Ormiston Villa (1798), erected by Edward Burd (1750–1833) near Woodford (Figure 9), and Rockland (c. 1810) near Mount Pleasant (Figure 10).

The builder of Rockland, dry goods merchant George Thomson, remains enigmatic; his architect or builder is an even greater mystery. Thomson purchased the 26-acre tract where a large rock projected out over the Schuylkill in 1809 and probably erected his villa around 1810; it certainly existed by 1815, when it was sold to Isaac Cooper Jones, another Philadelphia merchant whose family held the house until its acquisition by Fairmount Park in 1870. Like most villas of its type, Rockland is a two-and-one-half-story, stucco-over-stone, nearly square structure with hipped roof and deck that originally held a balustrade, now unfortunately lost. But Rockland is unusual for what does survive. The three-bay main facade has an original portico with a semi-circular projection supported by six fluted columns and two pilasters. A semi-elliptical fanlight surmounts the double door entrance. Above the portico is a modified Palladian window. Nothing else from the Federal period in Philadelphia even approaches the sophistication of this composition, making Rockland a rare example. One wonders how many other houses boasted similar porticoes that have been lost to the human mind or the camera lens. We probably will never know, but for visitors interested in early American architecture Rockland is well worth a brief stop between tours of Mount Pleasant and Woodford.[8]

Figure 10. Elegant, classical Rockland (c. 1810), built by George Thomson near Mount Pleasant, originally had a roof balustrade—as did Ormiston—which provided spectacular views over the Schuylkill. As at The Solitude, a large parlor occupies most of the main floor with floor-to-ceiling windows that open onto a wide piazza overlooking the river below. Both Rockland and Ormiston confined the kitchen to the basement; food would be carried up the stair to tables set up in the parlor. At The Solitude the kitchen was in a separate building with underground access to the main house.

# BELLAIR

20th Street and Pattison Avenue,
Philadelphia, PA 19145

Architect unknown, c. 1714–20s;
restored by Erling Pedersen, 1934

Owned by the City of Philadelphia, 1929;
operated by Bicentennial Women '76, Inc.

Telephone for opening days and times,
610.664.8456

⚜ The paneling of the Bellair interior is a remarkable survival, particularly in the larger of the two ground floor rooms, which has two closets, one called in the early eighteenth century a "buffet," for the display of decorative porcelains and earthenware. In 1742 the owner of Bellair kept "17 Pieces of China in the Buffet."

Most early houses erected on the edge of the marshy lowlands at the mouth of the Schuylkill River have been lost. In the eighteenth century a visitor with letters of introduction could ride south from Philadelphia, perhaps stopping for refreshment at Joseph Wharton's justly famous country house, Walnut Grove, site of the Meschianza (the famous ball given by the British Army in Philadelphia during the Revolution), and then turn west from the Delaware River across the peninsula to the banks of the Schuylkill. Where Passyunk Avenue crosses the river today there once were clustered a group of houses belonging to the colonial elite: the Cadwalader, Morris, Rambo, Cox, Lord, Penrose, and Hannis families. Some of these were attached to working farms; several were country villas. Today the only surviving Passyunk Township house from the colonial period available to the public is Bellair, which sits back from the river on a patch of high ground overlooking what once was a working farm of 142 acres. Those fields are now a municipal golf course.

The exact date of Bellair—a name it acquired in the nineteenth century—is uncertain. It probably did not exist until the decade after 1714, when the successful Quaker merchant Samuel Preston (1665–1743 ) purchased the land. In that year he became Provincial Treasurer, a post he held until his death. He also served as a trustee of William Penn's estate.

The house we see today has five bays and is built of brick, laid in Flemish bond pattern with glazed headers. It rises two and one half stories with dormers; the only windows in the house are in the southwest facade, except one on the northeast side that lights the stair hall. The plan is typical of such houses of its date: central passage, two rooms on each floor; one room deep. The most distinctive feature of the facade is a balcony above the main entrance with a small coved hood projecting above the second

floor balcony door. Such balconies are said to have been common in colonial Philadelphia, and have been reconstructed from physical evidence at Grumblethorpe in Germantown, Harriton in Bryn Mawr, and the Peter Wentz House in Montgomery County.

The interior is handsomely paneled. The stair rises from the fully paneled central passage dividing the hall and parlor. Like the hall paneling, this stair is an unexpected survival from the early eighteenth century and compares favorably with the c. 1704 stair at Harriton in Bryn Mawr. The most elaborately paneled room is the larger reception room, or hall, with raised panels, bold bolection moldings, and double-door closets on either side of the fireplace. One of these has an elaborately carved interior.

We have no idea how Preston furnished Bellair. However, he sold the farm in 1735 to Alexander Woodrop, who died in 1742 leaving an inventory of property "At his Plantation in Passyunck Township." Sparse furnishing is typical of the period, as is the use of native walnut rather than imported mahogany. The inventory is not divided by room, but we can follow the appraisers around the house, beginning in the great hall, where they found six walnut chairs, one "Corner Elbow Chair," a small walnut table, a "Japann'd square Tea Table," a dozen prints painted on glass, and a good assortment of Chinese porcelain "in the Buffet." They then went up to the bed chambers, where they found a fully furnished bed (at £4 the most expensive item in the house), a set of "Old Silk Curtains and Furniture," two walnut chairs, three old chairs, an "old fashioned Walnut Chest of Drawers," and three lesser beds. Returning to the first floor, probably to the parlor, they found a walnut couch, five old chairs, a walnut table, more prints, and a map on the wall.

❀ The southwest facades of Bellair and its kitchen building are laid in Flemish bond pattern with glazed header bricks. The second floor balcony and hood—both recreations—are distinctive features of this house erected in the early years of the eighteenth century.

# HISTORIC BARTRAM'S GARDEN

54th Street and Lindbergh Boulevard, Philadelphia, PA 19143

Builder, John Bartram, c. 1730 incorporating an earlier structure; additions c. 1765–c. 1815

National Historic Landmark, 1960

Owned by the City of Philadelphia, 1891; operated by the John Bartram Association, 1893

Telephone for opening days and times, 215.729.5281

❧ Some family estate inventories have survived to guide the refurnishing, and a few key objects with family association have been returned to the house. Most notable of these is the medicine chest (c. 1775–95)—sometimes called a "physic chest"—shown here in a bed chamber; this chest descended in the family and is attributed to John Bartram's brother James Bartram, a cabinetmaker of Chester County, Pennsylvania.

This unusual and important site includes one of the earliest house museums in America, purchased by the City of Philadelphia in 1891 as a park honoring its famous resident builder, Quaker John Bartram (1699–1777), first American-born botanist, and his son, William Bartram (1739–1823), who established America's first botanic garden there.

The elder Bartram began acquiring land on the lower Schuylkill in 1728 with an initial purchase of 112 acres to which he gradually added. Here he created a world-renowned farm and garden. Most of the land he farmed, but a few acres to the south east of the house he terraced for the cultivation of North American plants, many of which he gathered on collecting trips that ranged as far afield as Florida. Within a few years Bartram had a brisk trade in shipping roots and seeds to wealthy Englishmen. So great had his fame become by 1765 that George III appointed him Royal Botanist with an annual stipend of £50. Linnaeus called him "the greatest natural botanist in the world."

The younger Bartram continued his father's explorations in the Carolinas, Georgia, and Florida and with his brother operated the garden and nursery, shipping roots and seeds throughout the United States and Europe. Gradually they added greenhouses and increased their sale of live plants, which could be ordered from the catalogues they produced.

The house itself probably incorporates a seventeenth-century Swedish structure

🌳 The house of Quaker botanist John Bartram on the west bank of the Schuylkill River is built of local stone (Wissahickon schist), which he quarried himself and carved with rough simulations of Georgian console brackets and ionic columns.

built by Mans Jonasson which John Bartram expanded c. 1730 following his second marriage. He would later recount that he had "Split rocks, seventeen feet long, and built four houses of hewn stone split out of the rock with my own hands." By 1770 he had extended the house again, even carving decorative stone window surrounds that were probably inspired by wooden dormer console brackets found on Philadelphia Middle Georgian houses. Clearly the house owes much of its character to the unique genius of its builder and the organic evolution of its form over time, reflecting as it does additions by several generations of the Bartram family.

By the 1840s the nursery business had begun to fail, and John Bartram's descendants were forced to give up the property to the railroad entrepreneur Andrew Eastwick in 1850. He appreciated the importance of the original house and garden, but for all his early success in business his years at the site proved ill-fated. He erected a thirty-six-room Italianate villa designed by Samuel Sloan (1815–1884) on the grounds, but suffered financial reverses; the house was later destroyed by fire. Eastwick's gardener, Thomas Meehan, became a nurseryman and city councilor; he persuaded the City of Philadelphia to acquire the site. Today the house and garden are jointly operated by The John Bartram Association and the Fairmount Park Commission.

❧ A small room on the ground floor is furnished as a study with an eighteenth-century comb-back Windsor chair and American tavern table, c. 1750. On the desk is a copy of William Bartram's *Travels* (Philadelphia, 1791); on the stool is a dried Franklinia blossom, one of the exotic American plants John Bartram discovered and named for his friend Benjamin Franklin.

# THE WOODLANDS

40th Street and Woodland Avenue,
Philadelphia, PA 19104

Architect unknown, c. 1780s

National Historic Landmark, 1967

Owned by the Woodlands Cemetery
Company; operated by The Woodlands
Trust.

Telephone for opening days and times,
215.386.2181

◈ The south facade with its giant-order portico overlooks the Schuylkill, although the railroad that contributed to the destruction of so many river-front villas in the nineteenth century has disturbed the view of "the verdant mead, the spacious lawn, Schuylkill's lucid stream, the floating bridge, the waves here checked by the projecting rock, there overshadowed by the inclining trees" described in one 1809 account.

◈ The first floor plan of The Woodlands shows how the rooms flow together for entertaining large groups of guests. Notice the circular domed reception vestibule, the saloon with its apsidal ends, and the oval parlor and dining room.

Architecturally The Woodlands is one of the premier Neo-Classical residential structures of the Federal period in America. Yet it is little appreciated in Philadelphia where so many lesser houses compete for attention. Thomas Jefferson called the house and grounds "the only rival I have known in America to what may be seen in England," and the artist William Birch remarked, "it is charmingly situated on the winding Schuylkill, and commands one of the most superb water scenes that can be imagined."

William Hamilton (1745–1813), creator of The Woodlands and grandson of the Philadelphia lawyer Andrew Hamilton—who defended John Peter Zenger against the charge of seditious libel in the famous freedom of the press case of 1735—inherited the property in 1747. It then consisted of 356 acres and a "comfortable and fair sized house." He would later acquire an additional two hundred acres and expand the house. A loyalist during the Revolution, Hamilton only narrowly escaped conviction for high treason and confiscation of his property.

Prudence dictated that Hamilton maintain a low profile after the Revolution. During 1784–86 he lived in London, chiefly engaged "in viewing the best Houses." He proudly reported, "I have scarcely omitted visiting any thing . . . that I have ever heard of as worthy of notice." His correspondence strongly suggests that he approached a London architect to provide plans to expand his house, a design that totally obliterates the house he inherited. Requesting plans from an architect who never came to America would not have been unusual for a wealthy Anglo-American of the time. The British architect John Plaw designed William Bingham's town house on south Third Street in 1786, and Henry Ashley Keeble provided plans for gates and lodges for Bingham that were erected at Lansdowne in 1798.

We do know that the present house results from a building campaign that took place mainly in late 1788 and 1789. With frustration familiar to all who build in any age, Hamilton wrote of his supervisor in the fall of 1788, if he "pays so little attention to my . . . directions I must in my own defense immediately on my return give up all thoughts of removing to the Woodlands during this year of our Lord. Should that be the case, I shall as soon as I return Home discharge every workman and shut up the house until the spring."

Both the interior and exterior of the resulting house owe much to the Late Georgian Neo-Classicism associated with Robert Adam. The carefully proportioned and symmetrical exterior is set in a picturesque landscape, causing Julian Ursyn Niemcewicz to declare in 1797 that "it is the villa Borghese of Philada. Its situation is one of the most beautiful that one could see." The interior is entered through a circular domed vestibule, which provides circulation in all directions: ahead to the saloon with its apsidal ends and "French" doors opening out onto the portico overlooking the gardens and the Schuylkill beyond. To the east is the parlor, to the west the dining room, both made oval by the curving of the interior walls and floor-to-ceiling bay windows on the ends, which take maximum advantage of the views in every direction. Behind the oval rooms are two smaller square parlors that, according to one account, "may justly be called two large cabinets of gems. . . . The walls are decorated with the works of several

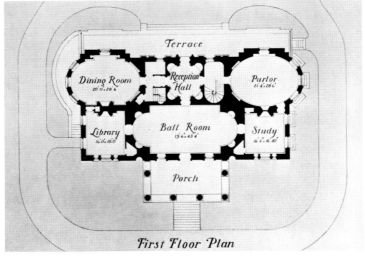

Terrace

Dining Room
20'0"x28'6"

Reception
Hall

Parlor
21'4"x28'6"

Library
16'0"x18'0"

Ball Room
19'6"x43'4"

Study
16'4"x16'10"

Porch

First Floor Plan

of the ancient painters, from the Italian, Dutch, and Flemish schools, many of which are of great merit." Niemcewicz tells us that the interior was "arranged and decorated in a style rare in America; there are pictures, medallions, bronzes, etc."

Hamilton died in 1813. His heirs and subsequent owners of The Woodlands did not maintain the garden, the greenhouse, or the villa itself. In 1840 the house and 78 acres were turned into a rural cemetery as a means of "removing the dead from the midst of the dense population of our cities, and placing them in operation with the beautiful works of nature; thus making them the means of preserving open spaces and some of the finest park scenery near our town which otherwise would be prostrated in the progress of building improvements." The cemetery company continues in operation and now encourages the careful restoration of the house and surrounding grounds. This long-term project is gradually returning William Hamilton's house to its former glory.

⚜ The domed vestibule has four statuary niches and must immediately have alerted visitors that this is something new in American architecture. Directly ahead is the grand saloon, from which three sets of "French" doors with fanlights provide access to the portico and the river views beyond. To the east is the oval parlor, to the west the oval dining room.

❧ The grand saloon with its apsidal ends. At each end are paired niches originally intended to hold a stove and a classical statue: a marble figure of Antinous at one end and a bronze Apollo in pursuit of Daphne at the other. Hamilton never finished the embellishment of this room, which he intended to be decoratively painted in the Neo-Classical style; the windows were to be hung with drapery which he purchased from the booty stripped from noble houses by the revolutionary French government for sale in America.

# SWEETBRIER

Lansdowne Avenue, Fairmount Park West, Philadelphia, PA 19131

Architect unknown, 1797; extensively damaged by fire, 1875; restored by Erling Pedersen, 1927

Owned by the City of Philadelphia, 1868; operated by The Modern Club

Telephone for opening days and times, 215.222.1333

❧ The south parlor has floor to ceiling windows and a Robert Wellford type Federal mantelpiece, and is furnished with objects on loan from the Philadelphia Museum of Art, most notably the block-front Massachusetts bureau that descended in the Breck family. All the other furniture originated in Philadelphia and is early nineteenth century. The porcelain tea set is English Spode, c. 1810.

"Sweetbrier is the name of my villa," wrote the prosperous merchant and erudite civic leader Samuel Breck (1771–1862) in 1830. It is "situated on the right bank of the Schuylkill" with a view "animated by its great trade carried on in boats of about thirty tons, drawn by horses." For more than forty years he lived in the house he commissioned in 1797. "It is a fine stone house, roughcast, fifty-three feet long, thirty-eight broad, and three stories high, having out-buildings of every kind suitable for elegance and comfort."

The land came as a gift from Breck's father-in-law, John Ross, whose estate The Grange is now a house museum discussed elsewhere. The Schuylkill site had the additional advantage of being far enough from the city to escape the terrible epidemics of yellow fever that killed thousands of Philadelphians between 1793 and 1800, but the decision to live out of town did not protect the Brecks' only child, Lucy, who died from an outbreak of typhus in 1828. Nor was Sweetbrier only a summer retreat; Breck lived there year round until 1838, when he sold the property and returned to the city.

Breck was born in Boston, educated in France, and favorably inclined toward the many French émigrés who sought safety in Philadelphia, and the cosmopolitan Breck household hummed with activity. Breck recalled, "Congress held its sessions in Phila-

✤ Samuel Breck's Federal style Sweetbrier on the west bank of the Schuylkill (1797) is stuccoed with simple quoins. The house burned in 1875 while being used as a restaurant, and the exterior has been much altered over the years. A portico probably embellished this front, and a piazza spanned the east facade overlooking the 400-foot lawn that stretched down to the river.

delphia until the year 1800, and gave to the city the style and tone of a capital. All the distinguished emigrants from France took up their abode there. The French Revolution was a paroxysm of rage . . . and kept by its fury many of the ablest sons of France abroad. I knew personally Talleyrand, Beaumais, Vicomte de Noailles, the Duc de Liancourt, Volney, and subsequently Louis Philippe . . . and his two brothers, the Ducs de Montpensier and Beaujolais." Nearby were former governor Penn's Lansdowne, John Penn's The Solitude, and Judge Peters's Belmont. The full sun of Federalism smiled on Philadelphia, the more democratic age of Jefferson and Jackson unanticipated in the future.

Ultimately Samuel Breck is remembered as a minor player in the momentous events of nation forming, but his extensive diary gives us trenchant views on the comings and goings of the movers and shakers of his age. Like William Lewis of Strawberry, Breck took advantage of his brief tenure as a Pennsylvania State Senator to introduce in 1821 a bill for the emancipation of those slaves in the state not yet free. Into his last years he bitterly opposed sectional conflict and had little patience with Southern separatists. At the age of ninety he declared at a public meeting, "I was a man when [the United States] were formed, and God forbid that I should live to witness their downfall!" He died the following year, cheering with his last strength a northern military victory—certain to the last that the Union would endure.

   &#10087;   Breck describes the main passage on the ground floor of Sweetbrier as being "a fine open space for every breeze that blows." On November 17, 1830, he records, "the weather is so sweet and there has been such an entire absence of frost to produce ice, that I gathered in the garden this morning a very pretty bouquet . . . placed in a tumbler of water."

# CEDAR GROVE

Lansdowne Avenue, Fairmount Park West, Philadelphia, PA 19131

Architect/builder unknown, c. 1748; enlarged 1798–99; moved and restored 1926–27

Owned by the City of Philadelphia, 1926; operated by the Philadelphia Museum of Art

Telephone for opening days and times, 215.684.7922

Cedar Grove is one of the oldest houses open to the public in Fairmount Park and one of the last to be erected there. Built in the mid-eighteenth century by recently widowed Elizabeth Coates Paschall as a summer retreat for herself and three children, the house stood about four miles from Philadelphia at Harrogate near Frankford. Originally a two-and-a-half-story stone farm house with gable roof and pent eaves, this modest structure served the Paschalls for two generations until inherited by Sarah Morris, wife of Isaac Wistar Morris, in the late eighteenth century. Isaac (whose brother built The Highlands, now a house museum) doubled the size of Cedar Grove and gave the expanded house a commodious gambrel roof with a large lunette window in the gable—virtually the only hint that the entire house does not date from half a century before.

On the death of Isaac Morris, Sarah regained possession of what his will calls their "annual Summer residence in the Country (called Cedar Grove)." It continued to pass down in the family virtually unaltered—except for the piazza across the north and west fronts. In 1888, however, the construction of new railroad tracks nearby made the

Cedar Grove, originally erected near Frankfort, Pennsylvania in the eighteenth century, was moved to Fairmount Park in the 1920s. Summer home of the Paschall-Morris family for five generations, it is furnished with objects that descended in the house.

The parlor of the earlier section of the house (c. 1748) is shown here set up for dining. The mahogany table (c. 1785), the swell-front sideboard (c. 1795), and the arm chair and side chairs (1760–90) all have a history of Morris ownership. The portrait in the manner of Thomas Sully is of Isaac P. Morris, who summered at Cedar Grove from 1831 to 1867. The floor covering is a painted floor cloth.

house uninhabitable, causing Lydia Thompson Morris and her brother to close it and move the two-hundred-year accumulation of family objects to their home in the Chestnut Hill section of Philadelphia. It was Lydia Morris who offered the house to the city and paid to have it taken down, re-erected in Fairmount Park, and refurnished with original family objects.

While Cedar Grove itself may be considered by some to be of modest architectural interest, the house is noteworthy for the Paschall-Morris objects kept together over so many generations. This sets Cedar Grove apart from the other Fairmount Park house museums and raises it into a special category with Wyck, Cliveden, and Andalusia—houses where original objects survive in context, a circumstance regrettably rare in America. For example, there are at Cedar Grove a high chest and dressing table made c. 1725 for Catherine Wistar of Germantown that descended in the Wistar family (they were appraised for £4 in Caspar Wistar's 1752 estate inventory) and hence to the Wistar-Morris union that brought them to Cedar Grove. Sets of "chest of drawers & table" were popular in Philadelphia from the late seventeenth century well into the eighteenth, although this is the only Philadelphia pair from the "Queen Anne Style" period known to survive. Such sets—and their more common Georgian cousins—were always bed chamber furniture. The opportunity to see objects of this quality displayed in their historic context makes a visit to Cedar Grove a particular treat for individuals interested in American decorative arts.

⊷ Elizabeth Paschall's bedroom contains some of the most important objects at Cedar Grove. The walnut side chair with its solid splat, shell-carved crest and knees, curved slip seat and "claw foot" (1750–90) sits next to the justly famous Wistar-Morris American black walnut (*Juglans nigra*) high chest and dressing table (c. 1725). The looking glass frame is c. 1790. The bed, made for Elizabeth Paschall, has sat in this location since the mid-eighteenth century.

# LEMON HILL

Kelly Drive and Sedgley Avenue,
Fairmount Park, Philadelphia, PA 19130

Architect/builder unknown, 1799–1800;
restored by Fiske Kimball, 1925–26

Owned by the City of Philadelphia, 1844;
operated by the Colonial Dames of
America, Chapter Two

Telephone for opening days and times,
215.232.4337

Lemon Hill is justifiably one of the best known Schuylkill River villas open to the public as a house museum. Erected at the very close of the eighteenth century, the house occupies a spectacular site overlooking both the river and the heart of the modern city; its Adamesque Federal architecture celebrates with restrained elegance Philadelphia's apogee as cultural center and political capital of the new nation.

The house stands on land previously owned by the financier Robert Morris (1734–1806), signer of the Declaration of Independence, who succumbed to bankruptcy brought on by real estate speculation in the years following the revolution. Here, on an estate he called The Hills, Morris built a villa and developed extensive greenhouses. This house had burned by the time the successful businessman Henry Pratt (1761–1838) purchased the land at a sheriff's sale in the Spring of 1799, but the "large & Elegant Green House with a Hot House of 50 feet Front on each side" survived and continued to be thought worthy of comment by visitors to the city. One tourist in 1829 recorded, "it is filled to overflowing with the choicest Exotics: the Chaddock Orange of different kinds & the Lemon loaded with fruit." Pratt retained the greenhouse and erected a new house for himself, which was completed in 1800.

The greenhouse and surrounding pleasure garden are gone now, casualties to decades of concessionaires who maintained a beer garden and restaurant there after the city acquired the property in 1844 to protect the Fairmount Water Works from industrial development (see pages 8–11). Porches had been erected across the main facades of the house and everything allowed to decay. All this changed in the 1920s, however, when the new Philadelphia Museum of Art was sited on the nearby water works reservoirs. Lemon Hill then became the residence of the museum's director. He happened to be the brilliant architect and historian Fiske Kimball, who renovated Lemon Hill in 1926 and occupied it for three decades (see pages 15–16).

The extraordinary architectural feature of Lemon Hill is its stack of three oval rooms, one above the other, with double-hung windows that allow access to the exterior and the view to the Schuylkill below. The ground floor oval served as dining room, the first and second floor ovals as parlors. Such high style Neo-Classical rooms were rare in America of 1800. Those in James Hoban's White House in Washington, D.C. and Charles Bulfinch's Joseph Barrell house (1792–93) in Somerville, Massachusetts are usually cited as earlier examples. Nonetheless, William Hamilton's nearby The Woodlands with its sophisticated plan of elliptical dining room and parlor, apsidal-ended saloon, and circular vestibule already reflected the Late Georgian or Adamesque taste that had become popular in Britain during the American War (see the discussion of The Woodlands, pages 78–81.)

The visitor approaches the house from the north and climbs a tall double stair to a wide double door with sidelights and a fanlight reminiscent in scale to the slightly earlier, London-made example at Physick House. The interior is plain but satisfying. The front passage—again like that in the Physick House—has a gray and white checkered marble floor leading to the first floor oval parlor with its curved mahogany doors

⊛ Successful businessman Henry Pratt commissioned Lemon Hill in 1799. Its Federal simplicity is relieved on the north facade by a wide entrance with sidelights and fanlight. The second floor Palladian window is probably both old-fashioned and oversized, but from the interior it provides one of the most appealing features of the house. The double stair that ascends to the main floor is a successful creation of Fiske Kimball, who renovated the house in 1926.

⊛ The floor plan of Lemon Hill shows the oval parlor that is echoed on the other two floors. This stack of oval rooms is one of the earliest American examples of such a high style Neo-Classical design.

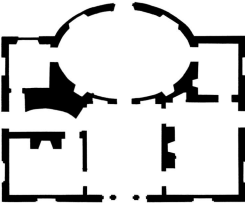

❦ The "Palladian Hall," so named in modern times for the dramatic window of that type that admits light to the second floor passage, is shown here furnished as a sitting area with American-made furniture: mahogany bookcase, c. 1800, maple settee, c. 1820, and piano by the New York maker John Geib, Jr., c. 1815.

and mantels. If decorative plaster ceilings ever existed at Lemon Hill, they have been lost; their absence in a house of this period is a genuine disappointment. To the east an elegant winding stair with statuary niche ascends to the second floor, where the passage over the entrance is dramatically lit by a tall Palladian window. But unlike that in nearby Mount Pleasant, the Palladian window rests directly on the floor to provide maximum light and a view of the garden below—even when the viewer is standing at a distance from the window. The effect is dramatic and gives a great illusion of space.

The property is managed by the Colonial Dames of America, Chapter Two, and is furnished with Federal-period fine and decorative arts belonging to that society or on loan from the Philadelphia Museum of Art and other institutions. These include a few objects known to have been owned by Henry Pratt.

The first floor oval parlor is furnished with Federal-style American objects arranged in formal fashion around the walls. The mahogany doors and fireplace mantels are curved to follow the line of the walls. The portraits are of Judge John K. Kane and Jane Leiper Kane, both painted by Thomas Sully, c. 1832. The carpet is a modern reproduction laid wall-to-wall as would have been typical in a high style house of the time.

# MOUNT PLEASANT

Mount Pleasant Drive, Fairmount Park East, Philadelphia, PA 19121

Thomas Nevell, Master Builder, 1763–65; restored 1926, 1976

National Historic Landmark

Owned by the City of Philadelphia, 1869

Telephone for opening days and times, 215.684.7922

Captain John Macpherson is one of those colorful figures of colonial America so beloved by authors of historical fiction. A native of Edinburgh who turned to the sea, Macpherson appears in Philadelphia at the height of the bitterly contested French and Indian War (1755–63), which pitted the French and Spanish, their North American colonies, and their Indian allies against the British, their American colonies, and their Indian allies. Assuming command of the 20-gun privateer *Britannia*, he captured several rich prizes and in the process lost an arm, suffered nine other wounds, and made a fortune—all in the course of two years. Then he retired and began investing his profits in Philadelphia real estate.

But the prospect of rich pickings in the French and Spanish West Indies proved too great a temptation. Macpherson returned to sea in 1760–62, capturing several more prizes. In 1761, having determined to establish himself as a man of prominence in his adopted city, Macpherson acquired two tracts of land overlooking the east bank of the Schuylkill River a short ride from the city. With the war concluded by the Treaty of Paris (February 10, 1763), he was ready to create an appropriate expression of his new wealth—if not social position. As architect he selected master builder Thomas Nevell (1721–1797), who would give him one of the premier Middle Georgian country houses of the region. John Adams describe the result as "the most elegant seat in Pennsylvania."

Nevell had been trained by Edmund Woolley, builder of Independence Hall, and having proved himself "an ingenious House Carpenter" became one of a group of talented contemporaries—including Benjamin Loxley, Gunning Bedford, and Robert Smith—who were leading members of the Carpenters' Company. With drafting board skills and familiarity with Middle Georgian Style architectural pattern books, Nevell would later found Philadelphia's first school of architectural drawing, thereby becoming an important link in the succession of high style British design in the city. On July 27, 1763 Nevell recorded in his account book under Captain Macpherson's name: "one Jeniral plan for all The Buildings at [the] plantation," for which he charged one pound, and "two difrant plans & Elivations for his Country Seat," at six pounds. By September Nevell had charged Macpherson for the centerings to complete the distinctive chimneys at Mount Pleasant, and on March 23, 1764 he records that Robert Smith and John Thornhill had valued his work on the Schuylkill frontispiece at twenty-five pounds. The Macpherson family appears to have occupied the house in May 1765, when Nevell charged eight shillings for "hanging 4 Luking glasses."

Mount Pleasant is the best surviving example of Philadelphia's Middle Georgian country houses of the 1760s. Here we are fortunate; it may also be the best that ever was—and it exists largely unchanged. Its contemporary twin, Port Royal, built for Edward Stiles (c. 1765), has been dismantled and the remaining bits incorporated into Winterthur Museum. Benjamin Chew's Cliveden in Germantown (c. 1763–67) happily survives and will be discussed elsewhere, as will nearby Woodford, which is included in this group because of its later additions. What sets these houses apart is the application of Palladian design principles and vocabulary, particularly the geometri-

cally precise adherence to symmetry and proportion, as articulated by British archi-tects and conveyed to America largely through architectural books and builder's guides.

The role of architectural pattern books in shaping Middle Georgian Philadelphia taste is dramatically obvious at Mount Pleasant. Just as Macpherson was moving into his new house, he sold Nevell a copy of Abraham Swan's *A Collection of Designs in Architecture* (London, 1757) which illustrates simple five-bay Palladian facades with

The east front of Mount Pleasant demonstrates the symmetry, proportion, and decorative vocabulary of Philadelphia architecture of the Middle Georgian Style. Master builder Thomas Nevell designed and erected the house for the successful French and Indian War privateer Captain John Macpherson (1763–65).

The second floor passage is pure architecture. As in the drawing room, a false door balances the opposite one that enters a chamber. The Palladian, or Venetian window is duplicated at the other end, flooding the space with light in both morning and afternoon while providing a free flow of cooler country air in the sultry Philadelphia summers.

Nevell's crew completed the "Drawing Room" in November, 1764; it runs the full depth of the ground floor. This view looks east and shows the false doors installed to balance the passageway doors on the opposite wall. The portrait attributed to John Trumbull is of Macpherson's son Major John Macpherson, who died in the attack on Quebec during the American Revolution. Both the slip-covered mahogany camel-back sofa in the foreground and the mahogany desk and bookcase between the windows originated in Philadelphia, 1760–90.

The great chamber on the second floor overlooks the garden and the Schuylkill below and has been furnished as a sitting room. This is the most lavishly decorated room in the house, with "buffets" for the display of porcelain that are surmounted by interrupted pediments. The carving generally follows the *rocaille* taste advocated by Abraham Swan. The portrait hanging on the richly carved chimney breast is of Mary Keen (1730–1767). The extraordinary mahogany library bookcase is based on one illustrated in Thomas Chippendale's *The Gentleman and Cabinet-maker's Directory* and may be from the shop of "the ingenious John Folwell."

hipped roofs, dentil cornices, quoins defining corners, and centered projecting pavilions—some with Doric-order pitched pediment frontispieces with fanlights—surmounted by Palladian windows (see illustrated glossary, page 222). Had a hands-on client and his practical architect/builder put their heads together over Swan's *Designs* and brought forth Mount Pleasant? And had the builder said he'd like his own copy? We'll never know for certain, but the possibility seems plausible.

All that said, Mount Pleasant is not merely a pattern book knock-off ; nowhere does Swan suggest the massive cluster of arched chimneys or the modified bell roof lines of the flanking service buildings that Nevell calls "Pavilions." The entire composition has a tight, broad-shouldered, self-assured symmetry, but the details—dormer shape and the lack of a raised brick frame around the windows, and much of the interior carved woodwork, for instance—follow Philadelphia practice rather than slavishly mimicking British pattern books.

The fates that protected Macpherson on the quarter deck deserted him ashore. He and his wife became estranged, she died in 1771, and his first-born son fell in battle during the American attack on Quebec in the early days of the Revolution. He was resident at Mount Pleasant off and on during this period, but mostly he leased the house to others and in 1779 sold it to General Benedict Arnold, military governor of Philadelphia after the British evacuation. Arnold and his new wife, Peggy Shippen, probably didn't live there before his attainder for treason. In 1791 General Jonathan Williams purchased Mount Pleasant at a sheriff's sale; his family lived there until the City of Philadelphia acquired the property in 1869.

# LAUREL HILL

Edgeley Drive and Fairmount Avenue,
Fairmount Park, Philadelphia, PA 19121

Architect unknown, c. 1767 with later
additions; rehabilitated 1901, 1976

Owned by the City of Philadelphia, 1869;
operated by Women for Greater
Philadelphia

Telephone for opening days and times,
215.235.1776 or 215.627.1770

❧ The octagonal room occupies the entire
ground floor of the addition built after
Philip Syng Physick's daughter, Sarah
Randolph, inherited Laurel Hill in 1837. The
piano forte in the foreground is by John
Broadwood & Son, London, 1808; the
portrait is of William Rawle after Henry
Inman.

Not all houses erected along the banks of the Schuylkill in the eighteenth century
exude the self-conscious pretension of Mount Pleasant, Lansdowne, or Belmont,
whose owners also maintained city houses but probably viewed their country estates as
year around "seats." More typical of the seasonal retreats is a group of east bank houses
like The Cliffs (c. 1753; destroyed), Woodford (c. 1756), and Laurel Hill (c. 1767).
The basic form of this group is a two-story, three-bay symmetrical facade, with hipped
roof and raised basement.

Laurel Hill is architecturally interesting because it reflects the Middle Georgian
influence of nearby Mount Pleasant applied to what is otherwise a modest (22′ × 32′)
three-bay vernacular villa. The dentil cornice and projecting pedimented pavilion with
pedimented frontispiece of Mount Pleasant and Port Royal are here executed in less
monumental scale. The house we see today is the result of three building campaigns:
the central block of the original house erected after 1767, the single-story addition to
the east that appears c. 1800, and the two-story octagonal wing after 1837.

Rebecca Rawle and her second husband, Samuel Shoemaker, erected the central
section of Laurel Hill at the time of their marriage in 1767. She had inherited the land
from her first husband, Francis Rawle, who purchased the vacant 31 acres in 1760, a
year before he died in a hunting accident. Samuel Shoemaker (1725–1800), success-

ful Quaker merchant and civic leader, served as councilman, alderman, mayor, and representative to the Provincial Assembly. When revolution descended on the city, Shoemaker remained loyal to the Crown, serving in the civil government appointed by Sir William Howe during the occupation. When the British army evacuated in 1778, Shoemaker and other prominent loyalists fled for their lives. The Americans confiscated Shoemaker's property—including his life rights to his wife's property at Laurel Hill—and eventually sold them to Major James Parr. Rebecca Shoemaker reacquired the house and land from him after the Treaty of Paris (1783) that recognized the independence of the United States. The Rawle-Shoemaker family owned the property until 1828, when it was sold by William Rawle to Philip Syng Physick, whose daughter in turn sold Laurel Hill to the City of Philadelphia in 1869. After being used for several decades by Fairmount Park as employee housing, Laurel Hill was leased to the Colonial Dames of America, Chapter Two, in 1901; they renovated the house and for several years made it available for visitors—probably the first attempt at a house museum in Fairmount Park. In 1976 Women for Greater Philadelphia reopened the house.

❧ The main facade of Laurel Hill reflects three building campaigns: the Middle Georgian central block erected c. 1767, the one-story wing added c. 1800, and the octagonal, two-story wing erected after 1837.

# WOODFORD

33rd and Dauphin Streets, Fairmount Park East, Philadelphia, PA 19132

Architect unknown, c. 1756–59, 1772; restored by John P. B. Sinkler, FAIA, 1927–30

National Historic Landmark, 1967

Owned by the City of Philadelphia, 1869; operated by the Naomi Wood Trust

Telephone for opening days and times, 215.229.6115

In 1769 the owner of Woodford insured his "Country Seat . . . about 4 miles from this city" for £350. The house, described as being " about 10 years old . . . one story high . . . raised about 4 feet & half from the ground" with "stone steps at the front door & Tuscan frontispiece" appears to have been a typical vernacular, hipped-roof, three-bay Philadelphia house over a raised basement in the Early Georgian style. It was probably erected in the 1750s for William Coleman, the civic leader and sometime judge of whom Benjamin Franklin said, "he had the coolest, clearest head, the best heart, and the exactest morals of almost any man I ever met with."

Coleman died in 1769 and his estate sold the "Country Seat" and twelve acres to Alexander Barclay, comptroller for the port of Philadelphia; he died in 1771, bequeathing Woodford to his wife's sister and her husband, David Franks. The Frankses

❧ The main facade of Woodford (c. 1750s) assumed its present Middle Georgian appearance after the addition of a second floor in 1772. The house has been used to exhibit the Naomi Wood Collection of early American fine and decorative arts since 1930.

❧ The "neatly finished . . . Tabernacle frame pediment mantle" in the drawing room survives unchanged from the 1750s and greatly contributes to the display of exceptional Philadelphia-area objects from the 1760–90 period, particularly the mahogany desk and bookcase (attributed to John Elliott), camel-back sofa, and tea table.

needed more space for their large family and promptly raised the roof at Woodford to add another floor. To reinsure the house they called in Gunning Bedford from the Contributionship for the Insurance of Houses from Loss by Fire. His description discusses the new second story with "a way out on Roof" with balustrade, modillion cornice, and the frontispiece, now with a "venision [Venetian] window over it." That the Frankses would have updated their house with Middle Georgian Palladian vocabulary is not surprising; the premier Philadelphia example in that style (Mount Pleasant) and a modest vernacular house already tricked out with similar embellishments (Laurel Hill) were nearby to provide inspiration.

David Franks remained loyal to the Crown during the Revolution. Like Samuel Shoemaker of Laurel Hill, he fled, first to New York and then to London, and was forced to sell Woodford at a loss. Eventually Woodford came into the hands of the Wharton family, who sold it to the City of Philadelphia in 1869. For many years Fairmount Park used the house as the headquarters for Park guards until approached in 1927 by the estate of Naomi Wood (1871–1926) with an offer to restore the house to house Miss Wood's collection of American decorative arts. It has been so used since 1930 and is well worth visiting for both the house and the collection.

☙　The parlor is arranged as a dining room to display Federal objects of the 1790–1810 period. The mahogany shelf clock on the Philadelphia bureau is from the shop of Abner Jones of Weare, New Hampshire. Over the American liquor chest-on-frame is a New England inlaid mahogany pipe and tobacco box. Four of the side chairs with vase backs were sold by the Philadelphia cabinetmaker Jacob Wayne, 1796, for which the bill of sale survives.

# STRAWBERRY MANSION

33rd and Dauphin Streets, Fairmount Park East, Philadelphia, PA 19132

Architect unknown, 1788–89, incorporating an earlier structure; wings, c. 1821–32; restored by Erling Pedersen, 1930–31

Owned by the City of Philadelphia, 1867; operated by the Committee of 1926, opened to the public 1931

Telephone for opening days and times, 215.228.8364

✤  The wings added by Joseph Hemphill have massive Neo-Classical crests with carved brackets.

In the 1860s the City of Philadelphia purchased one by one the elegant country seats and villas along the banks of the Schuylkill, adding them to Fairmount Park. Some existing buildings the city demolished; others sheltered Park employees or provided amenities for urban dwellers who flocked to the Park in ever-increasing numbers as the grid of densely populated streets marched northward along Ridge Avenue. Strawberry's fate included use as a restaurant serving chicken dinners and ice cream with strawberries. A city family could journey up the river by steamboat and disembark at Strawberry landing for an outing in the sun and fresh air; in later years a trolley provided similar access for even less cost.

A century earlier Strawberry—or Summerville as then known—had been the private retreat of William Lewis (1751–1819), a bright light of the Philadelphia bar thrust into early prominence by the loss of so many elder statesmen who sided with the Crown during the American Revolution. Staunchly in favor of independence, he nonetheless defended Quakers and other non-jurors accused of treason for failure to renounce George III and pledge allegiance to the revolutionary Pennsylvania government. His most important accomplishment came in March 1780, with the passage of an act he had drafted "for the Gradual Abolition of Slavery in Pennsylvania," the first such law in the United States. A firmly committed abolitionist, Lewis served for many years as counsel for the Pennsylvania Society for the Abolition of Slavery, and worked openly to protect the civil liberties of free African Americans.

Summerville reflects an even more complex building history than its near neighbors Laurel Hill and Woodford. The first house on the site, probably a three-bay stone farm house erected by William Coxe in the 1750s, passed to William Lewis in 1783; he

❀   The five-bay center section of Strawberry Mansion is William Lewis's Summerville (1788–89), which incorporates an earlier farm house. The overwhelming wings were added by Joseph Hemphill (c. 1821–32), who greatly expanded the house to permit large-scale entertaining.

🌳 The entire ground floor of one Hemphill wing is occupied by a formal reception room in high Neo-Classical style. Here is exhibited a suite of late Neo-Classical gilded furniture in the Restoration style that became popular in the reign of Charles X and the early years of Louis Philippe. It was made in Paris for Philadelphian George Cadwalader, c. 1835, and is an extraordinary survival.

then extended the house and thereby created the center section of what we see today (1788–89). From the exterior Summerville seems untouched by Georgian sophistication; and some images even suggest that there was a lean-to porch across the entire front that may date from the Lewis period. Inside, however, Lewis added a central passage with four statuary niches defined by reeded and carved Federal woodwork, in which he probably kept the four portrait busts known to have been in his estate. Off either side of this passage are double doors with fanlights that open into reception rooms; these had mantels with applied decoration in the Late Georgian or Federal style. After Lewis's death the property passed to U. S. Representative Joseph Hemphill (1770–1842), who added the overwhelming three-story Neo-Classical wings to meet the needs of his lavish entertaining. During the subsequent century Strawberry gradually declined. Hemphill became insolvent, and subsequent absentee owners leased the property until it became a part of Fairmount Park—the resort of day-tripping picnickers.

The Sesquicentennial of 1926 ultimately proved to be the salvation of Strawberry. Following that celebration, Fiske Kimball, Director of the Philadelphia Museum of Art, suggested to Elizabeth Price Martin, head of the Women's Sesquicentennial Committee, that the ladies turn their attention "to secure an unrivaled permanent display of Colonial things in a chain of the old mansions of Fairmount Park." Strawberry Mansion offered a site of sufficient scale to permit the Committee not only to renovate the house, but to furnish several period rooms with appropriate decorative arts. Their objective has not been to restore the Lewis or Hemphill interior, but to create a sympathetic setting for the display of fine and decorative arts assembled by the Committee in the subsequent decades.

Four houses on the east bank of the Schuylkill are particularly important for their decorative arts exhibitions, and all might be visited in a single day: Mount Pleasant, Woodford, Lemon Hill, and, of course, Strawberry Mansion. These supplement the extraordinary decorative arts holdings of the Philadelphia Museum of Art and realize Fiske Kimball's concept of period settings in original context. As discussed elsewhere, the west bank of the Schuylkill offers similar opportunities. (For a discussion of Fiske Kimball and the Fairmount Park houses, see pages 15–16.)

❧ The cross passage created by William Lewis (whose portrait hangs over the parlor fireplace) has Federal woodwork, including four wall niches for portrait busts or other figures.

# GERMANTOWN

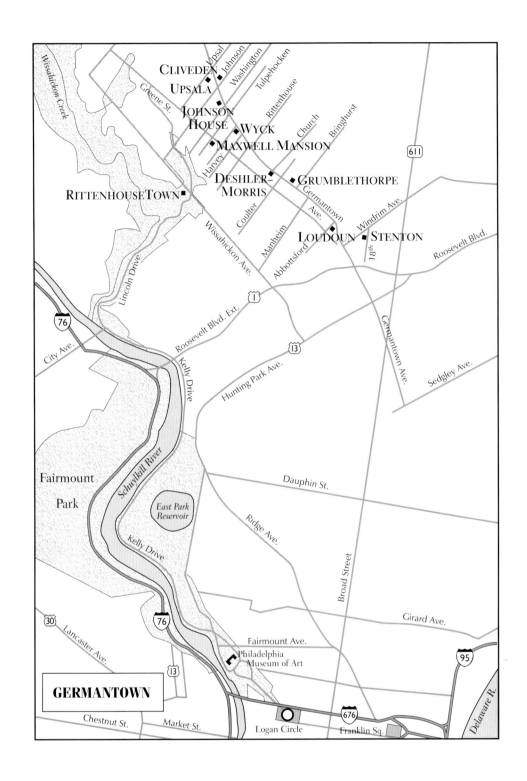

❧ Upsala. The Johnson family has returned many objects to Upsala, including the c. 1790 mahogany dining table, one end of which is here stored in the main passage as it might have been in the early nineteenth century and a tall-case clock by the Irish maker James Gordon of Ballymoney (1824). See page 122.

The Swedish naturalist Peter Kalm records visiting what is now the Germantown section of Philadelphia in the mid-eighteenth century. "After a ride of six English miles we came to Germantown; this settlement has only one street but is nearly two English miles long. It is for the greatest part inhabited by Germans, who come from their country to North America and settle here because they enjoy such privileges as they are not possessed of anywhere else." The first settlers of Germantown consisted of a small group of Rhindlander pietists from Krefeld, a town between Dusseldorf and the Netherlands border, who had been proselytized by English Quakers and attracted to Pennsylvania by William Penn's liberal religious policies. They arrived in 1683 and immediately began settling in the "German Township," a tract of land north of Philadelphia granted by Penn that ultimately amounted to 5,700 acres. By 1690 the population was 175 "of whom all but eight or ten were Dutch," a circumstance that would gradually change over the next century.[1]

In fact, by the time Kalm described Germantown, English-speaking residents probably amounted to half the population. When Germantown Academy opened in 1761, English-speaking students outnumbered the German-speaking ones, and by 1809 classes taught exclusively in German had been eliminated. The first Germantown English-language newspaper began publication in 1830; two years later the Philadelphia, Germantown & Norristown Railroad connected Germantown to Philadelphia; and the establishment of steam-driven textile mills in the later decades of the nineteenth century brought thousands of English-speaking mill workers to the community. The railroad—extended to Chestnut Hill in 1854—proved to be the most significant of these changes; it effectively made Germantown a Philadelphia suburb accessible to the newly wealthy mercantile class, for whom former farms were subdivided into building lots. As Sidney George Fisher remarked, the houses built on these lots are "in every variety of taste and size. . . . They are the results of railroads which enable anyone to enjoy . . . ventilation, clean lines, space, healthful pursuits, and the influences of natural beauty, the want of which are the sources of so much evil, moral and physical, in large towns."[2]

The influence of Anglo-Georgian architecture, as we shall see in the following pages, also began to have an impact on traditional Germanic forms in the mid-eighteenth century, as wealthy Philadelphians began to summer at the higher elevation of Germantown. Chief Justice William Allen, for example, whose house called Mount Airy lives on in name only, summered in Germantown in the 1750s, and a decade later Benjamin Chew built **Cliveden** after spending a summer at Mount Airy. Not only did Philadelphians find the air cooler in Germantown, but those who would escape the scourge of yellow fever sought safety there, and many villas appeared in the waning years of the eighteenth century.

One of the most important of these is Loudoun, erected for Thomas W. Armat in 1800 by the builders Peter L. Berry and John Ardis. In 1846 Anna Armat married

Cliveden. A pier glass attributed to James Reynolds, c. 1770, hangs above a serpentine-front chest of drawers by the Philadelphia cabinetmaker Jonathan Gostelowe (1774–1795). The red leather-covered "back stool" is one of a set attributed to Thomas Affleck and believed to have been part of the furniture made for Governor John Penn. There are nine of these at Cliveden. See page 116.

Gustavus G. Logan, who was descended from James Logan of Stenton and John Dickinson, thus bringing to Loudoun furniture and paintings with extraordinary provenance and importance to the history of Philadelphia. Their daughter, Maria Dickinson Logan, died in 1939 and bequeathed Loudoun, its contents, and an operating endowment to the City of Philadelphia in memory of her mother. Loudoun had everything: a distinguished history, architectural integrity, and the undisturbed accumulation of several generations of the same prominent and prosperous family. But tragedy struck. Just after this book had been launched—and a photographic session at Loudoun scheduled—a bolt of lightning set the house afire. While the flames raged through the 200-year-old tinder-dry attic rafters, volunteers moved first floor contents out onto the lawn; what could not be removed suffered extensive smoke and water damage. As of this writing, efforts are underway to reopen Loudoun, but for the time being the public is deprived of a much admired Germantown house museum.[3]

**Getting to Germantown.** The modern visitor can approach the ten house museums of Germantown via bus by traveling north from City Hall on Broad Street, then northwest along Germantown Avenue, arriving first at **Stenton** (a few blocks north east on Windrim Street) and hence on up to **Upsala** and **Cliveden**. It is also possible—but not recommended except for the extremely hardy—to take a train to Wayne Junction station, which is near Stenton, and then walk *uphill* for more than two miles, returning to center city by train from the Upsal Station.

The most agreeable and flexible approach to Germantown is by private automobile, beginning at the Philadelphia Museum of Art and following Kelly Drive along the east bank of the Schuylkill River through Fairmount Park to the point where it intersects Lincoln Drive, which winds along Wissahickon Creek through some of the most beautiful scenery in Philadelphia. Just before you exit the Park the restored structures of **RittenhouseTown** will appear on the left (northwest) side, where you will want to visit the only surviving early German stone houses of the type once common in the area. Just after Lincoln Drive leaves the Park you turn right (northeast) on Johnson Street, which intersects Germantown Avenue one city block below **Cliveden** and **Upsala**. From this point you can begin working your way down Germantown Avenue to the **Johnson House**, with a highly recommended detour on Tulpehocken Street to see **Maxwell Mansion**, and then return to Germantown Avenue for **Wyck**, the **Deshler-Morris House**, **Grumblethorpe**, **Loudoun** (if it has been reopened), and then **Stenton**, for which a slight detour on Windrim Street will be required. From Stenton, pick up U.S. Route 1 (Roosevelt Boulevard) back to Kelly Drive or cross the Schuylkill to the Expressway (I 76) back into Center City or northwest to the Pennsylvania Turnpike.

All these houses—plus a stop at the Germantown Historical Society near the Deshler-Morris house—will obviously require more than one day, even for the most dedicated pilgrim. It would be wise to select the houses you most want to see and visit them first, back-tracking to others as time allows. Keep in mind that you will be visiting houses that in several instances are furnished with original family objects that deserve more than a quick walk through, and virtually all the Germantown houses have important museum collections for persons with interest in decorative arts as well as architecture. (Also remember to check on opening days and hours; not all houses have the same schedule.)

Fortunately there are several attractive places for lunch or dinner in Chestnut Hill, which sits astride Germantown Avenue approximately two miles north of Cliveden, and if a member of your party has limited capacity for an entire day of house museums, Chestnut Hill also offers a wide range of interesting shops worthy of a morning or afternoon stroll.

# RITTENHOUSETOWN

206–207 Lincoln Drive, Philadelphia, PA 19144

Architects/builders unknown, c.1690s–c.1720

National Historic Landmark

Owned by the City of Philadelphia, 1891; operated by the Friends of RittenhouseTown

Telephone for opening days and times, 215.438.5711

RittenhouseTown grew up around the mill of William Rittenhouse (1644–1708), who migrated to Philadelphia from Holland with his wife and children in the mid-1680s to found (on September 29, 1690) the first papermaking business in British North America. This was a capital intensive activity, and Rittenhouse went into partnership with William Bradford, the only printer in Philadelphia and a logical consumer of his paper, and two others. They leased twenty acres in the picturesque, steep valley of Monoshone Creek near the intersection of modern Lincoln Drive and Wissahickon Avenue. Of the approximately forty structures erected on the site between 1690 and 1891, seven buildings remain.

Architecturally, much of the appeal of RittenhouseTown is the opportunity to experience the only early eighteenth-century complex of German buildings surviving in Philadelphia. In the early nineteenth century such buildings existed in large numbers in Germantown, but virtually all of these have been demolished or altered beyond recognition. Fortunately, John Fanning Watson has left us in his *Annals* an account from his observations in the 1820s: "Most of the old houses in Germantown," he wrote, "are plastered on the inside with clay and straw mixed, and over it is laid a finishing coat of thin lime plaster. . . . They are but one story, so low that a man six feet high can readily touch the eaves of the roof. Their gable ends are to the street. The ground story is of stone or of logs—or sometimes the front room is of stone, and the back room is of logs, and thus they have generally one room behind the other. The roof is high and mostly *hipped*, forms a low bed chamber; the *ends* of the houses *above* the first story are of boards or sometimes of shingles, with a small chamber window at each end. Many roofs were then tiled."

Several of the earlier structures that have survived share high roofs, clay-straw insulation, casement windows, corner chimneys, informal interior plans, and asymmetrical window placement. Unfortunately, many of these characteristics of late medieval German construction have been concealed by later construction in the nineteenth century, when the mills converted from paper to textiles. Gradually, as mills came to depend less on water power, the RittenhouseTown mills declined. In the 1880s and 1890s the land became part of Fairmount Park. The Park Commission demolished the mills but preserved the older houses that had sheltered the Rittenhouse family for nearly two hundred years. During the Bicentennial two of the houses were restored and opened to the public, and the Friends of Historic RittenhouseTown now continue the restoration and interpretation.

For visitors headed to the house museums of Germantown via Kelly Drive, Wissahickon Drive, and Lincoln Drive, a preliminary stop at RittenhouseTown is directly on the route and will help introduce one of the most historically rich neighborhoods in Philadelphia.

✿   The rural setting of RittenhouseTown, a German paper mill town founded by the Rittenhouse family in
1690, is preserved by the surrounding Fairmount Park; it introduces modern visitors to the architecture
of the earliest Germantown settlers.

# CLIVEDEN

6401 Germantown Avenue, Philadelphia, PA 19144

Design attributed to Benjamin Chew and William Peters, 1763–67

National Historic Landmark, 1962

Owned by the National Trust for Historic Preservation, 1972; operated by Cliveden, Inc.

Telephone for opening days and times, 215.848.1777

The Treaty of Paris ended the French and Indian War in 1763. The French no longer threatened from Canada; the commerce of Britain's loyal colonies flourished; the thunderclouds of revolutionary discontent rumbled so softly in the distance that few could hear their ominous warning. On the Schuylkill River during that summer of peace, retired privateer John Macpherson began a grand Palladian house. And in Germantown Benjamin and Elizabeth Chew with their children enjoyed the loan of William Allen's country house, Mount Airy, while the Chief Justice journeyed to London. So smitten were the Chews by the neighborhood—and so concerned by the outbreak of yellow fever in Philadelphia the previous summer—that they purchased eleven acres on the east side of Germantown road for £650. Allen wrote to them, "it gives me pleasure to hear that your abode [at Mount Airy] contributed to your heath and that you are like to build and be my neighbor."

Benjamin Chew (1722–1810), a Maryland-born lawyer sent to Philadelphia to read law with Andrew Hamilton, spent a year at Middle Temple in London, and on returning to Philadelphia eventually became the Penn family lawyer, attorney general, and Chief Justice of the Supreme Court. At the age of forty and about to build a country house, Chew had solidly established himself among the Philadelphia elite. A lucrative law practice, salaries from his official positions, and income from inherited farms in Maryland and Delaware provided well for his growing family.

Chew's first wife, Mary Galloway, with whom he had four daughters, died young. Two years later he married Elizabeth Oswald, who would bear him two sons and seven more daughters. The Chews' new house would be filled with young children for the first decade of its existence—all attended by ten servants who moved seasonally back and forth between their elegant Philadelphia town house next to Samuel Powel's on south Third Street and the more informally furnished country house in Germantown. This pattern continued with the second generation of Chews at Cliveden, and some insight into the Philadelphia practice of moving furniture with the family comes from a surviving letter of instruction: "I have said nothing in my mem[orandum] about chairs, it seems hardly worth while to move the mahogany but you know, we have ten here. All the Windsor had best come. The other East India Sofa too. It will help out the be[st] parlor. . . . We do not want Tables except from the Nursery."

Like Macpherson, Chew had set out to build a Middle Georgian house that followed Palladian design principles and vocabulary, particularly the geometrically precise adherence to symmetry and proportion, as conveyed to America largely through architectural books and builder's guides. Whether Chew drew the plans—perhaps with the help of his friend William Peters of Belmont—or revised the suggestions of his master mason (John Hesser) or master carpenter (Jacob Knor) can only be a source of speculation. The surviving drawings are unsigned and clearly illustrate the evolution and gradual simplification of a five-bay Palladian facade with dentil cornice and pedimented projecting pavilion with pitched-pediment frontispiece.

Cliveden is less fully developed in execution than Mount Pleasant and Port Royal, however; it has a gable roof and consequently no balustraded roof deck, and there is no

For most of its history the handsome Middle Georgian country house of Chief Justice Benjamin Chew (erected 1763–67) remained in family hands. It was acquired by the National Trust for Historic Preservation in 1972. Because of its architectural significance, historical associations, quality of surviving decorative arts, and continuity of ownership, Cliveden is one of the premier house museums in America.

Palladian window centered over the door in the shallowly projecting pavilion. Cliveden also seems less formal because the main facade is exposed stone, laid in courses of almost perfect regularity, and not stuccoed and scored. (The gable ends and rear wall are constructed of rubble stone stuccoed and scored to simulate blocks of cut stone.) Chew's blending of Palladian formality with well-established Germantown building practices may relate to his often quoted remark about the "plainness of my building." But then Chew adds back two Palladian attributes rarely found elsewhere in Philadelphia: five large, imported urns on the roof and a semicircular colonnade (the latter added in 1776, enclosed in the mid-nineteenth century) that joins the pedimented kitchen dependency to the main house. (The three-and-one-half-story Middle Georgian Jacob Duche Mansion, erected c. 1764–68 on the east side of south Third Street, supported *six* urns, but it is impossible now to determine which house was so embellished first. The house was demolished c. 1819–23.) Curiously, Chew does not construct a similar colonnade to the flanking laundry dependency—a clear violation of Palladian orthodoxy that today detracts not at all from our enjoyment of the house.

The interior plan also follows Middle Georgian pattern books. The large reception hall separated by a screen of columns and four other rooms on a ground floor appears

One of the small rooms off the entrance hall, seen here through its pedimented doorway, is interpreted as Mrs. Chew's sitting room, or "cabinet." The room is dominated by a mahogany desk and bookcase, 1765–90.

The main hall of Cliveden features an impressive screen of columns through which visitors must pass to reach the parlor on the right or the parlor/dining room on the left. Jacob Knor, Chew's master carpenter, called this the "Dorick Intablature." The portraits are of Joseph Turner (1701–1783) and his niece Margaret Oswald, sister of the second Mrs. Benjamin Chew. The handsome Philadelphia lyre-base mahogany tables beneath the portraits date from c. 1810. The guns are a Colonial Revival touch that recalls the Battle of Germantown, October 4, 1777.

in Abraham Swan's *A Collection of Designs in Architecture* (London, 1757), the reputed source for Mount Pleasant. On either side of this hall are small rooms or cabinets; behind the screen of columns are the stairs and passage to the back door, the formal parlor, and the dining room. In the mid-19th century the house was extended by an addition reached through the former back door—and a window on the half-pace landing of the stair which became a door—and the colonnade leading from the dining room to the kitchen dependency was enclosed. Otherwise the plan remains much as it was in the 1760s.

The Chews enjoyed Cliveden for a decade before the full fury of the American Revolution appeared out of the early morning fog on October 4, 1777, in the person of General George Washington and the Continental Army advancing down the Germantown road (the "Great Road") to engage the British. Falling back from the Americans, several companies of the British 40th Regiment turned the house into a fortified position from which they could not be dislodged, greatly contributing to the failure of Washington's attack. The Valley Forge encampment followed.

Returning to Philadelphia after the British withdrawal, Benjamin Chew visited his devastated country house. "I would retire to Cliveden for a time if it was habitable," he wrote in the summer of 1778. "At present it is an absolute wreck, and materials are not to be had to keep out the weather." Thus discouraged, he sold the property in 1779, only to reconsider his action and repurchase Cliveden in 1797. For the next 175 years the Chew descendants maintained the house, gradually consolidating there objects from other family properties, each generation—especially in the years following the Centennial of 1876—thus embellishing the palpable sense of continuity and history that makes Cliveden a popular historic site with visitors today.

The parlor contains several pieces of important Chew furniture, most of which came to Cliveden from the city house. The mahogany sofa attributed to the Edinburgh and London-trained cabinetmaker Thomas Affleck (1740–1795), thought to have been made for Governor John Penn, c. 1765, is the most famous object in the house. The armchair is also attributed to Affleck. Over the sofa and to the right of the fireplace hang looking glasses from the Philadelphia shop of James Reynolds, c. 1771. The painting surrounded by the tabernacle frame over the fireplace depicts the siege of Cliveden; it is a recent acquisition.

# UPSALA

6430 Germantown Avenue, Philadelphia,
PA 19144

Architect unknown, 1798; restored by
George C. Johnson, AIA, 1944

National Register of Historic Places, 1972

Owned and operated by The Upsala
Foundation, Inc., acquired 1944

Telephone for opening days and times,
215.842.1798

On October 4, 1777 George Washington's Continental Army advanced down the "Great Road" to surprise the British Army encamped at Market Square in Germantown. Near Cliveden they unexpectedly stumbled onto six companies of the British 40th Regiment of Foot, who had bivouacked behind the house. The British barricaded themselves in Cliveden and the Americans began what would be an unsuccessful siege that included a battery of cannon firing from land that had been owned and farmed by the Johnson family for four generations.

John Johnson (1774–1825) inherited this land in 1797 and commenced a Federal style house that would continue in Johnson family hands until 1941. Frustratingly little is known about the design, construction, and subsequent history of the five-bay, center-hall, two-and-one-half-story house set back 100 feet from Germantown Avenue. We do know that when the tax assessor for the United States Direct Tax of 1798 visited the site he recorded under "A List or Description of each Dwelling-house . . . owned, possessed, or occupied on the first Day of October, 1798" that John Johnson's stone house and kitchen were "Shingled the first of October and half the Garrett floor laid," which suggests he visited a house under roof but not yet completed.

Typical of those in Germantown houses, the main facade is constructed of exposed Wissahickon schist finely dressed into uniform blocks called ashlar. The kitchen wing is rubble masonry. Instead of a Middle Georgian, pedimented frontispiece, Upsala has a wood portico with fluted Doric columns supporting a nicely detailed cornice and pediment. The marble lintels with key stones over the windows and belt course between the floors contrast agreeably with the ashlar and provide horizontal definition to the facade. The denticulation and modillions of the cornice are more refined than those seen on mid-eighteenth-century examples such as those at Cliveden.

The interior plan consists of four rooms of nearly equal size on each floor, entered from a wide central passage. If the refined Federal details of the exterior do not alert the visitor that Upsala differs from earlier Germantown houses of similar scale and quality, the interior leaves little doubt. Like Middle Georgian Delaware Valley houses, the ground floor passage is lighted by a fanlight over the front door. Wainscoting extends to chair-rail height and the division between the front and back passage is defined by an arch, but here the fluted pilasters with gouge-work stops are much lighter and the wide arch and vestigial keystone are attenuated. Rather than the boldly carved wood frieze and cornice of a Powel House passage, Upsala has lighter cast plaster decoration. The wainscoting is carried into the rooms off the passage and each room is given a decoratively gouge-carved fireplace surround that has survived two centuries, a major fire, removal for sale, and reinstallation—all in remarkably good condition.

Of the nine children born to John and Sarah Wheeler Johnson, seven never married, and four lived on in the house after Mrs. Johnson's death in 1852. The sole survivor of these died in 1880 and Upsala passed to a brother, whose son Dr. William Norton Johnson (1858–1937) inherited. He died with considerable debt; his widow

✤ Erected in 1798, Upsala is one of the finest Federal-style houses in the Germantown section of Philadelphia. It remained in the builder's family for nearly 150 years until acquired by a volunteer committee and opened as a house museum.

was forced out of the house in 1941; and the contents were dispersed at public auction. Left empty and defenseless, Upsala fell prey to a group of neighborhood boys who set it afire in 1942. The roof and third floor, stair, and decorative plaster were extensively damaged. To prevent demolition for construction of a supermarket directly opposite Cliveden, a group of community leaders headed by Miss Frances Anne Wister (founder of the Philadelphia Society for the Preservation of Landmarks) acquired the property and established a foundation to restore, refurnish, and operate the house.

⟐ Room use changed over time in early houses. By 1826 the Johnsons were using the four ground floor rooms as a front and back parlor, a library, and a dining room. This is the library, which is furnished with a variety of objects dating from the early nineteenth century, here set up for afternoon tea. The door provides access to the dining room, which has been redecorated with a French scenic wallpaper. The fireplace surround is typical of those used throughout the house.

# JOHNSON HOUSE

6306 Germantown Avenue, Philadelphia, PA 19144

Architect/builder, Jacob Knor (attributed), c. 1765–68

National Register of Historic Places, 1972

Owned by the Germantown Mennonite Historic Trust, 1980; operated by the Johnson House Historic Site, Inc.

Telephone for opening days and times, 215.438.1768

To appreciate how remarkable Cliveden must have appeared to Germantown residents of the 1760s, it is instructive to visit its nearby contemporary the Johnson House. Both are constructed of Wissahickon schist ashlar, and they may even share in Jacob Knor the same master builder. Both are two-and-one-half-story, five-bay houses with center hall and gable roof, although Cliveden is seventeen feet wider. Here the similarities taper off. The Johnson House enjoys no park; it is sited squarely on the dusty street to leave the maximum space for the family's tanning business at the back. It also squats close to the ground, not elevated on a high basement. The main facade is symmetrical, but rather than a projecting pedimented pavilion and frontispiece, the Johnson House continues the vernacular Germantown tradition of a heavy pent eave across the front and side that accentuates the horizontal line. The eave is interrupted over the simple front door by a projecting pedimented hood rather than by a balcony as at Bellair, Grumblethorpe, the Peter Wentz House, and Harriton. The door and window casings are traditional and the cornice is a simple box with bed and crown molds, rather than Cliveden's decorative cornice with modillions and dentils. In fact, the Johnson House is of most interest because it is such an unaltered survival of the once common form of Germantown house.

John Johnson, Sr. (1708/9–1794), son of Dirk Jansen, an early Germantown settler

An architectural screen consisting of an entablature supported by two pilasters divides the central passage, the narrower front segment and the back that widens to accommodate the stair. The back door leads to what originally was a piazza open on the south side, separating the kitchen from the main house. This has been enclosed to create another service room or pantry.

126    GERMANTOWN

with associations with Wyck, commissioned the house and completed it in 1768. According to family tradition, the elder Johnson gave it to his son, John Johnson, Jr. (1748–1810), after his marriage in 1770. Like many houses facing Germantown road, the Johnson House fell into the line of fire during the Battle of Germantown. Caught in the house when fighting erupted at nearby Cliveden, the Johnsons immediately sought safety in the cellar while the battle swirled around the house. It took one direct hit from an American cannon on the northwest wall, several doors and windows were shot out, and a board fence—behind which a company of Americans formed a firing line—was riddled by British return fire. (This fence, like the front doors of Cliveden, became Battle of Germantown relics and often were brought out for exhibits in the late nineteenth and early twentieth centuries.)

Prior to the Civil War, the Johnson House was a station stop on the Underground Railroad, which aided fugitive slaves to attain freedom in the free states and Canada. This theme has been developed for the current interpretation of the site.

The Johnson House, c. 1765–68, is a remarkable late colonial survival that owes more to Germantown building traditions than to the Middle Georgian Palladianism of nearby Cliveden. The dormers date from the mid-nineteenth century and the street level has been raised slightly around the ground floor. Wooden benches originally flanked the front entrance, and the front door—probably original—is a two part "Dutch" door that allows the top half to be opened for the circulation of air while the bottom half provides a barrier to roaming livestock and domestic pets. The original exterior color scheme was white trim with reddish brown doors.

# EBENEZER MAXWELL MANSION

200 West Tulpehocken Street,
Philadelphia, PA 19144

Architect, attributed to Joseph C. Hoxie,
c. 1859

National Register of Historic Places, 1971

Owned and operated by Ebenezer
Maxwell Mansion, Inc.

Telephone for opening days and times,
215.438.1861

On the eve of the American Civil War, the diarist Sidney George Fisher recorded, "Germantown is lined with cottages & villas, surrounded by neat grounds, trees, shrubbery & flowers, many of them costly & handsome, all comfortable and pretty. They are in every variety of taste and size and there are hundreds of them. . . . They are the results of the railroads which enable anyone to enjoy the pleasures of country life and at the same time attend to business in town. . . . The advantages are so obvious that this villa & cottage life has become quite a passion and is producing a complete revolution in our habits." The full thrust of steam had come to Philadelphia. Steam to power the modern Germantown textile factories, steam to transport the expanding middle class out of the congested city—out to "neat grounds, trees, shrubbery & flowers."

John Fanning Watson lamented in 1856, "Germantown now, is no longer Germantown as it was! It goes on in building fancy cottages for city business men." One of these was Ebenezer Maxwell (1827–1870), who in the space of a single decade arrived in Philadelphia with a small inheritance, became successful as a dry goods commission agent, married Anna Smith (1831–1912), fathered two children, and moved to rapidly expanding Germantown, where, after renting for two years, he commissioned the house that today bears his name.

Maxwell would probably be startled to hear his speculative venture in suburban development called a mansion, since it is neither very large nor particularly stately. Nonetheless, Maxwell was fortunate to have a competent architect, probably Joseph C. Hoxie (1814–1870), who gave him a suburban villa right out of the pages of a pattern book by Samuel Sloan (1815–1884). Hoxie had designed the Second Presbyterian Church across the street and Sloan had designed a nearby house for one of Maxwell's friends. Whoever the architect, he created a sturdy yet picturesque amalgamation of the Gothic and Second Empire decorative styles then popular with newly prosperous Americans of the Victorian age.

The house is mainly Wissahickon schist, which continued to be the building material of choice in Germantown, and the exterior trim is wood, painted and sanded to simulate cut stone in color and texture. As would be expected at the time, the house boasted gas lighting, hot-air central heat, and a "Wood bathtub tinned with varnished Copper. Hot & Cold Water introduced. Water closet fixed as usual," according to the November 11, 1859 insurance survey. For interior decoration the Maxwells relied mainly on graining, marbling, stenciling, wallpaper, and carpets laid wall to wall rather than costly hardwoods, marble, and decorative plasterwork. Such fugitive surfaces are easily destroyed and have had to be replaced since the house became a museum—a long and costly process.

Three years after occupying their new house, the Maxwells completed a larger house nearby, moved there, and in 1862 sold their first house at a profit to the William Hunter, Jr., family. (Mr. Hunter was a successful businessman. Unfortunately for him he died in 1867, but for the curators a century hence his estate inventory provides a fair idea of

❧ The Ebenezer Maxwell Mansion
(c. 1859) in the Germantown section of
Philadelphia is an excellent example of the
Victorian-era picturesque suburban villa
erected for the prosperous middle class,
able for the first time to commute by rail
from their center city businesses.

how the house was furnished within a decade of its construction.) The subsequent owners made modest changes, and the house gradually declined during the tenure of the last reclusive resident, who lived there for ninety years. With the ground floor barricaded and only the faint flicker of gas light to be seen from second floor windows, the house and its overgrown gardens gave off a decidedly eerie appearance. Because of its similarity to the Second Empire house drawn by the famous cartoonist Charles Addams, neighbors began to refer to it affectionately as the "Charles Addams House."

In the late 1950s and early 1960s local residents working through the Germantown Historical Society blocked repeated efforts to demolish the house, first for a filling station, then for expansion of a nearby retirement home. Rallying support to purchase a mid-nineteenth-century house and turn it into a museum did not have immediate public appeal, even in Germantown, where residents have traditionally provided leadership for the Philadelphia preservation movement. Fortunately, preservationists across America were discovering the nineteenth century. The Victorian Society in America (founded in 1966) had established its national office in Philadelphia, and several pioneering books extolling the merits and reevaluating Victorian architecture and decoration by Philadelphia scholars had appeared. These developments improved the environment for what nonetheless remains a grass roots effort to create at the Ebenezer Maxwell Mansion the first house museum of the Victorian period in Philadelphia.

❦   The parlor has been furnished along the lines of the William Hunter, Jr. inventory of 1867, which mentions wall to wall carpet, "4 fine stuffed chairs," two sofas, 4 reception chairs, 2 ottomans, a card table, a walnut center table, a French plate looking glass in gilt frame, nine assorted oil pictures, "3 sets curtains and lambrequins," a walnut what not, 3 bronze statues, and a piano. The recreated curtains and lambrequins are based on a design published in *Gleason's Pictorial Drawing Room Companion* (November 1854).

# WYCK

6026 Germantown Avenue, Philadelphia, PA 19144

Architect/builder unknown, c. 1690; alterations by William Strickland, 1824; restored by John M. Dickey, FAIA, 1974–76

National Historic Landmark

Owned by The Wyck Charitable Trust, 1973; operated by The Wyck Association, 1981

Telephone for opening days and times, 215.848.1690

The word to describe Wyck is continuity—a sense of being uninterrupted in time. Continuity cannot be retrospectively created by the artifice of curators and consultants who may homogenize a house in the process of preserving it for the future. Continuity requires generations of a family who build, tear down, and alter to suit their needs or whims, each leaving behind objects that may range greatly in age, style, and quality—not unlike the accretion of a coral reef. Among Philadelphia's museum houses one senses continuity at Cliveden, Andalusia, Cedar Grove, and Stenton, but nowhere else is it so palpable as at Wyck.

For nine generations spanning nearly three centuries, Wyck sheltered the Quaker Wistar-Haines family, beginning c. 1690 with Hans Milan's small stone house. The subsequent building history of the rambling two-and-one-half-story stuccoed stone house is complex; and the result is prepossessing without being architecturally imposing. In 1736 Milan's son in law, Dirk Jansen, built a stone house in front of Milan's, and in 1771–73 Reuben Haines I pulled down Milan's original house and erected a larger 29′ × 50′ house separated from Jansen's by a carriageway. By 1799 the two houses had been joined, with the ground floor of the connecting section left open as a covered

✿ Wyck sheltered nine generations of the Wistar-Haines family of Germantown. The stucco coating ("Ruff Casting and Plastering"), first applied to the stone in 1799 and recently restored, unifies the house, built in several stages spanning c. 1690 to 1824.

✿ The museum staff has been careful to preserve the eclectic accumulation of family objects from all periods and styles that came with the house. In the library the Greek Revival niche, over the marble mantel and coal grate, resulted from extensive alterations suggested by William Strickland in 1824.

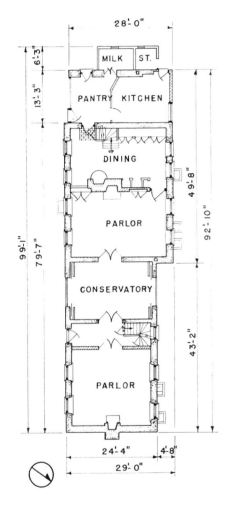

28'-0"
6'-3"
13'-3"
MILK   ST.
PANTRY   KITCHEN
DINING
PARLOR
CONSERVATORY
PARLOR
99'-1"
79'-7"
92'-10"
49'-8"
43'-2"
24'-4"   4'-8"
29'-0"

The Wyck floor plan, reproduced from Tinkcom and Tinkcom, *Historic Germantown*. By permission of The American Philosophical Society.

breezeway. In 1814 Reuben's wife could report, "I am seated in [a] most delightful hall where we live almost entirely. It is 20 feet wide with two huge barn like doors [that] open to the yard in front and the garden [in] back—it is always cool here." In 1844 sliding glass doors were added to make it a hall for all seasons.

In 1767 Wyck had passed to Catherine Jansen Wistar (1703–1786). She lived mainly in Philadelphia with her husband Caspar Wistar (1696–1752), who became wealthy in trade and the manufacture of glass in New Jersey; they probably made little use of the house. But, as happens so often in the history of Philadelphia's eighteenth-century houses, yellow fever plays a role at Wyck. In the epidemic of 1793 Reuben Haines I and his wife Margaret Wistar Haines, who had inherited in 1786, both died of yellow fever, prompting their son, Reuben Haines II, to move out from Philadelphia to reestablish the family in Germantown full time. Here he founded a successful brewery which his son, Reuben Haines III (1786–1831), continued. He also participated in a wide range of social, civic, and scientific causes.

Reuben Haines III launched the next building campaign at Wyck after learning that most of the floor joists needed replacement. "The joice under the front parlour were rotten in my father's time," he wrote to his wife, "but he supported the ends of them by beams that are in their turn decayed and I feel little inclination to '*patch the patches*' when by a little more trouble and expense we can render the old mansion good enough to serve during the period of our joint lives be that prolonged to the greatest extent of our wishes."

To correct the deficiencies Reuben turned to William Strickland (1788–1854), who had been trained by Benjamin Henry Latrobe and was just emerging as one of America's leading architects. Strickland made virtually no exterior modifications, but rearranged the interior so it would function as a single house rather than two old structures joined. On the ground floor the family now had four large rooms that could be combined or closed off according to their need. Haines wryly remarked, when reproached by his wife over the extent of the alterations, "Thee very well knows few if any [persons] ever begin a career of vice! or commence the repair of an old building! that stop exactly at the point they intended. It is not therefore to be expected I should prove myself different from all other mortals, and had thee been exposed to the same temptations thee would probably have fallen into the same errors."

For her own part, Jane Haines laid out an ornamental garden to the north of the house, including twenty types of roses. For 150 years subsequent generations of the family, and now the The Wyck Charitable Trust, have maintained her planting scheme, making it one of the oldest documented gardens in America still under cultivation.

✿ The dining room that William Strickland created from the kitchen of the earlier house contains the Federal mahogany dining table made by Jacob Super for Reuben and Jane Haines in 1812. It is set with an extraordinary Tucker porcelain dinner service made in Philadelphia c. 1828. The mahogany Philadelphia tall-case clock by Edward Duffield, c. 1740–60, belonged to Caspar Wistar.

# DESHLER-MORRIS HOUSE

5442 Germantown Avenue, Philadelphia, PA 19144

Architect/builder unknown, c. 1773, incorporating earlier structure

National Historic Landmark, 1965

Owned and operated by Independence National Historical Park (acquired 1948, opened 1949)

Telephone for opening days and times, 215.596.1748 or 215.597.8974

During the battle of Germantown (October 1777) British General Sir William Howe occupied as his headquarters the recently built house of merchant David Deshler on Germantown road opposite Market Square. Sixteen years later, in one of those marvelous twists of fate that occasionally occur in history, Deshler's house became the summer home of President George Washington, who temporarily sought refuge there from the yellow fever then ravaging his capital. "I have taken a house in Germantown," Washington wrote, "commodious for myself and the entertainment of company." Latter-day publicists would label it "the first summer White House."

Deshler originally erected a modest summer cottage. By 1772 he decided to build a more formal five-bay, two-and-one-half-story stuccoed stone house with gable roof, "Modillion and Frett" cornice, and pedimented "plain Dorick Frontispiece." His new house sits squarely on the street, conservative and unremarkable. No Schuylkill River villa Middle Georgian fripperies here; it is the *beau ideal* of a prosperous merchant's house of the time. Even the interior, regardless of wainscoting to the chair rail and paneled chimney breasts, lacks carved embellishments, which would have represented an additional and unnecessary expense. Deshler described it as sitting in "an airy, high Situation, commanding an agreeable Prospect of the adjacent Country," with

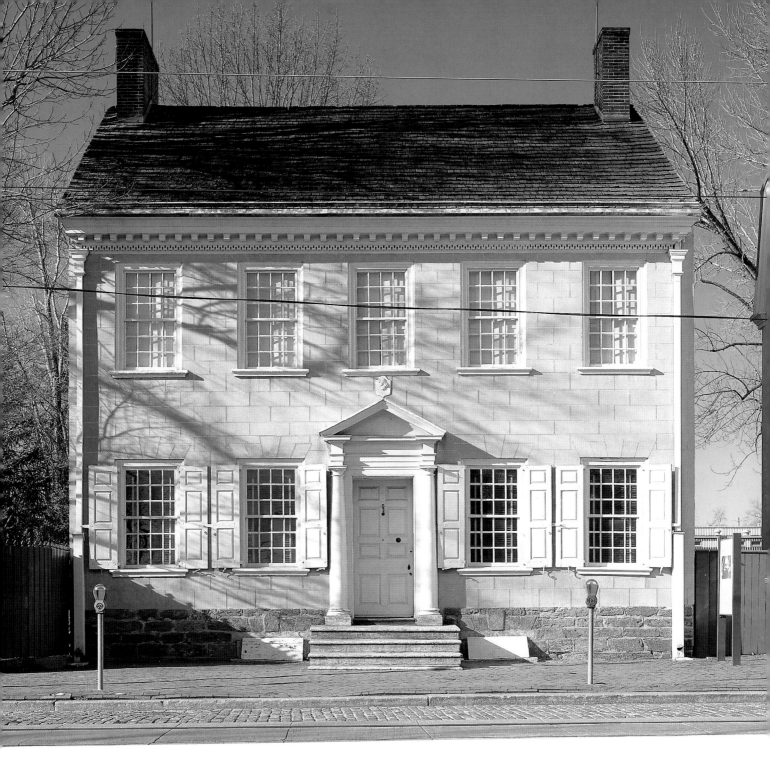

🌳   The Deshler-Morris house, built c. 1773 by the successful merchant David Deshler, became Sir William Howe's headquarters during the Battle of Germantown and President George Washington's summer residence in 1793 and 1794 during yellow fever outbreaks in Philadelphia.

🌿   According to Isaac Franks's inventory, the "Left hand Room" when rented to President Washington included chintz window curtains and green Venetian blinds, a looking glass, four girandoles (branched candle holders), two dining tables, two arm chairs, and eight "Stuffd Bottom Chairs." The Park Service has added a "crooked leg" with "claw foot" mahogany sofa attributed to Benjamin Randolph and originally made for Robert Morris's house in Philadelphia, which might have been used by Washington while it served as the President's House. The portrait is of Isaac Franks (1759–1822) and is inscribed, "To friend Isaac Franks, Gilbert Stuart." It is unlikely that an oriental carpet would have been used in this location and season. Washington favored grass "floor matting from China" in the summer.

two acres of orchard of "the best grafted Fruit, of various Kinds, and a large Garden paled in."

Following Deshler's death in 1792, the successful broker Isaac Franks acquired the house. He rented it to President Washington for a few months in 1793 and 1794—the president paid a pro rata of the $400 annual rent. After Washington left, Franks billed him $2.50 "for Cleaning my house and putting it in the same condition the President rec'd it in." Fortunately Franks rented the house partially furnished and made a detailed inventory, which survives to provide National Park Service curators a primary source for refurnishing the rooms as they might have been during Washington's stay. We also know that Washington moved two wagon loads of furniture from the President's House in 1794, which would have supplied many items that are obviously missing from the Franks inventory.

Franks sold the property in 1803 to John and Elliston Perot, and their eldest daughter and her husband, Samuel B. Morris, acquired it from Perot's estate in 1836. The Morrises were the first owners to live in the house year round, and their descendants remained there without interruption until Elliston P. Morris donated the property to the federal government, as a memorial to Elizabeth Canby Morris and Marriott C. Morris, and for the benefit and inspiration of all future generations of visitors.

❧ The small room adjoining the left parlor is interpreted as a tea room, a use suggested by the Franks inventory, which listed a card table, four Windsor chairs, and assorted tea paraphernalia "in the Closett." The table shown here (c.1765) originally belonged to James Smith (1719?–1806) from York, Pennsylvania, who signed the Declaration of Independence. The Windsor chairs carry the stamp of Gilbert and Robert Gaw, who were partners in Philadelphia, 1793–1800.

❧ The "Right Hand Room" contained a dining table, a breakfast table, six chairs upholstered in chintz, 72 pieces of "Nankeen China," and other assorted food service items. The mahogany Philadelphia table shown here dates from 1780–1800; the chairs are attributed to the shop of Daniel Trotter (1747–1800). The passage floor between the right and left rooms is covered with a painted floor cloth.

# GRUMBLETHORPE

5267 Germantown Avenue, Philadelphia, PA 19144

Architect/builder unknown, 1744; alterations and additions, 1808; restored by G. Edwin Brumbaugh, FAIA, 1957–67

National Historic Landmark

Owned and operated by the Philadelphia Society for the Preservation of Landmarks, 1940

Telephone for opening days and times 215.843.4820

❧ The brick-floored kitchen in the rear ell has been restored to its eighteenth-century appearance. Originally this room was separated from the main house by an open passage.

The sons of Hans and Katrina Wüster who immigrated to Pennsylvania from Hillspach near Heidelberg, Germany in the early eighteenth century became prominent citizens of Philadelphia and Germantown. One son, Caspar, anglicized his name with an "ar" and lived at Wyck; the other son, John, elected "er" and became the builder of Grumblethorpe. Both houses are now museums, and keeping straight the Wister and Wistar branches of the family is one of those genealogical niceties in which Philadelphians delight. Like the Wistars who lived at Wyck for nearly three hundred years, the Wisters remained at Grumblethorpe from 1744 until acquisition of the house by Landmarks in 1940—nearly two hundred years.

Referred to in the eighteenth century as "Wister's big house," Grumblethorpe—a name it acquired in the nineteenth century—was built by John Wister (1708–1781) as a summer retreat from his town house on High Street between Third and Fourth Streets in Philadelphia. The six-bay main facade of the two-and-one-half-story house is built of dressed stone in typical Germantown fashion; the other walls are irregular rubble stone. Behind the twelve-room main house is a long two-story ell containing the kitchen and other rooms added over several generations.

In 1808 the third owner of Grumblethorpe, Charles Jones Wister (1782–1865), decided to modernize the house by removing the pent eaves and balconies, closing one door, adding dormers, and installing a late Georgian frontispiece with fanlight. As at

❀ The garden facade of Grumblethorpe (1744) shows the kitchen ell and Charles Jones Wister's workshop added in the early nineteenth century. The pent eave and balcony on the main house were recreated by G. Edwin Brumbaugh during the restoration of 1957–67.

Wyck, the exposed stone was then stuccoed. These changes were reversed nearly 150 years later when architect G. Edwin Brumbaugh—working for Landmarks—recreated the two front entrances, pent eaves, and balconies that exist today.

From the mid-eighteenth century, wine merchant John Wister had maintained an orchard at Grumblethorpe that included apples, plums, peaches, and cherries, in addition to a large vegetable garden. Daniel Wister (1738–1805), living in the tenant house next door, began to cultivate ornamental bulbs and annuals in the years immediately prior to the Revolution; his diary records setting out beds of tulips, blue and white hyacinths, narcissus, polyanthus, jonquils, and violets. History neglects to tell us whether the Wisters' housekeeper was weeding flowers or vegetables on that fateful morning of October 4, 1777 when British General James Agnew—who had been billeted at Grumblethorpe for about a week—rushed from the house at the sound of the American attack on Cliveden. Noticing the housekeeper about her task, Agnew warned her to seek shelter in the cellar—advice she ignored. Shortly later the fatally wounded officer returned to Grumblethorpe, where he died on the parlor floor.

In the nineteenth century, once Charles Jones Wister had renovated the house, retired from his business, and moved to Germantown full time, the garden became an even more important ornamental feature of the Grumblethorpe property. In addition to agriculture and horticulture, Charles Wister dabbled in a wide range of natural sciences. He kept regular weather records, collected minerals, made and repaired clocks, and in 1834 erected an observatory from which he observed the eclipse of the sun and the transit of Mercury, having first established the "meridian of Grumblethorpe" as "six seconds west of the Philadelphia State House [Independence Hall]."

Charles Jones Wister, Jr. (1822–1910) never married and lived at Grumblethorpe all his life, continuing many of his father's interests, especially the garden. After his death the Wister heirs did not wish to live at Grumblethorpe, and Landmarks purchased the house in 1940.

The ground floor passage is divided into front and back halls by an elaborate doorway dating from 1744; the stair is an early nineteenth-century replacement for the original winding stair.

# STENTON

4601 North 18th Street, Philadelphia, PA
19140

Architect/builder unknown, 1727–30

National Historic Landmark, 1965

Owned by the City of Philadelphia, 1908;
operated by the National Society of
Colonial Dames, 1899

Telephone for opening days and times,
215.329.7312

In the summer of 1714 forty-year-old James Logan confided to a friend, "I am about Purchasing a Plantation to retire for I am heartily out of love with the World." After he acquired several hundred acres of land on the Germantown Pike four miles north of Philadelphia, work began in earnest on his house in 1727 and was completed in 1730. "Now," he could write, "if I can make philosophy my mistress for life, it is the only choice in my power that can give me the prospects of any comfort." The "plain, cheap farmer's stone house" he intended to build had also become "a large brick house . . . 51 ft. by 40, two good Stories in height, very convenient, & not unsightly. . . . I have proposed to call ye place Stenton after the Village in E. Lothian where [my] father was born."

A quarter of a millennium later, James Logan's Stenton is one of the earliest, best preserved, and most believable house museums in Philadelphia. It is a joy to anyone who appreciates authentic early American architecture and decorative arts, and it should be on every list of "must see" sites in the region.

The son of Scottish parents who became Friends and ultimately settled in England, James Logan (1674–1751) entered trade where he came to the attention of William Penn, who invited the precocious young man to come to America as his secretary. He rapidly became irreplaceable as the Penn family's agent and over the subsequent half century held virtually every position of trust in the proprietary government. Like Thomas Jefferson in a subsequent generation, Logan's innate curiosity, brilliant intellect, and mastery of languages made him a voracious consumer of books. He assembled one of the finest libraries in colonial America, preserved to this day by the Library Company of Philadelphia.

Stenton would not excite much comment if it were set down behind a rose-covered, mellow brick wall in an English market town. It might be the Early Georgian residence of a successful merchant or the rectory of a prosperous parish church. For its time and place, however, the house is far more sophisticated than its surviving Delaware Valley contemporaries such as the Trent House (see pages 166–69). For comparison we might fervently wish that Isaac Norris's nearby and slightly earlier Fairhill had also survived the British army patrol dispatched to burn it *and* Stenton. Fortunately we have one of the these important houses.

Stenton's five-bay main facade is symmetrical and well laid in Flemish bond with a brick belt course; the lesser facades are asymmetrical, laid in English bond. There is nothing unusual here. But at Stenton subtle brick pilasters define the corners and the main entrance with its transom and sidelight windows, which originally were sheltered by a hood. The window openings are relieved by segmental arches and the frames hold sash, still something of a novelty in Philadelphia at the time; earlier houses used casement windows with the glass held in place by lead cames. There also are no exterior shutters. Logan specified interior blinds that fold back into the window reveals, a feature the Trent House has in common with Stenton. (Even high style Middle Georgian houses in Philadelphia would continue to rely on exterior shutters to repel thieves and control light.) The hipped roof once had a balustraded gallery, a cupola, and a copper weather vane. During James Logan's time a defining and protective brick

❧ Six generations of Logans occupied Stenton, the house in Germantown erected by James Logan (1727–30), before it was opened as a museum by the National Society of Colonial Dames and acquired by the City of Philadelphia in the early twentieth century.

wall enclosed the house and its immediate garden; this was removed by his grandson, Dr. George Logan, in the early nineteenth century.

Stenton is a double-pile house with a central passage and four rooms on each floor. But here the passage is more of a reception space—complete with practical brick floor and fireplace—designed both to control and to impress visitors, who might range from colonial grandees and native American tribal delegates to tenant farmers. Off this hall are the parlor and rooms variously used as family sitting room, dining room, and lodging or bedrooms. It is now generally believed that James Logan kept his library on the second floor, although it is likely that there were bookcases in several locations in the house, since Logan's lameness tended to confine him to the ground floor.

After Logan's death, Stenton passed to his son, William, and then to his grandson, Dr. George Logan, who with his wife Deborah Norris Logan lived full time at Stenton. It is Deborah Logan, diarist, antiquarian, and friend of John F. Watson—Philadelphia's first preservationist—who encouraged the family to protect the house from substantial change. Consequently, when Stenton passed to the City of Philadelphia after six generations of Logan ownership, it remained largely as known by earlier generations. Thanks to a century of dedicated care by the National Society of Colonial Dames, that trust has been maintained.

On the eve of the American Civil War, Sidney George Fisher visited Stenton and recorded in his diary, "There are not many places in America like Stenton." Few visitors today would disagree.

❧ The "Hall and Entry" with its brick floor and elaborate woodwork opens into a fully paneled parlor with a fireplace surround of Valley Forge marble. According to James Logan's estate inventory, the hall contained "1 Large Black Walnut Table, 8 Leather Bottomed Chairs, a Tea Table, and 1 Large Black Walnut Table & Stand." The oval oak table shown here is English, c. 1680–1700. The portrait is of Isaac Norris of Fairhill after Sir Godfrey Kneller (1649?–1723).

❀    Above the first floor parlors are two chambers of equal size divided by large folding doors. According to James and Sarah Logan's estate inventories (1752, 1754), the near room contained the most valuable bed (£30), hung with yellow wool damask which has been reproduced for the bed hangings, curtains, and upholstery in the room. The far room is believed to have housed James Logan's extensive library, which having been bequeathed to the people of Philadelphia, would not have been included in his estate inventory. The blue and white checked cotton slip cover (which matches the curtains and bed furniture in the room) is based on a document found at Stenton. The Philadelphia mahogany chest-on-chest between the doors is one of several Logan family objects that have been returned to the house since it opened to the public.

# DELAWARE RIVER

ANDALUSIA

GLEN FOERD

PENNSBURY MANOR

TRENT HOUSE

BURHOLME

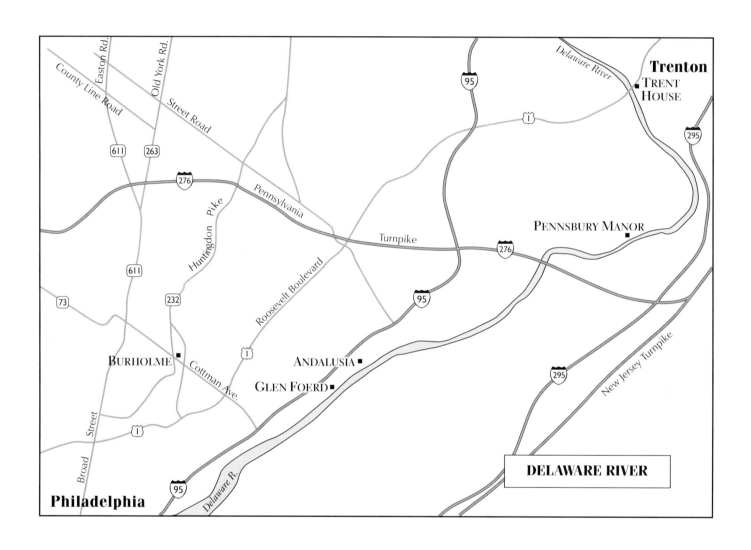

❧   Glen Foerd. The extent of the Foerderer alterations can be appreciated in the Georgian Revival grand stair, with its fifteen-foot diameter, domed skylight forty feet above the ground floor. This view looks past the double manual Haskell pipe organ into the art gallery wing, also added in 1902–3. See page 158.

In this age of dependence on the private automobile, it is difficult to imagine how readily nineteenth-century Philadelphians used the Delaware River for transportation and what they encountered on the way north toward Trenton. In the spring of 1853, for example, Aaron and Nathan Stein booked passage for Burlington, New Jersey on the steamboat *Edwin Forrest*, which departed from the foot of Arch Street. According to their journal, after passing the Kensington shipyards and the Richmond coal wharves, they reached "the open country interspersed with villages . . . encircling [Philadelphia] with an ornamental border of *scallop-eaved* cottages!!!"

> Some of these retreats from the heat and toil of a city life in summer, seem to be the very perfection of elegance; the most favorable ground being generally chosen, you see them for the most part, gradually sloping away from the river, from which the house is approached by wide gravel walks. Viewed from the upper deck, the Plan of these residences and grounds lie like a Map before the eye. Steamboats, and other craft, occasionally passed us in our upward voyage, and the bells pealed a merry salute as the boats presented a broadside to each other.[1]

The Delaware River rises in the Catskill Mountains of New York, joins its east and west branches at Hancock on the Pennsylvania line, rushes south through the Delaware Water Gap, passes Easton, and from the falls at Trenton is a long extension of the bay and ocean beyond. Below Trenton the river widens and is tidal and the banks flat and fertile—in all a topography to encourage landed estates.[2] It was here, twenty-five miles north of the proposed city of Philadelphia, that William Penn's deputy governor had set aside 8,431 acres for the proprietor's use and on which Penn constructed in 1683 a brick and frame house facing the river. Over the next century and a half—as the Stein brothers observed—the banks of the Delaware became lined with landed estates and summer villas, many featuring handsome examples of virtually every architectural style.

Probably the most famous individual drawn to the banks of the Delaware was Joseph Bonaparte (1768–1844), eldest of Napoleon's brothers, who had been placed on the throne of Naples and the Two Sicilies and in 1808 proclaimed King of Spain and the Indies. Following the collapse of the Empire and the Battle of Waterloo, Joseph fled to America, where he adopted the title Comte de Survilliers. He occupied rented houses in Philadelphia, including Lansdowne on the Schuylkill, prior to purchasing and developing a grand estate of more than 1000 acres at Point Breeze near Bordentown, New Jersey, across from Pennsbury, where he lived more or less continuously from 1817 to 1832. That Bonaparte chose to settle on the Delaware River rather than the Schuylkill was probably determined by the availability of larger tracts of land and its proximity to both Philadelphia and New York (Figure 1).

The grounds at Point Breeze were elaborately landscaped, with ten miles of carriage

Figure 1. Point Breeze, the estate of Joseph Bonaparte. This view of the house is attributed to Charles B. Lawrence (fl. 1813–37), a portrait and landscape painter born near Bordentown. New Jersey Historical Society, gift of Mrs. J. W. Mailliard, 1957.

drives, vistas, rare trees, gazebos, tree houses, gardens, fountains, and an artificial lake half a mile long. In addition, Bonaparte's art collection was the finest in America at the time. There were several statues by Canova and more than 150 paintings. The bulk of the collection consisted of minor Dutch works taken from Holland by the Spaniards and taken from Spain by Joseph. But there were also Murillos, a Titian, a Van Dyck, a Velasquez, a Raphael, and several family portraits by David. Foreign visitors and American guests alike were impressed by what they saw, although one American found the art too explicit for her taste. "The walls were covered with oil paintings," she reported, "principally of young females with less clothing about them than they or you would have found comfortable in our cold climate." As for the copy of Antonio Canova's nude statue of Pauline Bonaparte Borghese, "the Count called our attention and asked us to admire it . . . enumerating all her charms one after another and demanding our opinion of them . . . , it was impossible to get him away without our prudery exciting more attention than would have been pleasant" (Figure 2).[3]

It is no longer possible to journey up the Delaware by steamboat, and it is difficult to imagine the pretty scene described by the Steins. Industrialization has dealt a cruel blow to this rich architectural and horticultural legacy; for miles up the river the summer villas and great country houses have been swept away. Occasionally a private oasis can be glimpsed from the river, but Bonaparte's house at Point Breeze is gone and Pennsbury, demolished in the eighteenth century, has been replaced by a recreation.[4] For these reasons, the survival of **Glen Foerd** and, especially, **Andalusia** are all the more precious. As for the **Trent House**, the river context has been lost by the intrusion of modern highways. Nonetheless, the trip is worth the trouble for the house and collection, which relate so closely to the few Early Georgian Philadelphia houses that survive.

**How to Reach the Delaware River House Museums.** In the nineteenth century a visitor to Glen Foerd, Andalusia, Pennsbury, and the Trent House would probably have ventured north by river boat, but even if you have access to a boat, there are no longer safe landings. An expedition north will probably follow Interstate 95 from Center City all the way to Trenton, exiting as appropriate. It is not recommended that you attempt to navigate State Road, which runs parallel to the Delaware, nor should you even head north without obtaining detailed travel instructions and confirming that the houses you want to visit will be open. None of the riverfront houses are easy to locate without directions from the nearest Interstate 95 exit, and none offer luncheon facilities. There are several restaurants within walking distance of the Trent House, however, and if you have time to drive up New Jersey Route 29 to Lambertville or Pennsylvania Route 32 to New Hope—both of which are attractive roads—there are numerous restaurants and antique shops in this popular resort area.

Figure 2. The Delaware River from the terrace of Point Breeze, Joseph Bonaparte's estate north of Philadelphia. Thomas Birch, c. 1818. Birch (1779–1851), son of the artist William R. Birch, was a marine, landscape, and portrait painter. Private collection.

# ANDALUSIA

1237 State Road, Andalusia, PA 19020

Architects, Benjamin Latrobe, 1806–7; remodeled and expanded, Thomas U. Walter, 1833–35

National Historic Landmark

Owned and operated by The Andalusia Foundation

Telephone for opening days and times, 215.639.2077

One of the Philadelphia merchants attracted to the banks of the Delaware was John Craig, who in 1795 purchased a farm located halfway between Pennsbury and the city. Here he erected a relatively modest house in 1797–98. As Craig's fortunes flourished, he approached the fashionable architect Benjamin Henry Latrobe to improve and expand the house—which became the mansion Andalusia, although Craig did not live to see the architect's design realized. Craig died in 1807, leaving a wealthy widow with several children, one of whom, Jane, married Nicholas Biddle.

Nicholas Biddle (1786–1844) came from a respected family of means whose roots extended deeply into the earliest Quaker settlements of the Delaware Valley. After graduating from Princeton and reading law, Biddle accompanied as secretary General John Armstrong, newly appointed United States minister to France. During the three years he spent in Europe, Biddle witnessed Napoleon's coronation as Emperor, met the artists Jean-Antoine Houdon and John Vanderlyn, and visited Greece—which aroused in him what was to be a lifelong interest and appreciation of classical architecture.

In 1811, Biddle married Jane Craig. Her mother died in 1814, and from the close of the War of 1812 until 1819—when Biddle's responsibilities as president of the Second Bank of the United States kept him in Philadelphia—the young family moved to Andalusia in the spring and remained there almost continuously through the fall. This pattern seems to have been fairly typical of country villa families of the eighteenth and early nineteenth centuries. Except for brief periods Andalusia did not become a year-round residence of the family until the 1930s.

By 1833 Biddle was ready to expand the Craig villa to match his economic success and rising position. For this he invited the young architect Thomas Ustick Walter (1804–1887), whose revised design for Girard College Biddle had already supervised as chairman of the trustees. Walter, a native Philadelphian, had been trained by William Strickland. Eventually he would become the dean of mid-nineteenth-century American architects and a founder of the American Institute of Architects. In the 1850s he would cap his career by designing the wings and dome of the United States Capitol, arguably the most identifiable building in the United States. Andalusia would be his most famous residential commission.

Biddle and Walter considered making the house into a miniature Parthenon, with what architectural historians call a peripheral octastyle plan; that is, a single row of columns around the perimeter with eight across the pedimented ends. Walter, however, favored the simpler and less expensive hexastyle structure (six columns across) based on the surviving fifth-century B.C. Doric-style Temple of Theseum in Athens. Only Biddle had actually seen these temples, of course, but Walter owned the seminal book of American Neo-Classicism, James Stuart and Nicholas Revett's *Antiquities of Athens* (London, 1762, and later editions).

Work on the house progressed through 1834. Walter's design enveloped the Craig house and created two new parlors in the front, overlooking the river. Floor-to-ceiling windows permitted easy warm weather access directly onto the porches, which the family always referred to as the piazzas. In addition, the third floor was enlarged and

🌀 The east front of Andalusia was added by architect Thomas Ustick Walter (1804–1887). On March 20, 1835, with all the columns in place, Walter rowed out to the middle of the Delaware to obtain the full effect of what he had wrought. "The building shows nobly from a distance," he recorded, "the proportions of the Doric order are so massy that they require to be seen from a distance."

The "yellow" parlor at Andalusia contains objects acquired by several generations of Biddles. The interiors are consciously maintained as they were in the 1950s when the family was in residence. These photographs show the rooms in summer: curtains have been removed and slipcovers installed on upholstered furniture. The marble mantel is probably Italian; the white-and-gilt over-mantel mirror was made for the house in the 1830s. Acting as agent for his parents, Edward Biddle acquired the chandelier from the Paris firm of Thomire & Cie in 1836. The maple sofa table on the right, with painted slate top, carries the label of Anthony G. Quervelle, master Philadelphia cabinetmaker of the 1820s and 1830s.

two-story wings added across the land-side front to provide a kitchen (to the north) and library (to the south). The main rooms created by Walter's extension of Andalusia were the formal parlors—the "yellow" and the "ottoman"—overlooking the Delaware. Their handsome plaster ceiling medallions, cornices, and pilasters; classically detailed marble mantels; and French chandeliers have caused these rooms to be among the most published in America.

Walter's contribution to Andalusia extended beyond the house. In the park he expanded the billiard house and designed a suitably picturesque riverside Gothic ruin. Graperies were erected in the garden, and nearby a Gothic cottage—so richly embellished during the 1980s by Nicholas Biddle's great-grandson—provided housing for long-term guests.

In 1839 Biddle resigned from the Second Bank of the United States, expecting to spend the balance of his life raising Guernsey cattle and thoroughbred horses and cultivating grapes and the *Morus multicaulis* mulberry for feeding silkworms. Black clouds of economic depression hung over the country, however, and two years later the bank failed—and most people blamed Biddle. Speaking of Biddle after his fall, Sidney George Fisher would record in his diary, "there have been few instances of a more complete reverse of fortune. I was never among those who praised him or admired him extravagantly in his prosperity, and I think now that the censure, the abuse, the hatred which accompanied his downfall were quite excessive and unmerited as the fulsome adulation which was offered to him by the whole community during the period of his power."

Broken financially, Biddle relinquished his city house and moved year-round to Andalusia, itself saved from the maelstrom of his declining fortunes by Mrs. Biddle's trustees, who purchased Andalusia with funds from John Craig's estate. Biddle died in 1844, and Mrs. Biddle continued to summer at Andalusia, as did succeeding generations of the family. This use protected the property from serious change. For sixty years following Mrs. Biddle's death her children retained joint, undivided ownership; this helped to preserve the house from being modernized in one of the several styles of the Victorian period that obliterated so many eighteenth- and nineteenth-century American country houses. Joint ownership ended in the early twentieth century, at which time the preservation and careful embellishment of Andalusia as it had been known by the family over nearly two centuries became a trust to be passed to future generations.

❧ The painted-and-gilt bookcases of the library are among the most important examples in the Grecian style to survive in the United States. They house Nicholas Biddle's considerable library, including his edition of the Lewis and Clark journals. The sofa is wood-grained and gilt-decorated similarly to the bookcases. The statue is of Napoleon I in his coronation robes. Young Nicholas Biddle observed the coronation of Napoleon as emperor while in Paris on December 2, 1804; he would later become a friend of the exiled Joseph Bonaparte who lived at Point Breeze up the Delaware.

# GLEN FOERD

5001 Grant Avenue, Philadelphia, PA
19114-3199

Architect unknown, mid-nineteenth
century; renovations by William J.
McAuley, 1902

National Register of Historic Places

Owned by the City of Philadelphia, 1984;
operated by the Glen Foerd Conservation
Corporation

Telephone for opening days and times,
215.632.5330

The financier and philanthropist Charles Macalester (1798–1873), today remembered as the benefactor of Macalester College in St. Paul, Minnesota, was one of the Victorians drawn to the banks of the Delaware above Philadelphia. He retired from business in 1849 and the next year purchased 1000 acres fronting on the river with the unpromising name of Poquessing Creek, which in the local Native American language meant "Land of Many Mice." Consequently, Macalester renamed the area Torresdale after a family seat in Scotland. The house he commissioned commands a spectacular view up river toward Andalusia, and south across to Riverside and Rancocas Creek in New Jersey. He named it Glengarry.

Italianate-style houses are generally commodious, which accounts for the vast number erected by architects like John Notman, Samuel Sloan, and John Riddell for newly affluent Victorian businessmen in towns such as Riverside and Bordentown. Macalester's Glengarry consisted of an imposing three-story, square, stucco-over-masonry Italianate structure with octagonal lantern and porches on the east and south sides. Nearby he erected a stone building for the generation of illuminating gas, an ice house, a Gothic gate house, a sixty-foot-high stone water tower, and five greenhouses. Following the death of Macalester's daughter, the house remained empty for two years before being acquired in 1893 by Robert and Caroline Foerderer. They commissioned extensive renovations and renamed the house Glen Foerd.

Robert Foerderer's fortune derived from a method he perfected of treating goat skins to make them pliable; his factory in the Lower Frankford section of Philadelphia employed 3,000 persons processing 40,000 goat skins a day to be fashioned into women's shoes. Turning his wealth to politics, he served as a U.S. Representative at large (1900) and then Representative of the Fourth Pennsylvania District (1902).

As architect Foerderer chose the now obscure Philadelphian William McAuley (fl. 1884–1904), who is principally known as co-author of *Old Colonial Architectural Details in and Around Philadelphia* (1890). His extensive labors and Foerderer's wealth brought forth the Georgian Revival gentleman's estate that exists today. They removed the Italianate lantern and added a porch with new porte cochere to the west facade. Most dramatically, they carved out space in the middle of Macalester's house for an appropriately grand approach to a new two-story art gallery inspired by the Tate Gallery in London. The gallery was designed to display a ready-made collection of paintings purchased by Foerderer in 1899, many of which later proved to be "from the school of" or "formerly attributed to"—but nonetheless they are highly decorative.

After Foerderer died in 1903, his widow completed the house and continued over the next three decades to acquire fine arts and decorative embellishments, which in 1934 passed to the Foerderers' daughter, Mrs. William T. Tonner. Raised by acquisitive parents and now equipped with ample resources, a discerning eye, and confidence in leading dealers, she seriously collected works by William Blake, old-master prints, rare books—particularly Bibles—silhouettes, glass, porcelain, and furniture. Some of Mrs. Tonner's treasures remain at Glen Foerd; most have been transferred to the Phila-

✿ Glen Foerd on the Delaware River in the Torresdale section of Philadelphia was erected by the banker and philanthropist Charles Macalester, c. 1850, and substantially expanded by the industrialist Robert Foerderer, 1902–3.

delphia Museum of Art, Muhlenberg College, and the Lutheran Theological Seminary. Mrs. Tonner lived at Glen Foerd until her death in 1971. She had established a trust transferring the house, collections, and an endowment to the Lutheran Church in America with the stipulation that they were to be used by the church or "for the benefit and service of the entire Torresdale general community." The church used the estate as a conference center for a decade before relinquishing it to the Fairmount Park Commission. The Commission entered into an operating agreement with a volunteer group known as the Glen Foerd Conservation Corporation, which manages the house. Operating support for the house and grounds, which occupy a spectacular site on the Delaware, comes primarily from leasing the property for weddings and corporate dinners.

The 25′ × 50′ art gallery at Glen Foerd, inspired by the Tate Gallery in London and designed by William McAuley (1902), houses a collection of paintings Robert Foerderer purchased. The fireplace is "Old Convent" Sienna marble; the walls above the wainscoting are covered with damask. For nearly seventy years Mrs. Foerderer and her daughter Mrs. William Tonner added to the collections of paintings, prints, porcelain, carpets, and furniture.

# PENNSBURY MANOR

400 Pennsbury Memorial Road,
Morrisville, PA 19067

Recreated by R. Brognard Okie, AIA,
1938–39.

National Register of Historic Places

Owned and operated by the Pennsylvania
Historical and Museum Commission

Telephone for opening days and times,
215.946.0400

Granted the charter for Pennsylvania by Charles II, William Penn (1644–1718) established an American colony based on religious toleration, representative government, and ethnic diversity; in the process he had every expectation of making his family wealthy. Appropriate to a gentleman proprietor of such stature, Penn's agents identified 8,431 acres on the Delaware River approximately 26 miles north of the new town of Philadelphia. Here Penn would create an English country seat. "The Country Life," he wrote, "is to be preferr'd; for there we see the Works of God; but in Cities little else but the Works of Men."

Intending ultimately to live in America, Penn actually spent little time here. During his first visit (1682–84) work commenced on the manor house, which he occupied briefly in the summers of 1683 and 1684 before returning to England; while away he ordered the construction of "a kitchen, two larders, a wash house & room to Iron in, a brewhouse & in it an oven for bakeing, & a stable for twelve horses." Penn returned in 1699 accompanied by his wife Hannah and daughter Letitia; they lived at Pennsbury in those months of 1700 and 1701 when the Delaware River was free of ice. In Philadelphia they occupied the Slate Roof House. All during this period there was a flurry of construction at Pennsbury Manor. Then William Penn sailed away, never to return.

Throughout the eighteenth century, the estate—left in the care of a skeleton staff—steadily declined. The family would not or could not live there, yet resisted offers to buy the house, although all but 300 acres were gradually sold. On the eve of the Revolution, Richard Penn acquired the remaining property and demolished his grandfather's house in preparation for building a Middle Georgian country house on the Delaware as John Penn had done on the Schuylkill. Then the Revolution intervened, and in 1792 the site passed out of Penn family hands.

The story might well have ended here were it not for the Friends' Historical Society of Philadelphia, the Welcome Society (descendants of those who accompanied Penn on his voyage to America), and a few antiquarians, such as John Fanning Watson. Pilgrims continued to visit the site throughout the nineteenth century, often carrying away relics. In the 1880s the Pennsylvania Bicentennial spawned an unsuccessful effort to acquire the site as a park; fifty years later, as the 250th anniversary approached, a similar effort finally led to the acquisition by the newly established Pennsylvania Historical and Museum Commission of ten acres surrounding the house site.

Intending initially to create a park, the state soon announced that the house and outbuildings of Pennsbury Manor would be recreated as a symbolic memorial to William Penn. Since there were no detailed drawings or even reliable images of the house, and historical archaeology was yet in its infancy, the reconstruction would be short on scholarly documentation and long on the artistic imagination of its architect. R. Brognard Okie (1875–1945), a native of the Delaware Valley and one of the earliest architects to specialize in Pennsylvania colonial and vernacular structures, had been responsible for the Betsy Ross House and the vastly popular High Street colonial replicas for

✿　　The recreated Pennsbury Manor on the Delaware River twenty-six miles north of Philadelphia is a memorial to William Penn, founder of Pennsylvania. Erected in 1938–39 from designs by architect R. Brognard Okie, it sits on the location of Penn's seventeenth-century country house.

the Sesquicentennial Exposition of 1926. At Pennsbury Manor he had his most enduring and controversial commission, the merits of which are debated to this day.

In the 1930s the success of Colonial Williamsburg loomed large in the minds of Harrisburg officials, who saw Pennsbury as a Pennsylvania rival to the recreation of the Virginia Governor's Palace. Architectural authenticity seemed less important than "pageant architecture" designed to engage the public in participatory history. The infant historic preservation movement, then led by the American Institute of Architects and the growing cadre of federal government historians who had been honing their skills at Yorktown and similar sites, had begun to question the wisdom of reconstructions or recreations. Out of the controversy surrounding the use of depression-era public relief program funds for the Pennsbury project would come a prohibition against reconstruction or recreation. Decades later, the Pennsbury experience would shape the decision by Independence National Historical Park not to recreate Benjamin Franklin's house or the Slate Roof House, both of which are better documented than Pennsbury Manor.

In the final analysis the 23 structures on the 43-acre Pennsbury Manor site, like the recreations at Colonial Williamsburg, tell us as much about twentieth-century perspective on the past as they do about seventeenth- or eighteenth-century reality (see pages 16–17). In subsequent years, however, the curators of both Pennsbury and Williamsburg have reinterpreted their restorations, reconstructions, and recreations more accurately to reflect modern research into room and textile use, furniture and arrangement, as well as analysis of both interior and exterior paint colors. Even allowing for the limitations of a recreated setting, Pennsbury Manor is in the hands of professional historians, curators, and guides who help provide visitors with a worthy memorial to Pennsylvania's founder.

✤    The furnishings and interpretation of Pennsbury Manor are intended accurately to reflect not only the Penn inventories but the most recent research into late seventeenth-century Anglo-American interiors. The rooms are arranged to portray the domestic life of William Penn and his family and servants, and to shed light on the social history of the period. This view looks from the "Governor's Parlor" into the "Governor's Withdrawing Room" (to the left) and the "Entrance Hall" through the door to the right.

# TRENT HOUSE

15 Market Street, Trenton, NJ 08611

Architect/builder unknown, c. 1719;
restored by J. Osborne Hunt, 1934–36

National Historic Landmark, 1970

Owned by the City of Trenton, 1929;
operated by the Trent House Association

Telephone for opening days and hours,
609.989.3027

✤ One parlor is set up as a dining room,
in which the original furnishings included a
corner cupboard, a black walnut looking
glass, an oval table, one arm chair, and two
dozen side chairs, but no window curtains
or carpets. The Trents owned card tables
japanned in gold and large pier glasses
"with Sollopt [Scalloped] Shells gilt" valued
at £14.

To the eye of a savvy seventeenth-century merchant, the head of navigation on the Delaware River offered a gilt-edged opportunity. Whoever controlled the surrounding land could profit from building a grist mill, operating a ferry, and selling building lots after founding a town. William Trent (1653–1724) was such a man. He emigrated from Scotland to Philadelphia in the 1680s and by the earliest years of the eighteenth century had become one of the leading merchants of the city, exporting tobacco, flour, hides, pelts and hardwoods in exchange for brandy, wine, rum, molasses, dry goods, and slaves. Although an Anglican and vestryman of Christ Church in Quaker-dominated Pennsylvania, Trent served on the Governor's Council, sat as a member of the Pennsylvania assembly, and eventually sat as a justice of the Supreme Court.

In 1714 Trent purchased 800 acres straddling the Assunpink Creek ("stone in the water") at the Falls of the Delaware. The house that now bears his name is believed to have been erected c. 1719. Trent and his second wife spent summers there until 1721, when they moved permanently to the new township of Trent's Town. Exchanging leadership in Pennsylvania for similar positions in New Jersey, Trent represented Burlington County in the New Jersey Assembly (1722) and became its speaker (1723). He also served as Judge of the Court of Common Pleas in Hunterdon County and Chief Justice of New Jersey. Suddenly, on Christmas Day 1724, he died.

❀   The house, erected c. 1719 by the founder of Trenton, New Jersey, is one of the finest surviving Early Georgian domestic structures open to the public in the Delaware Valley.

❦ The Trent bed chambers had fully furnished beds with matching window curtains of various materials and colors, "Searsuccar," "Yellow Sattin," "Callico," and a "bedstead & green Linen Curtains." Such textile use is found in only the wealthiest early eighteenth-century Delaware Valley households. Mrs. Trent's room, for example, contained a dressing table and looking glass, a chest of drawers, a "Black Armed Chair & Small Ditto," a bedstead and "blue camlet curtains," a Dutch stand, an old tea table, "3 pr. Searsuccar Window Curtains"—and no carpets.

Who designed and built Trent's house is unknown, although it is logical to assume that the builders came from Philadelphia. One irresponsible writer without a shred of documentary proof attributes the house to the master carpenter James Portues (d. 1736) because of an earlier—also unsubstantiated—attribution of the Slate Roof House to him. But while we may never know who designed the house, it ranks among the most important surviving Early Georgian houses in the Delaware Valley.

An early description of the Trent property mentions "a large well built brick dwelling house, 38 by 48 feet, two story high, four rooms on a floor, with a large handsome stair case and entrys thro' the house, with cellars under the whole building, and a courtyard on each front of the house, the one fronting down the river Delaware to the ferry, thro' a large handsome avenue of English cherry trees, the other fronting up the river to Trenton." The five-bay north and south brick facades are laid in Flemish bond, and a lantern tops the hipped roof above a simple cornice with unembellished modillion blocks.

Following Trent's death the house passed through the hands of several owners, one of whom substantially remodeled and expanded it in the mid-nineteenth century by adding a Greek revival wing and portico, enlarging the size of window lights, replacing doors, removing the lantern, replacing the roof, and painting the brick. In this form it came to the City of Trenton as a 1929 gift from Edward Ansley Stokes, who required only that the house be "restored to the original condition in which it was built" and "forever kept and preserved in good and proper condition." The early 1930s were not propitious for civic preservation efforts and little could done to restore the house until grants became available from federal emergency relief agencies. Then the additions came off and the lantern was reconstructed, although the lower Greek Revival roof line appears to have been retained.

The city determined "that the Trent House should be maintained primarily as an historical museum and gradually be refurnished as it was in William Trent's time, *following the guidance of an extant inventory of William Trent's estate*" (emphasis added). This decision, remarkable for the time, set a high standard for the recreation of the interiors that proved difficult in execution. The inventory dated from two years after Trent's death while his widow still lived in the house, and the survival of this document might yet permit the furnishings committee to realize their goal. Nonetheless, by enlisting the aid of several patriotic societies and generous donors, the original committee assembled a remarkable collection at a time when such could still be readily assembled.

The Trent House is geographically the most distant destination included in this book, but one well worth visiting for the quality of the decorative arts and as one of the few surviving Early Georgian houses erected by the Philadelphia merchant class—which included James Logan, Isaac Norris, Samuel Carpenter, and William Trent. It should be viewed in context with Stenton, Hope Lodge, and the recreated Pennsbury.

# BURHOLME

## RYERSS MANSION

7300 Central Avenue, Philadelphia, PA
19111

Architect unknown, c. 1859; extensive
alterations by Zantzinger, Borie &
Medary, Architects, c. 1920

National Register of Historic Places, 1976

Fairmount Park Commission, 1905

Telephone for opening days and times,
215.745.3061

⚓ The parlor of Burholme is furnished
with Ryerss objects to reflect the eclectic
taste of one prosperous Philadelphia family
of the late nineteenth century. A portrait of
Joseph Waln Ryerss hangs over the
fireplace.

Sited on a hill in its own 70-acre park in the Fox Chase section of Philadelphia, Burholme commands such a panorama of the surrounding communities that it nearly became a fortification when the Confederate States Army under Robert E. Lee invaded Pennsylvania in 1863. Today the Italianate house is open as a museum and also serves as a local public library.

On January 1, 1859 the 82-acre farm that would become Burholme became the property of Joseph Waln Ryerss (1803–1868), scion of the distinguished Waln family of Philadelphia that included the textile manufacturer Robert Waln (1765–1836) and his son the author Robert Waln (1794–1825). Ryerss named his country estate Burholme after the Waln ancestral seat in England. A successful East Indian and China trade merchant in his own right, Ryerss turned to railroads. By 1859 he held the presidency of the Tioga Railroad, running eight locomotives and 130 cars over thirty miles of track from Morris Run in Tioga County, Pennsylvania to New York State, mostly transporting coal. Railroad consolidation would soon absorb such independent lines, but in the 1850s they still had the potential to make their officers and directors wealthy.

❧ Burholme (c. 1859), erected by Joseph Waln Ryerss and greatly embellished by his son Robert Waln Ryerss, now houses the Ryerss Museum and Library, which is particularly rich in Asian decorative arts.

Less than a decade later (1868) Burholme passed to Joseph Ryerss's son, the lawyer Robert Waln Ryerss, who spent the next quarter century filling the house with a remarkable collection of fine and decorative arts inspired in part by the collecting interests of his father and grandfather. The younger Robert Waln had visited China in the early nineteenth century and wrote one of the earliest accounts of that country by an American.

In 1865, at the age of 64, Robert Ryerss married his housekeeper, Mary Ann Reed. He died eight months later, leaving no children; his will provided Mary with a comfortable annuity and "during her life the free use, possession and enjoyment" of Burholme. He also directed that "my country seat . . . be used as a Public Park, the . . . house to be fitted up as a Public Library and reading rooms in which are to be placed my books, and one or more rooms reserved for my pictures, old china, silver, glass and furniture and other curiosities as my wife . . . may designate, as a museum." Mrs. Ryerss relinquished her life rights to the property in 1905 and the Fairmount Park Commission of the City of Philadelphia opened the museum and library to the public in 1910.

Today picturesque Burholme reflects several building campaigns. The original three-story, five-bay, hipped-roof house (c. 1859) is stuccoed stone with a veranda on three sides; the lantern or belvedere is believed to have assumed its present form in the late 1880s. Originally a center-hall plan, the ground floor has been converted to use as a museum and the second floor as a library. To accommodate these uses, all interior partitions were removed and columns inserted. The Fairmount Park Commission c. 1920 constructed a museum addition to better house and display the Ryerss collections. Most recently, the ground floor rooms have been refurnished with family objects in an effort to suggest their appearance before the removal of the partitions.

The extensive collection of Asian objects collected by several generations of the Waln-Ryerss family are displayed in museum fashion in a wing added to the house c. 1920.

# NORTHERN *and* WESTERN SUBURBS

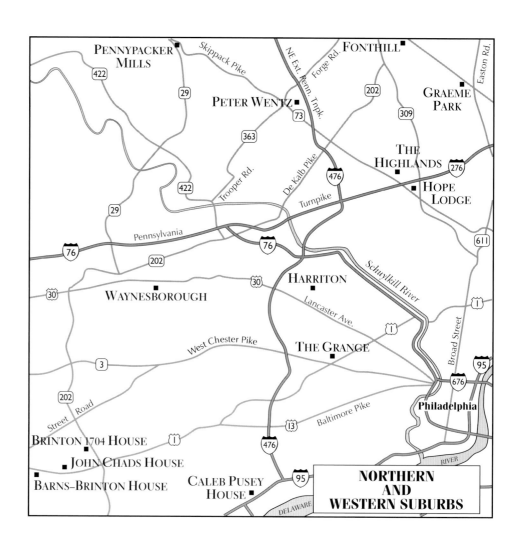

The Columbus Room ceiling is encrusted with decorative tiles set directly into the concrete. Mercer erected forms covered with sand into which tiles were pressed face down, allowing the backs to project. Concrete was then poured. Mercer remarks, "we feared sagging of vault forms and the fall of heavy tiles set in this manner." But "when we pulled out the platform props, the platforms collapsed and tons of earth and sand fell, exposing the tiles, after which the loose sand was washed off with a hose." The "ROLLO STAIRS" are so named because Mercer's dog ran up them while the concrete was wet, leaving his paw prints on the treads. See page 192.

The suburban counties that surround Philadelphia are liberally dotted with house museums that can easily be reached by automobile from Center City. Since the major roads tend to radiate out, it is often easier to target a group of houses. For that reason they are described here in clusters, anyone of which could easily require a full day to see. Beginning counter clock wise from the Delaware River at Trenton, Philadelphia's "home counties" are Bucks County, Montgomery County, Chester County, and Delaware County. Until the development of railroads in the nineteenth century, and the construction of multi-lane highways in the post-World War II decades, these were rich farming regions settled by German, Welsh, English, and Scots-Irish families attracted by William Penn's liberal policies and the promise of inexpensive bottomland. Today, unfortunately, that rich loam is likely to be nourishing suburban lawns rather than fields of grain to feed herds of milk cows or pigs being fattened for the market. Nonetheless, residents of all these counties are setting aside open spaces and acquiring historic buildings—those who would plant oaks arrayed against the forces of immediate gratification. Many of the historic house museums now open to the public are a

⚜ Harriton. In 1704 Rowland Ellis built Harriton (formerly called Bryn Mawr) in what is now Lower Merion Township, Montgomery County, at the center of his 690-acre grant from William Penn; it later became the home of Charles Thomson, Secretary of the Continental Congress. In the 1920s a modern bedroom and service wing were added to the original T-shaped structure. The house and sixteen acres now belong to the township and are administered by a private not-for-profit group. See page 202.

Peter Wentz Farmstead. The unusual Wentz house paint scheme discovered by Frank S. Welsh, a microscopist who specializes in historic architectural finishes, continues into the chambers, where it can be seen behind an eighteenth-century Pennsylvania walnut wardrobe with inlaid decoration. See page 196.

result of this environmental awareness and the desire to preserve the best of the past for future generations.

The Delaware River properties to the northeast are in Bucks County (and across the river in Mercer County, New Jersey); these, except for **Fonthill** in Doylestown, are discussed in the Delaware River section. Fonthill (1908–10), its related Moravian Pottery and Tile Works (1910–12), and the Mercer Museum (1914–16) of the Bucks County Historical Society deserve to be seen together and will require a full day in themselves. A two-day tour might include the Delaware River houses as far north as Trenton, an overnight stay in the Lambertville/New Hope area, and the second day spent in nearby Doylestown, returning to Philadelphia in the afternoon.

Another two-day tour might focus on Germantown the first day, moving north on

Bethlehem Pike and crossing into Montgomery County, where several significant houses are encountered. The first of these are three properties in the care of the Pennsylvania Historical and Museum Commission: **Hope Lodge** (c. 1743–48), **Graeme Park** (1723–26), and **The Highlands** (1795–1801). These houses deserve to be visited for different reasons. Graeme Park is an extraordinary survival of an unmodernized eighteenth-century interior; Hope Lodge ranks as one of the finest surviving Early Georgian houses in the region; and The Highlands, a fine Federal house in its own right, has a garden that has been praised in the horticultural press for more than a century and a half. Also north of the city are two properties belonging to Montgomery County, the **Peter Wentz Farmstead** (1758) and **Pennypacker Mills** (1901–2, incorporating an earlier house), both of which have historical associations with the 1777 Battle of Germantown. The vernacular Wentz house has Germanic grace notes and provides an excellent foil to the Welsh, English, and Scots-Irish stone houses of the region; it also has an unusual, academically recreated interior paint scheme. Pennypacker Mills, an early house heavily influenced by the Colonial Revival Style popular at the turn of the century, is being maintained as an example of that style, created by Pennsylvania Governor Samuel W. Pennypacker. Like several houses in this area, it enjoys a beautiful rural setting.

The next group of houses is located in the area south of the Schuylkill River where Montgomery, Chester, and Delaware Counties meet. If you plan to visit Valley Forge, it is possible to cut south to Lancaster Avenue (U.S. 30), which will put you close to **Harriton** (1704) in Bryn Mawr, one of the earliest Welsh stone houses to survive, and which also became the retirement home of Charles Thomson, a leader in the American Revolution and secretary of the Continental Congress. In Chester County, near Paoli, there is **Waynesborough**, ancestral home of the Wayne family, which included General Anthony Wayne, one of most famous of George Washington's lieutenants. And in Delaware County there is **The Grange** (1850–51), the only Downingesque Gothic cottage open to the public in the Philadelphia area, which also has extensive gardens. Here, too, is the modest stone cottage known as the **Caleb Pusey House** (c. 1683–96), which may be the earliest house open to the public in the region and the only one actually known to William Penn.

The final tour would include the far western sites in Chester and Delaware Counties. These are best reached from Philadelphia by driving south on Interstate 95 and then northwest on U.S. 322 to U.S. 1. This puts you within striking distance of three early houses that can easily be visited in a day: the **Brinton House** (1704), the **Barns-Brinton House** (early eighteenth century), and the **John Chads House** (c. 1725). They are near the Brandywine Battlefield, which offers additional historic houses open to the public that are not discussed in this book. All these houses have the advantage of being close to the Brandywine River Museum—one of the finest art museums in Southeastern Pennsylvania—and numerous country inns that serve lunch. Ask your guides to recommend their favorites. This is an easy, albeit full day in the country only a hour away from Center City.

# HOPE LODGE

553 Bethlehem Pike, Fort Washington, PA
19034

Architect/builder, attributed to Edmund
Woolley, c. 1743–48

National Register of Historic Places

Administered by the Pennsylvania
Historical and Museum Commission
(1957) and Friends of Hope Lodge and
Farmar's Mill

Telephone for opening days and times,
215.646.1595

Many house museums in the Philadelphia area have been open to the public for decades; others, until recently, remained privately owned by families who appreciated the historical importance of their homes and furnished them in what today is called the Colonial Revival Style. This approach to decorating became popular in the late nineteenth and early twentieth centuries because it united the romantic associations of Colonial and Federal era decorative arts, reaction to Victorian excesses of the 1890s, and a growing clamor among design critics for Arts and Crafts simplicity.

Oriental carpets on highly polished soft wood floors, elaborate draperies and curtains—often silk—at windows, bedroom furniture forms in parlors arranged in comfortable "conversation groups," dining rooms with tables permanently ready for use, white or pastel color schemes, and bedstead frames with vestigial textile hangings—all are characteristic of the Colonial Revival decorative approach. Today, however, professionally-trained curators and administrators often reinstall these houses, banishing as historically incorrect the decor created by the last private owners or by well-intended volunteers who arranged museum houses as they might their homes.

The current interpretation of Hope Lodge attempts to bridge the gap between the findings of modern research into our colonial past and what the last private owners created in the 1920s. Aside from the obvious didactic opportunities of such an approach, preserving some Colonial Revival spaces encourages us to judge that decorative epoch on its own merits.

Hope Lodge is one of the architectural treasures of the Delaware Valley. Located near the Pennsylvania Turnpike and rapidly spreading suburban development, it nonetheless sits well back from Bethlehem Pike in its own protective rural park. The house is believed to have been built by Samuel Morris (1708/9–1770), prosperous Quaker grist-mill operator whose mill stood across Bethlehem Pike on the banks of Wissahickon Creek approximately thirteen miles from center city Philadelphia. Morris acquired the property from Edward Farmar in 1741. Farmar, a wealthy, Irish-born Anglican, had inherited vast family holdings in the Whitemarsh area and would seem a likely candidate to commission an Early Georgian house with obvious similarities to James Logan's Stenton of 1727–30. However, recent research strongly points to Morris as patron; his account books for the period 1743–47 include expenditures for labor and materials "at my new house" and he mortgaged the house and two acres in 1747 for the large sum of £750.

Even more intriguing are cash payments to Edmund Woolley between 1743 and 1746, the exact period when Morris's "new house" would have been under construction. Woolley (c. 1695–1771) emerges as one of the key figures in the history of Philadelphia Georgian architecture. An early member of the Carpenters' Company, his crew worked on the Pennsylvania State House (Independence Hall) off and on from 1732 into the 1750s. In 1735 he charged £5 for "drawing the Elivation of the Frount one End the Roof Balconey Chimneys and Torret of the State House With the fronts and Plans of the Two offiscis and Piazzas Allso the Plans of the first and Second

✿   Erected by Quaker grist-mill owner Samuel Morris, 1743–47, Hope Lodge is one of the most important surviving Early Georgian country houses in the Delaware Valley. The dormers were a later addition and the front door hood is a 1920s recreation by Paul P. Cret.

Isaac Ware explained in 1768 that a hall such as the one at Hope Lodge "serves as a summer room for dining, it is an anti-chamber in which people of business, or second rank, wait and amuse themselves; and it is a good apartment for the reception of large companies." The handsome tall-case clock is by the Philadelphia maker Thomas Stretch, c. 1750. According to Morris's inventory, the Prussian blue parlor contained a clock, a desk, a looking glass, a pair of andirons, two tables, and a half dozen rush bottom chairs. The unvarnished floors are not carpeted; Morris appears not to have owned floor or window coverings.

floors of the State House." What services he may have provided to Morris will probably never be known, but the house stands—as does Stenton—as mute testimony to the hand of a master builder who—like Woolley—knew his English pattern books.

The exterior form of Hope Lodge looks backward to Early Georgian Stenton rather than anticipating Middle Georgian Mount Pleasant or Cliveden. Like Stenton, it has a hipped roof and a two-story, symmetrical brick facade, here extended to seven bays, with narrow window openings relieved by segmental arches. (The dormers are a later addition, as may be the ground level exterior shutters which would have been redundant with interior shutters.) The protective hood over the central entrance was designed in the 1920s by Paul P. Cret to fill a gap in the belt course similar to the one at Stenton. Above the hood is a blind window with an arched head.

The interior plan features a center hall of unusual width that passes directly through the house with the stair set laterally—as suggested by Georgian pattern books —rather than rising along one wall in the back hall as at Stenton or Cliveden. This stair—trimmed with a ramped and pilastered dado—rises to the second floor, where it is confined by an open balustrade that allows light from second floor windows to penetrate to the enclosed first stair run. The hallway woodwork is of outstanding quality. The median point of the wainscoted hall is divided by a flattened arch that springs from fluted pilasters. The front reception rooms have round arched, double-leaf doorways set between fluted pilasters; the back hall doors are pedimented.

Following Samuel Morris's death in 1770 the house passed through several hands, often absentee owners, which preserved it from major structural or mechanical alterations. In 1922 Mr. and Mrs. William Degn acquired the house and proceeded to restore and embellish it as a setting for their extensive collection of eighteenth- and nineteenth-century decorative arts, which they arranged according to the tastes of the time. In her will Alice Degn bequeathed Hope Lodge "in perpetuity for the enjoyment and education of the people of the Commonwealth of Pennsylvania and others, as a museum and permanent exhibit typical of the architecture and furnishings of the Colonial period of America." Rather than remove all traces of the Degns' Colonial Revival interior, half the house has been interpreted according to Samuel Morris's estate inventory of 1770, and the other half following photographs of how the rooms appeared during the Degns' occupancy, 1922–53.

❧ The largest bed chamber is furnished with outstanding examples of Middle Georgian decorative arts, all of Philadelphia origin dating from c. 1760–90. According to Morris's inventory this room contained the best furniture: "a Chest of Draws £6," a "Looking Glass & Dressing Table £3.10," a "Half Dozen Damasked Bottom Chairs £3," and a "Feather Bed & Furniture £13.10." The high valuation for the bed "furniture" relates not to the wooden bedstead frame but to the textile hangings, which often came with matching window curtains, as has been reproduced here.

# GRAEME PARK

859 County Line Road, Horsham, PA
19044

Architect/builder unknown, c. 1723–26;
interior c. 1745–60s

National Register of Historic Places

Owned and operated by the Pennsylvania
Historical and Museum Commission,
1958

Telephone for opening days and times,
215.343.0965

Graeme Park has special appeal. Erected in the 1720s by Sir William Keith, a provincial governor of Pennsylvania, and greatly embellished on the interior with Georgian paneling by Dr. Thomas Graeme in the 1750s, the house ceased to be used as a residence in the 1820s; from then successive generations of the Penrose and Strawbridge families preserved it unaltered until given to the Commonwealth of Pennsylvania. It survives today in a form that its eighteenth-century occupants would recognize, and it provides the modern visitor with a house museum experience unlike any other in the Philadelphia area.

William Penn appointed William Keith (1669–1749) governor of Pennsylvania in 1717, and in 1721 he acquired over 1,200 acres located 17 miles from Philadelphia in what is now Horsham, Montgomery County. He called his new estate Fountain Low, although he remarked in 1722 that he had "no view to a Dwelling house or anything thats ornamental." Nonetheless, by 1726 a stone six-bay, two-and-one-half-story, gambrel roof house had been erected. Differing from the Early Georgian five-bay, center-hall, double-pile houses like James Logan's Stenton, Fountain Low is asymmetrical and draws its inspiration from an earlier three-cell English vernacular single-pile

❧ Constructed c. 1723–26 by William Keith, provincial governor of Pennsylvania, and named Fountain Low (because of its many natural springs), the estate later passed to Dr. Thomas Graeme, who renamed it Graeme Park. The house is frozen in time—preserved by its owners without substantial alterations for nearly 150 years before its acquisition by the Commonwealth.

❧ Dr. Graeme began spending summers at Graeme Park in the 1740s. Over the next two decades he greatly embellished the interiors. The parlor, shown here, boasts some of the finest surviving Georgian woodwork in the Delaware Valley. The door on the left is false to provide balance to the door to the right that opens onto the stair Dr. Graeme also installed. The faded—but once glossy white—paint dates to the eighteenth century. According to Elizabeth Graeme Fergusson, this room in 1778 had "old green worsted Window Curtains," a large carpet (the only one listed in the house), an eight day clock, harpsichord, three looking glasses (probably including the one described as having "a white frame, gauze cover"), assorted chairs and tables, twelve prints of birds, and twelve plaster heads of "the poets."

house type—that is, three rooms in a line, one room deep. On the ground floor there were three major spaces: parlor, hall (with the stair), and a kitchen. Recent analysis suggests that these interiors were not finished during Keith's lifetime.

Sir William fell out of favor with the Penn family and in 1726 found himself removed from office; he returned to England in an effort to recoup his finances and died in debtor's prison without ever returning to America. In the meantime, Lady Keith sold Fountain Low to her son-in-law Dr. Thomas Graeme, who renamed the house Graeme Park. A Presbyterian Scot, Dr. Graeme held the post of port physician for Philadelphia and sat as a justice of the Pennsylvania Supreme Court. He rented Graeme Park at first, but in the 1740s launched a long campaign of improvements that continued into the 1760s. Gradually the Keith rooms became a formal parlor, a office/ library, and—especially after a separate kitchen building was completed in 1763—a dining room. On the second floor there were three bed chambers; a new stair replaced the original winders. The most dramatic change to the house also occurred during this period, when Georgian paneling and marble or delft fireplace surrounds went into the parlor and best bed chamber.

Dr. Graeme died in 1772 and his well-educated and accomplished daughter Elizabeth inherited. In matrimony, however, she proved unfortunate. Against her father's wishes, she married an unpromising Scottish immigrant, Henry Hugh Fergusson, who remained loyal to the Crown during the Revolution and deserted his American wife to suffer revolutionary justice alone when the Americans reoccupied Philadelphia. Unable to punish Fergusson in person, the council seized Graeme Park and sold its contents at public auction. Like Rebecca Shoemaker at Laurel Hill, Elizabeth Fergusson later regained title to pre-marital property, but debts and ill heath forced her to sell. After the Penrose family acquired the estate they erected a Federal house near the Keith-Graeme house in 1810. They and their successors, the Strawbridge family, preferred to occupy the Federal house, thereby preserving the original house for future generations to enjoy.

Like the National Trust for Historic Preservation at Drayton Hall near Charleston, South Carolina, the Pennsylvania Historical and Museum Commission wisely has decided not to furnish Graeme Park but to interpret this unsullied survivor in terms of eighteenth-century use of space, proportion, and design.

❧    Directly above the parlor is the master bed chamber. In households of any pretension in the eighteenth century such rooms served a dual role, as a place both to sleep and to entertain close friends and family members. In 1778 there were two bedsteads in the room, one "with Curtains" and one "without Curtains . . . for the Servant Maid." The window curtains were "blue worsted." The delft tiles around the fireplace opening are reproduced from originals discovered in the house. Notice the matching closets with practical fanlights.

# THE HIGHLANDS

7001 Sheaff Lane, Fort Washington, PA 19034

Architect, attributed to Timothy or Josiah Matlack; builder, Christian Loeser, 1795–1801

National Register of Historic Places, 1976

Owned by the Commonwealth of Pennsylvania; operated by the Highlands Historical Society

Telephone for opening days and times, 215.641.2687

In 1805 a real estate advertisement offered a property "situate about 14 miles from Philadelphia" consisting of 300 acres and a "Mansion House . . . not exceeded by any in Pennsylvania; its situation is elegant and healthy, and the surrounding scenery beautiful." The house, "is of stone, 60 feet in front by 45 in depth, the entrance to the hall is by a flight of marble steps and the pediment in front is supported by marble Ionic pilasters. The hall is 14 feet wide, and in the center of the house, with an elegant and spacious mahogany staircase." The anxious seller was Anthony Morris; he called his property The Highlands.

Anthony Morris (1766–1860), a Quaker lawyer born to wealth and social position on the eve of the American Revolution, reached his majority at the time of the Constitutional Convention. Drawn to politics, he first served in the Pennsylvania legislature and then as special envoy to Spain for Presidents Madison and Monroe, 1813–17. During his first term in the Pennsylvania Senate the terrible yellow fever epidemic of 1793 struck Philadelphia, potentially endangering his young wife Mary Pemberton (1770–1808) and their two infant children, and prompting Morris to rent Hope Lodge

❀ The five-bay main block of The Highlands is essentially as built for Anthony Morris in the 1790s. The distinctive pediment supported by pilasters over the center three bays began to appear in Philadelphia at The Woodlands (1780s) and Library Hall (1789–90 ). Such Late Georgian facades can also be traced to the influence of Abraham Swan's *Collection of Designs in Architecture* (London, 1757), one of the most popular design books in eighteenth-century Philadelphia. George Sheaff added the balconies c. 1817–45; the servants' wing to the left was designed by Halfden Hanson for Caroline Sinkler and erected c. 1922.

❀ The justly famous gardens at The Highlands are the product of several families over two centuries. As early as the 1840s, Andrew Jackson Downing remarked that they were a "striking example of science, skill and taste applied to a country seat." The crenelated stone walls, grapery, green house, and gardener's cottage all date from the nineteenth century; in the early twentieth century Wilson Eyre redesigned the garden, adding statuary and reflecting pools.

in what is now Montgomery County as a refuge. As he later reflected, "my earliest wishes pointed to the Country as to the Scene of Safety, of Peace, and . . . (with such a family as I was bless'd with) Happiness on Earth." So he purchased land and commenced a house of his own for use in the summer. "But, a total ignorance of the Expenses of building and a too sanguine disposition in calculating on the value of the Estate left me by my kind Uncle Luke Morris, induc'd me to erect a Mansion in the Country, which . . . prov'd to be the Tomb of all my earthy Hopes." In 1808 Morris sold his country seat.

In 1813 The Highlands changed hands yet again, this time to the prosperous Philadelphia wine merchant and successful land speculator George Sheaff (1799–1851), who by 1817 had moved his wife and eight children permanently to the country. This family would make The Highlands their home for nearly a century. George Sheaff laid out to the east of the house a new two-acre garden containing "the choicest variety of fruits. The pleasure grounds, surrounding the house, are shaded with evergreens and well laid out" with a nearby heated "greenhouse and grape wall." Concerning this garden we have no less an observer than Andrew Jackson Downing, America's first nationally-recognized critic of architecture and horticulture, who remarked in *A Treatise on the Theory and Practice of Landscape Gardening* (New York, 1841) that the Highlands garden is a "striking example of science, skill, and taste, applied to a country seat . . . there are few in the Union, taken on the whole, superior to it." Sheaff is also responsible for the veranda across the north facade of the house (c. 1840), to which the family migrated in the hot summer months when they closed the south-facing formal rooms of the original house. Following the elder Sheaff's death, a division of the property left three of his children with those acres encompassing the house and gardens. They resided there until the last died in 1915 at the age of 94, leaving the house in poor repair and the gardens overrun.

But The Highlands was about to enjoy a rebirth at the hands of the heiress Caroline Sinkler (1860–1949), daughter of Emily Wharton of Philadelphia and Charles Sinkler of South Carolina. (Miss Sinkler never married. Her engagement to the promising young Philadelphia architect John Stewardson came to a tragic end with his death in a skating accident on the Schuylkill a few days before their wedding.) For many years she summered at Gloucester, Massachusetts, where her next-door neighbor happened to be the antiquarian and interior decorator Henry Davis Sleeper. His friendship and his house—called Beauport—greatly stimulated an interest in early American architecture and decorative arts that culminated in her purchase of The Highlands in 1917.

Caroline Sinkler possessed the means, taste, and contacts with practitioners such as Sleeper and her Gloucester architect Halfden Hanson to embellish and expand the house and gardens at The Highlands, and in the process to create one of the finest twentieth-century country estates centered on an important eighteenth-century house in the Philadelphia area. By the 1930s readers of books and magazines on early American houses and gardens could be sure of encountering photographs of The

Highlands, where, as one author remarked, "its present owner, in this heritage of house and garden together, has wisely employed what was best in the old along with cosmopolitan elements agreeable to the spirit of our own times."

By 1940 Miss Sinkler was spending more time in Philadelphia, and in 1941 she sold The Highlands for $1.00 to her niece Mrs. Nicholas Roosevelt (1884–1970), reserving life rights. Together with her husband, Mrs. Roosevelt spent summers at The Highlands—which they meticulously maintained as left by Miss Sinkler—and winters at their South Carolina plantation. In 1957 they deeded the property to the Commonwealth of Pennsylvania, and ownership passed upon Mrs. Roosevelt's death in 1970. Shortly thereafter the contents were dispersed by auction, leaving the house vacant. In 1975, however, a dedicated group of volunteers formed The Highlands Historical Society to assist with the on-going research, restoration, and maintenance of the property as a community asset.

❧ The Colonial Revival interior of The Highlands, even without its furnishings, still reflects the collaboration of Caroline Sinkler with decorator Henry Sleeper in the 1920s. They painted the checkerboard floor and installed the Zuber scenic wallpaper panels known as *Les Vues de l'Amérique du nord,* a design first printed in 1834.

# FONTHILL

East Court Street and Swamp Road,
Doylestown, PA 18901

Builder, Henry Chapman Mercer,
1908–10

National Historic Landmark, 1986

Owned and operated by the Bucks County
Historical Society

Telephone for opening days and times,
215.348.9461

For most of his life the anthropologist Henry Chapman Mercer (1856–1930) listened to a drummer only he could hear. He consequently comes down to us as a brilliant eccentric who bequeathed to the future a house of extraordinary vision and creativity. A lifelong resident of Doylestown, Pennsylvania, Mercer attended Harvard, where he fell under the influence of historian Charles Eliot Norton. Norton extolled the virtues of preindustrial arts and crafts and set Mercer on the path toward becoming one of the earliest proponents of historical archaeology and the study of American material culture. After law school at the University of Pennsylvania he embarked on a decade of foreign travel and archaeological excavation, supported by the largess of his wealthy widowed aunt, Elizabeth Chapman Lawrence.

By the 1890s Mercer began to focus on the collection and "wider meaning" of tools from the recent past, using techniques until then applied by archaeologists to ancient cultures. Mercer called it "archaeology turned upside down, reversed, revolutionized." This fascination with "tools of the nation maker" would be lifelong, ultimately leading to his patronage of the Bucks County Historical Society, where his collections are the core of the Mercer Museum, which now administers Fonthill.

Mercer also became intrigued by early Pennsylvania pottery, an interest that meshed with the growing American arts and crafts movement. Arguing that "art needs the touch of a human hand," Mercer determined to resuscitate the craft of decorative tile, to "master the potter's art and establish a pottery under [my] personal control." He sought out masters like William De Morgan, who had worked with William Morris, and John Briddes, who designed his kilns for what became Mercer's "artistic pottery," the Moravian Pottery and Tile Works. Unlike most such efforts, the pottery became profitable: Mercer offered a moderately priced and attractive product perfect for the mood of the times. Recognition followed, and his tiles began appearing in buildings such as the Museum of Fine Arts and the Isabella Stewart Gardner Museum in Boston, the Rockefeller estate at Pocantico Hills, New York, and the Pennsylvania State Capitol in Harrisburg.

In 1908, enriched by the estate of his aunt, Mercer began to build a mansion to contain his collections, to display the products of the tile works, and to demonstrate the potential of poured-in-place, reinforced concrete. The house would be "an interweaving of my own fancies blending with memories of my travels and suggestions from engravings." He recalled, "the house was planned by me, room for room, entirely from the interior, the exterior not being considered until all the rooms had been imagined and sketched, after which blocks of clay representing the rooms were piled on a table, set together, and modeled into a general outline. After a good many changes in the profile of the tower, roofs, etc., a plaster-of-Paris model was made to scale, and used till the building was completed." There are 44 rooms, 18 fireplaces, and 200 windows of every size and shape in Mercer's "concrete castle for the New World."

He called his new house Fonthill after an Essex County, Virginia, house belonging to a distant relative; "it seemed very appropriate on account of the fine spring rising here on a hilltop close to the northwest corner of the tower." Mercer knew well the

✤ Henry Chapman Mercer's Fonthill (1908–10) attempts to "combine the poetry of the past with the convenience of the present." Designed and built by Mercer, the house is constructed of poured-in-place concrete and is stylistically highly individual, "an interweaving of my own fancies blending with memories of my travels and suggestions from engravings."

history of James Wyatt's ill-fated and chaotic design for William Beckford in Wiltshire, England. That Fonthill (1795–1807) in the Gothic Revival style had ignominiously collapsed due to incompetent construction. Nonetheless, Mercer records, I "finally decided to use [the name] on the advice of an English friend of high authority."

Mercer supervised the construction himself. "From eight to ten unskilled day laborers at the then wages of $1.75 a day, and under my constant direction, built the house in three summers. I employed no architect to carry out my plans, and there were no skilled laborers employed in the construction proper, though afterwards a carpenter put in the doors and window sash, a mason set the tiles on the vertical walls and a painter put in the window glass. As a single exception to this, a potter set the ceiling tiles which were cast into the building during its construction."

Mercer argued the case for the plasticity of concrete and used the same material and construction techniques at the Moravian Pottery and Tile Works (1910–12) and what became the Mercer Museum of the Bucks County Historical Society (1914–16). For this he has been hailed as an innovative forerunner of the modern movement in architecture. Like many later buildings that used poured-in-place concrete, however, Fonthill suffers from environmental forces and defects traceable to design and construction that require constant conservation. Fortunately the Bucks County Historical Society is committed to the ongoing stewardship of Henry Chapman Mercer's vision that makes Fonthill, the Moravian Pottery and Tile Works, and the Mercer Museum a stimulating day trip.

⁂ The vaulted Dormer Bedroom, inspired by medieval Haddon Hall in Derbyshire, England, conveys the sense of castle-like romance and mystery that is so typical of Fonthill. Hundreds of framed prints from Mercer's collection hang throughout the house.

# PETER WENTZ FARMSTEAD

Skippack Pike and Schultz Road, PO Box 240, Worcester, PA 19490

Architect/builder unknown, 1758; restoration architect, John Milner

National Register of Historic Places

Owned and operated by Montgomery County, acquired 1969

Telephone for opening days and times, 610.584.5104

Even if George Washington hadn't slept at the Peter Wentz house it would stand on its own merits as worthy of being open to the public as a house museum. Constructed in 1758 by American-born Peter Wentz, Jr. (1719–1793), on land purchased by his German emigrant father in 1743, the two-and-one-half-story, five-bay, double-pile stone house with pent eave and balcony probably stood out in the eighteenth century as one of the larger dwellings in what now is Worcester Township, Montgomery County. The west front is built of dressed stone; the other walls are rubble stone. While the house shares much with Anglo-Welsh stone houses of the time, there are also appealing Germanic grace notes such as the German-language house blessing, the extensive use of five-plate stoves, and perhaps the painted decoration.

Following his failure to check the British advance on Philadelphia at Brandywine Creek in September 1777, Washington withdrew his army across the Schuylkill, which had the advantage of putting his army on the Philadelphia side of the river. Once he had determined to attack, he moved down Skippack Pike, pausing at Peter Wentz's house before striking southeast into the heart of Germantown, where the

✤   The Peter Wentz house (1758) has been restored to approximate its appearance in 1777, the year George Washington made it his headquarters before and after the Battle of Germantown. The painting scheme of black window and door frames, white sash, and black and white doors and shutters gives the first hint that Peter Wentz had an unusual sense of color. The pent eave, balcony, and stoop are reconstructions based on physical evidence.

✤   The cast iron stove in the ground floor bedroom is stoked through a hole in the back of the parlor fireplace. In lieu of wallpaper, the wall area below the chair rail is decorated with dots.

Americans hoped to surprise the British on October 4. (The collapse of that attack and the role of Cliveden on the events of that day are discussed in the Germantown house museum section.) The American Army retired back to Skippack Creek, and Washington returned to the Wentz house. They were there when news came of Burgoyne's surrender at Saratoga—an event that proved to be the turning point in the American Revolution.

Peter Wentz sold his farm in 1784 and ten years later Melchior Schultz acquired the property, thus beginning a 175-year tenure of ownership by that family. Architecturally the Schultzes made few changes. The pent eave, balcony, and original porch had disappeared by 1969 and had to be reconstructed, but much of the original interior trim and paneling survived. Here the restoration team using analytical techniques then relatively new made a major discovery: the original interior colors—yellow, salmon, and blue—differed from those thought at the time to be typical in Pennsylvania colonial houses. More dramatically it was determined that these colors had been applied in decorative patterns. Particularly under the chair rails the original painter had boldly applied commas, stripes, and dots. To the credit of the Montgomery County Department of History and Cultural Arts, these decorative patterns were restored and made a part of the wider interpretive program at the site that focuses broadly on eighteenth-century life and crafts in Montgomery County. In subsequent decades, the discovery and recreation of fugitive paint schemes at the Peter Wentz Farmstead has encouraged the widespread use of scientific analysis and the reevaluation of many house museum interiors in an effort to improve our understanding of the past.

The parlor is here shown as it might have been when a large company of guests were to be entertained—a special setup for the annual Christmas candlelight tour. No original furniture from the house has been identified, but Peter Wentz's estate inventory survives to provide guidance for the installation. Most of the objects are of English or American origin from the 1750–1800 period. Appropriate to the time and place, and confirmed by the Wentz and similar household inventories, there are no curtains at the windows and no carpets on the floor. Colors are recreated from a microscopic and chemical examination of the original surfaces.

# PENNYPACKER MILLS

Route 73 and Haldeman Road, Schwenksville, PA 19473

Architect, Arthur H. Brockie, AIA, 1901–2, incorporating an earlier structure, c. 1720

National Register of Historic Places, 1976

Owned and operated by Montgomery County, 1981

Telephone for opening days and hours, 610.287.9349

❧ The library at Pennypacker Mills reflects the late Victorian melange of Colonial Revival furniture assembled by Mr. and Mrs. Pennypacker. A sample of the Pennypackers' wallpaper has been discovered behind the bookcase, but it had not been reproduced when this photograph was taken.

The appeal of Pennypacker Mills to Samuel W. Pennypacker was more than the Philadelphia jurist could resist. The genealogical link he assumed to early Pennypackers, the undoubted antiquity of a colonial house perhaps dating to the 1720s, and its documented use by George Washington's army before and after the Battle of Germantown all conspired to elevate the antiquarian's heart rate and trigger a desire to own.

A native of Phoenixville on the Schuylkill near Valley Forge, Samuel W. Pennypacker (1843–1916) developed an early love of history; he later recalled how as a child he "hunted through the fields, which had been plowed for corn, for the implements lost or thrown away by the Indians," and as an adult the Centennial Exposition further stimulated his fascination with American history. He formed one of the largest and most important book and pamphlet collections on Pennsylvania history ever assembled and served for several years as President of the Historical Society of Pennsylvania. After two decades at the Philadelphia bar, Pennypacker was elected to the Court of Common Pleas and then nominated for governor of Pennsylvania, serving a single term (1903–7). Unfortunately his term in office was overshadowed by corruption on a scale beyond the imagining of avarice in the construction and furnishing of the new Harrisburg capitol building.

In 1900 Pennypacker Mills came on the market, a house "30 × 50 ft., in good condition, with 4 rooms and a large hall on the first floor, 7 rooms and a large hall on the second and an attic over the whole, a cellar and out kitchen." Judge Pennypacker assured the local Schwenksville newspaper, "Not a line of its ancient architecture will be changed, and the interior so far as essentials are concerned will not be robbed of one of its Colonial attributes."

Immediately Pennypacker hired Arthur H. Brockie (1875–1946), a graduate of the

University of Pennsylvania who on his return from the Spanish-American War studied in Europe and then established a practice specializing in residential commissions for prominent Philadelphians. By 1902 the press reported, "Learned jurist purchases colonial farmhouse overlooking the Perkiomen Creek and spares no expense in having it remodeled." In the process of transforming a simple farmhouse into a gentleman's Georgian mansion, Brockie removed all the original details and replaced them with stock millwork—floors, doors, windows, mantels, shutters—all made new, but in the "colonial style." A large service wing doubled the number of rooms. The Germantown landscape designers Thomas Meehan and Sons were brought in to lay out an English garden, which now having matured adds greatly to the overall appeal of what Pennypacker created.

By 1902 Mr. and Mrs. Pennypacker had moved into their perfect Colonial Revival retreat, comfortably furnished with a late Victorian melange of ladder-back and Windsor chairs, Native American artifacts, early baskets, clocks, oriental carpets, and kerosene lamps (there was no electricity at Pennypacker Mills until 1935). During Pennypacker's governorship the family lived in Harrisburg, moving to the country in the summers. After his retirement in 1907 they took up full time residence, from which the governor pursued his antiquarian and eleemosynary interests. Following his death in 1916 the family continued to use Pennypacker Mills until it was sold to Montgomery County in 1981 by Margaret Pennypacker, widow of the governor's only grandchild.

❧ Aided by Philadelphia architect Arthur H. Brockie, Judge Samuel W. Pennypacker converted a simple Pennsylvania colonial farm house overlooking Perkiomen Creek at Schwenksville, Pennsylvania into a Colonial Revival Georgian mansion, 1900–1902. The natural English garden was laid out by Thomas Meehan & Sons at the same time.

# HARRITON

Old Gulph and Harriton Roads, Bryn
Mawr, PA 19010

Architect/builder unknown, 1704;
restored by Robert L. Raley, 1970–76

National Register of Historic Places, 1985

Owned by Township of Lower Merion,
1969; operated by the Harriton
Association

Telephone for opening days and times,
610.525.0201

In 1682 the Welsh Quaker Rowland Ellis (1650–1729) received from William Penn a grant of 690 acres located twelve miles from Philadelphia in what is now the prosperous suburb of Bryn Mawr. The name Bryn Mawr derives from that first given by Ellis to his new house, erected in 1704 to replace the rude cabin built to shelter the farmer sent to prepare the land for cultivation. Ellis's plantation, located in the so-called Welsh Barony, a tract of 40,000 acres set aside for groups of Welsh Quakers who migrated to Pennsylvania, was part of a group that received 5,000 acres known as "Merion" after Merionethshire, Wales.

In the best colonial tradition, Ellis attempted to profit as speculator rather than farmer and ran into financial difficulty. In 1719 he sold Bryn Mawr to Richard Harrison, a Maryland planter from the Western Shore of the Chesapeake, who renamed the house Harriton and moved his family and slaves to Pennsylvania, where he raised tobacco on the surrounding fields, one of the northernmost documented examples of the plantation system in America. The house eventually came into the hands of Hannah Harrison, who married Charles Thomson (1729–1824), a man destined by fate to have his name appear on the Declaration of Independence and join the pantheon of founding fathers.

Harriton's principal justification as a house museum is its 35-year association with Charles Thomson, whom John Adams called "The Sam Adams of Philadelphia, the life of the cause of liberty." An Ulsterman by birth, Thomson emigrated to America, obtained a solid classical education, taught Latin and Greek at the institutions now known as the University of Pennsylvania and William Penn Charter School, and eventually moved into mercantile ventures. Radicalized by Crown policy in the 1760s, Thomson became an advocate of separation from Great Britain and Secretary of Congress, a post he held for fifteen years until retiring to Harriton in 1789 to busy himself with scientific agriculture and translating the Bible from the Greek.

Charles Thomson had moved in exalted circles; he shared the aristocratic conviction that a "country gentleman . . . enjoys that situation in life which in my Opinion is the most delightful." But unlike the planter grandees of Virginia with whom he came in daily contact, this former public servant would not retire to a Palladian country house. By planter standards Harriton is a rustic retreat, albeit furnished with Middle Georgian mahogany furniture.

Architecturally unencumbered by classical conventions, Harriton stands as a better-than-average vernacular, two-and-one-half-story stone farm house of the type erected throughout southeastern Pennsylvania, several of which are now house museums. In plan the original house forms a "T": a hall and parlor in front with a kitchen and stair extension to the rear. Across the main facade a pent eave and balcony shelter the window openings, originally set with leaded casements. The gable roof has three dormers and the eaves kick out at the cornice. When Charles and Hannah Thomson renovated Harriton in preparation for moving there, the pent eave and balcony were removed and sash windows replaced the casements.

It is probable that the Thomsons used the stair passage door, because the front door

☙   In preparation for country retirement, Charles and Hannah Thomson renovated Harriton by removing the pent eave and balcony and replacing the leaded casement windows with sash windows. The pent and balcony were recreated during the restoration in the 1970s. The balcony balusters copy the interior stair balusters; the successfully recreated chimney caps are based on early photographs of the Slate Roof House in Philadelphia.

❦ The parlor at Harriton is furnished with Middle and Late Georgian objects of the type known to have been owned by Charles and Hannah Thomson; many of these came to the house in the 1970s from a descendant of John Curwen, a near neighbor and friend of the Thomsons. The bolection molding, mantel shelf, and chair rail are recreations based on molding profiles discovered under twentieth-century plaster. The wallpaper is reproduced from a fragment that had been similarly covered.

opens directly into the great hall without the intervening convenience of a passageway. Used for a wide range of activities, including Thomson's study, the hall is the largest room in the house. According to one account, Thomson used the closets in this room for storage "with their doors always standing open and the books and papers tumbling out." The adjoining parlor had received the most modernization by the Thomsons and contained their best furniture. Across the stair passage the Thomsons converted the Ellis kitchen with its large cooking hearth into a dining room by erecting a new brick kitchen connected by a piazza to the back of the house. The upper floors contained the bed chambers, two of which have been furnished by the Harriton Association to the time of the Thomson occupancy.

After Thomson's death, Harriton sheltered tenant farmers until extensively expanded in the 1920s as a suburban gentleman's Colonial Revival estate. Faced with potential development of the site in 1962, neighbors formed the Harriton Association to assist Lower Merion Township to acquire, restore, and open the house and its sixteen-acre park to the public.

The robust, closed-string staircase at Harriton rises three floors and survives virtually unaltered from 1704, making it one of the earliest and most significant surviving examples in the Delaware Valley. Microanalysis of the handrail and bulbous turned balusters discloses that both were first painted the yellowish white shown here. Note also the painted baseboards; in eighteenth-century Philadelphia this element was commonly painted dark brown or black to reduce soiling from washing the unfinished wooden floors.

# THE GRANGE

Myrtle Avenue and Warwick Road,
Havertown, PA 19083

Builder/architect, John E. Carver, 1850–
51, incorporating an earlier house; porte
cochere by John McArthur, Jr., 1863

National Register of Historic Places, 1976

Owned by Township of Haverford,
Delaware County, 1974; operated by The
Friends of the Grange, Inc.

Telephone for opening days and times,
610.446.4958

Writing of a Gothic house design not unlike The Grange, Andrew Jackson Downing—America's first architectural critic with a national reputation—described it as "a sensible, solid, unpretending country house, with an air of substantial comfort and refinement, not overpowered by architectural style, but indicating intelligent, domestic life in the country." It is probably coincidental that Downing published his design in 1850 and the Philadelphia architect John E. Carver (1803–1859) submitted his drawings for The Grange later the same year, but the resulting house does survive as the only Downingesque Gothic country house in the Philadelphia area that is open to the public.

The history of this appealing house and its extensive gardens, which contain some of the largest specimen trees in Pennsylvania, stretches back to the earliest years of settlement. The Grange occupies a site seven miles from Philadelphia overlooking Cobbs Creek that, like Harriton, had once been part of the Welsh Barony granted by William Penn. Throughout the eighteenth century successive owners built, demolished, altered, and added to a house they variously identified as Maencoch ("red stone" in Welsh), Clifton Hall, and finally The Grange—so named in honor of the Marquis de Lafayette's chateau.

By the time John Ashhurst purchased The Grange in 1850 it had incrementally evolved over at least a century into a two-and-one-half-story, six-bay Georgian stone house. It must have seemed woefully out of date by early Victorian standards. Ashhurst (1809–1892), a wealthy dry goods importer, and his wife, Harriet Eyre Ashhurst (1816–1890), whose father owned The Grange, traveled extensively in Europe, and maintained an elegant Grecian townhouse next door to the Athenaeum overlooking Washington Square. Following the death of Mrs. Ashhurst's father, the Ashhursts rented The Grange as a summer retreat and eventually purchased the property, quickly thereafter hiring John Carver, who already had a reputation for his ecclesiastical designs in the Gothic style.

The most obvious addition is an octagonal entrance vestibule rising on the exterior to a high-pitched gable, which together with its handsome oriel window becomes the most decorative feature of the facade. The house is also surrounded by verandas, and the high-pitched roof and dormers have handsome verge boards. The tall chimneys add character and heighten the verticality of the entire composition. Downing tells us that "the broad and massive veranda—the full second story, overshadowed by the overhanging eaves—the steep roof, to shed the snow and afford a well-ventilated attic . . . are all expressive of the comparatively modest but cultivated tastes and life of substantial country residents." While structurally little changed on the interior—except for the addition of a central stair and rearrangement of the kitchen—the house received ornamental plaster ceilings and cornices in mid-nineteenth-century taste which were decoratively painted.

To architects and critics of the mid-nineteenth century, Gothic cottages with their irregular outlines and earth-tone colors were thought to blend well with the natural

The Grange, in Haverford Township, Delaware County, acquired its Victorian Gothic appearance in 1850–51 at the hands of architect John E. Carver; he completely recast a much earlier Georgian house to suit the new owner, John Ashhurst, merchant, banker, and manager of the Philadelphia and Reading Railroad. Carver's design called for pinnacles projecting through the dormer roofs and entrance vestibule gable roof. The shafts can be seen but without the pinnacles, which probably decayed in the twentieth century and have unfortunately been removed.

landscape. The Philadelphia diarist Sidney George Fisher wrote admiringly of Downing's influence over Americans and the introduction of Gothic style cottages, "which harmonizes so admirably with the surrounding natural objects & is so much more easily adapted to the purposes of a dwelling" than the Greek Revival style. One person, however, who recalled the house before it was "metamorphosed into a Gothic cottage" remarked unfavorably on the "deep, obtruding piazza [that now] surrounds the old-fashioned low ceilinged Grange."

With the exception of an addition for staff bedrooms and a porte cochere designed by John McArthur, Jr. in 1863, The Grange structurally survives largely as conceived by Carver and the Ashhursts in the mid-nineteenth century. It remained in the Ashhurst family until early in the twentieth century, when it was purchased by Mr. and Mrs. Benjamin R. Hoffman; they were the owners until the property passed to Haverford Township in 1974. The Hoffmans redecorated the interiors and devoted several decades to restoring and embellishing the ornamental gardens that remain one of the principal attractions of The Grange.

❧ The ongoing restoration of The Grange interior has uncovered decorative painting from the 1850s, as seen here on the parlor ceiling. The wallpaper is early twentieth century and probably survives from the redecoration by Mr. and Mrs. Benjamin R. Hoffman, c. 1913.

# WAYNESBOROUGH

2049 Waynesborough Road, Paoli, PA 19301

Architect/builder unknown, mid-eighteenth century, incorporating an earlier structure

National Register of Historic Places, 1973

Owned by Easttown Township, Chester County, 1980; administered by the Philadelphia Society for the Preservation of Landmarks

Telephone for opening days and times, 610.647.1779

Pennsylvania General Anthony Wayne ranks among the most famous of George Washington's lieutenants in the Revolutionary War. Son and grandson of military men—his grandfather served under William of Orange at the Battle of the Boyne and his father fought in the French and Indian War—Anthony Wayne (1745–1796) became an early and fervent advocate of American independence. When protest turned to open rebellion, he joined the Continental Army, participating in several major engagements. Following the Battle of Brandywine, however, Wayne's troops—encamped near his house at Paoli—were surprised and routed by the British Army in the so-called Paoli Massacre. A court martial cleared him of responsibility, and he further redeemed his reputation in 1779 by leading the American Light Infantry in the capture of Stony Point on the Hudson. After the Revolution, Washington called Wayne back to service against the Native American tribes of the Northwest Territory, whom he defeated at the Battle of Fallen Timbers (August 20, 1794).

For seven generations the Waynes lived on the same tract of land in Chester County. General Anthony Wayne's grandfather purchased the original 386 acres after migrating from County Wicklow, Ireland in 1724. This property passed to his son Isaac Wayne, subsequently to General Wayne in 1774, and henceforth until 1965, when William Wayne III sold the estate—by then long known as Waynesborough. Frustratingly little is known with certainty about the early history of the house at Waynesborough. It is probable that the present west wing existed by c. 1745 and the main

block by c. 1760, both erected during the tenure of General Wayne's father, but the evidence is largely circumstantial, which accounts for the wide range of dates that have appeared in print over the past century. The east, or kitchen, wing existed by the early nineteenth century and was later raised to a full two stories.

The main block of the two-and-one-half-story, five-bay house—with a center hall, double-pile plan—is built of the same undressed schist used for the earlier west wing. The walls rise directly from the foundation without water table or belt course. The double-leaf paneled front door is protected by a pedimented hood that appears to be original; both this hood and the simple box cornice have modillions that are virtually the only exterior references to the classical orders. Like many vernacular houses of its type in Chester County, Waynesborough is a balanced composition, but it is hardly symmetrical in the Palladian sense of the Middle Georgian houses of Philadelphia.

In 1902 the Colonial Revival struck Waynesborough in the person of the architect Thomas Mellon Rogers (1857–1928). Hired by William Wayne II, who had just inherited the property, Rogers, his drafting tools still stained from a "restoration" of Independence Hall, descended on Waynesborough to "improve" its Colonial aspects. Dormer windows were tricked out with elaborate pediments (now removed); fanciful chimney breasts, window sash, shutters, and chimney caps were installed; and the interior was scrubbed clean of much physical evidence that might have assisted later, more thoughtful and knowledgeable restorers who have since attempted to correct his romantic errors. For all this colonial revivalizing, Waynesborough remains one of the most popular house museums in Chester County, set as it is in a 16-acre park and furnished with objects appropriate to the General Wayne occupancy, some of which have a history of Wayne family ownership.

Waynesborough near Paoli in Chester County sheltered seven generations of the Wayne family, including General Anthony Wayne of Revolutionary War fame. The main section built of undressed local stone dates from the mid-eighteenth century, when the property belonged to Isaac Wayne (1739–1774).

The north wall of the room long known as the General Wayne Parlor is fully paneled and includes a display closet or "buffet." The coved-cheek fireplace has a surround and overmantel that boldly depart from academic proportions, although the joiner had in mind a classically-inspired composition. The rich use of Prussian blue pigment is typical of better rooms in eighteenth-century American houses; George Washington painted the west parlor at Mount Vernon a lighter version of this same color. The portrait of General Wayne that has long hung in this location is by the French-born artist Jean Pierre Elouis (1755–1840), who worked in Philadelphia from 1792 to 1794.

# BRINTON 1704 HOUSE

West Chester-Wilmington Pike,
Dilworthtown, PA

PO Box 1032, Chadds Ford, PA 19317

Architect/builder unknown, 1704;
restored by G. Edwin Brumbaugh, FAIA,
1954–58

National Historic Landmark

Owned and operated by the Brinton
Family Association.

Telephone for opening days and times,
610.399.0913 or 610.399.4588

The Brinton family is a prolific Chester and Delaware County clan that traces its American origins to the English Quaker emigrants William and Ann Bagley Brinton, who settled near the Brandywine in 1684. Nearly two hundred years later, in the mid-nineteenth century, one of their descendants, West Chester lawyer John Hill Brinton, began a genealogical quest that included interviews with elderly family members and others of the community concerning the surviving Brinton House. Writing in 1868 he remarked, "I thus relate these facts minutely in order that some future Brinton . . . may restore the old house to its primitive aspect." Fulfillment of this hope would not come for nearly a century.

Today the handsomely furnished and extensively restored Brinton House bears little resemblance to what the Brinton Family Association faced in the 1950s when Francis D. Brinton presented the house to the Chester County Historical Society with the proviso that it be restored. Two hundred fifty years and many owners—including family members—had radically altered the house built by the second William Brinton (1670–1751), son of the emigrant. In the nineteenth century the dormers had been replaced by a large gable with decorative barge boards and the entire house had been stuccoed and given a wrap-around porch with suitable Victorian embellishments. Chimneys were reduced, windows enlarged, inside stairs moved, and doors replaced. Finally, a large serpentine stone wing dating from 1881 had been attached to the northwest side.

To recreate William Brinton's house, the association engaged architect G. Edwin Brumbaugh (1890–1983). He removed the alterations of 250 years. Then, based on his reading of the physical evidence and the detailed notes of antiquarian John Hill Brinton, many of which predate the extensive nineteenth-century changes, Brumbaugh recreated the missing details. Brumbaugh had apprenticed with the early twentieth-century country house revival architects Mellor and Meigs and only gradually turned to historic building restoration, eventually becoming one of the most popular Delaware Valley practitioners of that specialty. But Brumbaugh was no proponent of the John Ruskin and William Morris "anti-scrape" school of preservation—which holds that later changes to a building are just as valid as the original fabric. He also believed with the wider public of the time that the Victorian era represented an unfortunate lapse in taste that should be excised from earlier buildings at every opportunity. As nearly as possible he returned the house to its 1704 appearance.

If the visitor's time permits, the Brinton House should be viewed in comparison with the nearby Barns-Brinton House and John Chads House. The Brinton House is representative of the larger type of Chester County English Quaker dwelling of the eighteenth century and would, consequently, have been more richly furnished than the others. Fortunately, the estate inventories of both William and Jane (1756) Brinton survive, along with an extraordinary "account of damage Waste spoil & destruction which done & committed by the army of the King of Great Brittain under the Imediate Command of Genl Howe at the Battle of Brandywine from Septr 11th to the 16th

The Brinton 1704 House built by William Brinton the younger represents the finest class of early Quaker English domestic structures erected in the Brandywine Creek area. It was restored by G. Edwin Brumbaugh in the 1950s for the Brinton Family Association.

✿ A bedroom on the first floor contains a fully furnished bedstead, a large walnut clothes press, a day bed with rush seat, and a walnut spice box with tear-drop drawer pulls—all dating from the early eighteenth century. The diamond-pane casement windows are based on fragments discovered during the restoration.

1777 to the property Real & personal Belonging to George Brinton" in the amount of £544.11.8.

Howe's army lived off the land during its advance on Philadelphia, and British foragers made a clean sweep of the Brintons' farm: four-and-a-half tons of hay, 200 bushels of wheat, corn, rye, buckwheat, and barley, plus a "Likely Young Mare," other horses, bullocks, cows, heifers, spring calves, sheep, and swine—to feed the invading army and their horses. Apparently the troops ransacked the house, taking away men's, women's, and children's clothing plus bedding, pewter, porcelain, and earthenware. The Brintons' walnut furniture didn't interest the British, but according to the accounting they ran off with one looking glass, destroyed three chairs, and damaged a "Desk Book Case and Case of Drawrs." These documents provide the Brinton Family Association with excellent guidance for furnishing the house to the time of William and Jane Brinton's occupancy, and an unusually fine collection of southeastern Pennsylvania furniture—displayed in an appropriate setting—makes the Brinton 1704 House and its near neighbors at Chadds Ford well worth an expedition.

❦ The hall is furnished with walnut Anglo-American wainscot chairs, a walnut settle upholstered in leather, and a gate-leg table. The Staffordshire inkwell is believed to have belonged to William Brinton the elder (1650–1700).

# BARNS-BRINTON HOUSE

U.S. Route 1, Pennsbury Township,
Chester County, PA 19317

Architect/builder unknown, early
eighteenth century; restoration architect,
John Milner, 1969–86

National Register of Historic Places, 1971

Owned and operated by Chadds Ford
Historical Society, 1969

Telephone for opening days and times,
610.388.7376

⚜ The Barns-Brinton House boasts some
of the best surviving early eighteenth-
century woodwork in Chester County.

Located on the south side of U.S. Route 1 near the Brandywine River Museum, this
two-and-one-half-story, hall-and-parlor plan house is unusual for being built of brick in
an area whose early settlers favored the readily available local stone—as at the nearby
John Chads House. The brick is laid in Flemish bond with glazed headers forming a
diaper pattern on the gables. During the restoration the pent eave and the casement
windows were successfully recreated.

The exact date of construction is uncertain. Presumably the blacksmith William
Barns erected the house after he acquired the land in 1710 and before he paid taxes on
his 104 acres *and* a building in 1715. In 1722 Barns petitioned for a license to establish
"a Publick House for ye accommodation of Man and Horse" because of the "great
concors of Travellers along ye Road [that] leads to Maryland, and likewise to Con-
estogo." The Chadds Ford Historical Society has consequently interpreted the house
as a tavern with the keeper in residence.

William Barns's tavern did not greatly differ architecturally from purely residential
hall-and-parlor plan structures of the period. Such a "Publick House" might be little
more than a common or tavern room (the hall) where overnight travelers joined local
farmers having a tankard of cider or ale and could then obtain a meal and a dry space to
sleep. On the second floor there is no door between the two chambers. This division
allowed the tavern keeper's family the use of the "parlor" on the ground floor with a
private stair to their chamber above. Travelers would have had separate access to the
hall chamber and the finished garret under the eaves.

The Barns-Brinton House is an extraordinary survival. Virtually all the original poplar woodwork (some of the best in Chester County) and most of the decorative iron hardware (butterfly and HL hinges, thumb latches, and the like) remain in place, requiring only modest replacement or repair during the restoration. Board partitions divide the interior rooms, and the stairs have newel posts, closed strings, and boldly turned balusters at the foot of enclosed winders. The fireplace walls are paneled on both floors; in the hall fireplace an original built-in seat survives; and in the chambers there are decorative ventilation grills above the closet doors—details that have been widely used as precedents for the restoration of other houses.

William Barns died intestate in 1731 leaving an illiterate wife, several children, and debts to seventy-eight creditors. Eventually James Brinton acquired the property and the house remained in that family as a private residence for a century. It then fell to use as a tenant farm until acquired by the Chadds Ford Historical Society in 1969.

❦ Erected by the blacksmith William Barns in the early eighteenth century and operated as a "Publick House for ye accommodation of Man and Horse" on the main road from Philadelphia to Maryland, the Barns-Brinton house has been restored and opened by the Chadds Ford Historical Society.

# JOHN CHADS HOUSE

Chadds Ford Historical Society, PO Box 27, Chadds Ford, PA 19137

Builder, John Wyeth, Jr., c. 1725; restoration architect, John Milner, 1970s

National Register of Historic Places, 1971

Owned and operated by the Chadds Ford Historical Society, 1969

Telephone for opening days and times, 610.388.7376

As the British Army advanced from the Chesapeake toward Philadelphia in the late summer of 1777, General Washington positioned his army of 11,000 men behind Brandywine Creek to make a stand against a superior force of 18,000 British and Hessian troops. Chester County native General Anthony Wayne stood opposite Lieutenant General Wilhelm von Knyphausen's Hessians at the ford crossing the Brandywine. According to some accounts, Wayne established his headquarters in the modest stone bank house of John Chads's widow, Elizabeth Richardson Chads. Once the British troops under Cornwallis flanked the American right, Wayne fell back leaving the ford to the British, who swirled through the small settlement and on toward Philadelphia.

John Chads inherited his land on the banks of the Brandywine from his father, who had emigrated from Wiltshire, England, in 1689. The house the younger Chads built overlooked the point where the road to Philadelphia crossed the river, and it is here that he established a ferry in 1737. Chads died in 1760 and his widow lived on in the house until her death in 1790.

The John Chads House is a three-bay, two-and-one-half-story bank house built of the local undressed "Brandywine blue" stone with which the builder, believed to be John Wyeth, Jr., took some obvious care; the larger corner stones have been selected to give the visual effect of quoins as well as to provide needed stability. The John Chads House is a remarkable example of an early vernacular Chester and Delaware County building type that continued to be built throughout the eighteenth and nineteenth centuries. But unlike most of these later houses the Chads House survives with most of its original fabric intact, including the oak floors, poplar paneled chimney breasts,

✤ The modest interiors have plastered walls without baseboards and corner fireplaces with built-in cupboards and shelves.

corner fireplaces and cupboards. Details such as the beehive oven or the pent eave that had to be recreated or proved too deteriorated to repair were clearly indicated by the physical evidence and could be restored with confidence.

The John Chads House is modestly furnished, in keeping with a house of this period and class, and should be visited together with its nearby early eighteenth-century contemporaries—the Barns-Brinton House and the Brinton 1704 House. Directly across the road is the handsome modern headquarters of the Chadds Ford Historical Society, which offers exhibitions on local history, and less than a quarter mile away is the Brandywine River Museum—in case the visitor has forgotten that this is the home ground of the prolific Wyeth family of artists.

The John Chads House is the archetypical early eighteenth-century Chester County stone bank house; most of its original fabric has survived intact after a quarter of a millennium and a full-scale eighteenth-century battle. The reconstructed beehive oven to the left is used for baking demonstrations.

# CALEB PUSEY HOUSE

15 Race Street, Upland, PA 19015

Architect/builder unknown, c. 1683–96; restored by John M. Dickey, FAIA, 1963–66

National Register of Historic Places, 1971

Owned by Delaware County; operated by Friends of the Caleb Pusey House, Inc.

Telephone for opening days and times, 610.874.5665

The Caleb Pusey House is probably the oldest surviving Anglo-American residential structure in Pennsylvania and the only one with documented William Penn associations. Architecturally it provides virtually the only unaltered example of the vernacular cottages erected by the earliest Quaker settlers in the first years of settlement that is open to the public.

The settler in question here is Caleb Pusey (1651–1727). Born in Chipping Lambourn, Berkshire, 68 miles west of London—a shoe last maker by trade and a Quaker by conviction—Pusey answered William Penn's call to opportunity in America by acquiring 250 acres located approximately a mile and a half upstream from the point where Chester Creek flows into the Delaware River. Before his departure from England in 1682, Pusey became an investor with several other Quakers, including Penn, in a grist and lumber mill to be erected on Chester Creek.

By prior agreement, Pusey would manage the mill and one of the other partners, Richard Townsend, would build it. Townsend records, "I set up a mill, on Chester creek; which I brought ready framed from London; which served for grinding of corn, and sawing of boards; and was of great use to us." Later historians have assumed that Pusey would have had little experience with construction and that Townsend directed the erection of both a structure for the prefabricated mill and Pusey's house.

Regardless of builder, Pusey's one-and-one-half-story house consists of two one-room sections built within a few years of each other. The stone work of the eighteen-inch-thick walls is rough, and the casement windows and batten doors are randomly placed; the roof is low pitched and covered with wood shingles. (During the eigh-

❧ The modest stone cottage erected by Caleb Pusey in two sections spanning the years 1683–96 is the oldest documented Anglo-American house in Pennsylvania.

teenth century part of the roof was raised to a gambrel to provide more headroom.) The interior has always been whitewashed, and it escaped being updated with gas, running water, or electricity.

In 1717 Pusey retired from the mill and moved to London Grove in Chester County, where he died ten years later. His house passed through several hands until acquired by the industrialist John Price Crozer in the mid-nineteenth century. To the credit of the Crozer family, whose textile mills were constructed on former Pusey land, they recognized the importance of the house and erected a protective wall around it, on which was placed a marker reading, "This is the Caleb Pusey House, built in 1683. William Penn often visited here." In the following decades several initiatives by the Delaware County Historical Society failed to attract support for restoration until the founding of the Friends of the Caleb Pusey House in 1961. This volunteer group, encouraged by the Pennsylvania Historical and Museum Commission, ultimately raised both state and private funds to restore the house and open it to the public.

The Caleb Pusey House is an important survival well worth a brief visit. For the cultural tourist it would be an excellent point to begin a study tour of Philadelphia area houses, particularly in context with the early stone structures in Delaware, Montgomery, and Chester Counties.

# ILLUSTRATED GLOSSARY
# OF ARCHITECTURAL TERMS

The five figures in this section illustrate the architectural terms used frequently throughout the book. Mount Pleasant and Powel House represent typical Middle Georgian country and town houses respectively. The remaining three drawings show roof types, brickwork bonding styles, and varieties of classical orders commonly used in Delaware Valley houses.

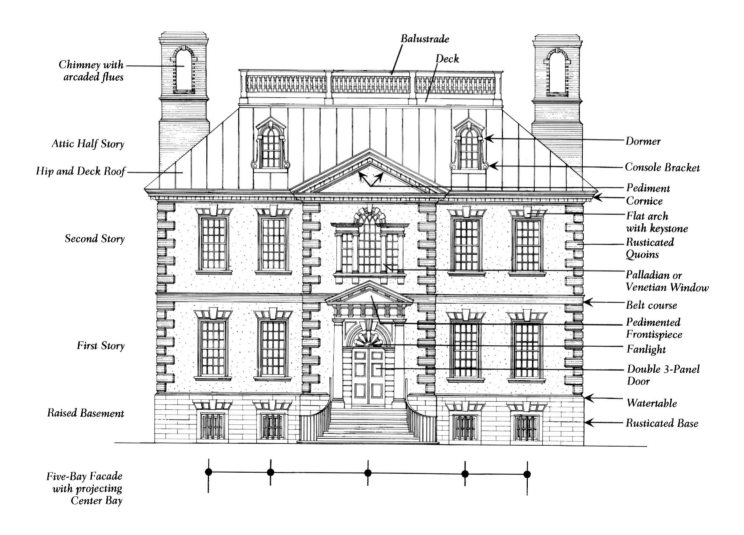

Balustrade

Deck

Chimney with arcaded flues

Attic Half Story

Hip and Deck Roof

Second Story

First Story

Raised Basement

Five-Bay Facade with projecting Center Bay

Dormer

Console Bracket

Pediment
Cornice

Flat arch with keystone

Rusticated Quoins

Palladian or Venetian Window

Belt course

Pedimented Frontispiece

Fanlight

Double 3-Panel Door

Watertable

Rusticated Base

Figure 1. Five-bay Middle Georgian country house (Mount Pleasant).

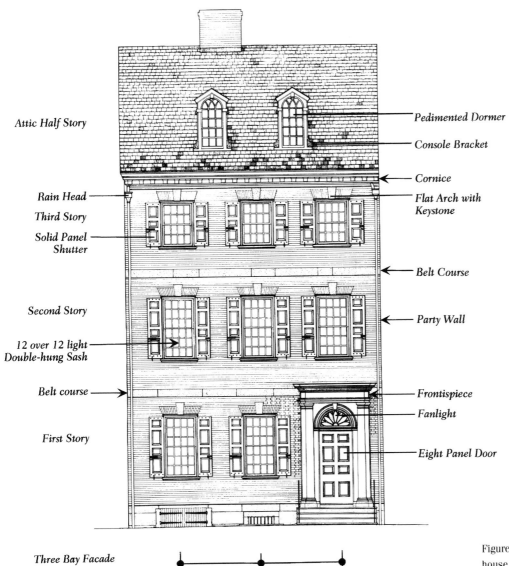

Attic Half Story

Rain Head
Third Story

Solid Panel
Shutter

Second Story

12 over 12 light
Double-hung Sash

Belt course

First Story

Pedimented Dormer

Console Bracket

Cornice

Flat Arch with
Keystone

Belt Course

Party Wall

Frontispiece
Fanlight

Eight Panel Door

Three Bay Facade

Figure 2. Three-bay Middle Georgian town house (Powel House).

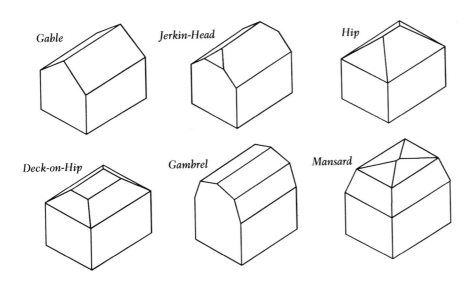

Gable    Jerkin-Head    Hip

Deck-on-Hip    Gambrel    Mansard

Figure 3. Roof types commonly used in the Delaware Valley.

**Common Bond**  Every sixth course or row of bricks is set with the short end (header) to the face of the wall. The headers tie the five courses of brick laid with the long end (stretcher) to the face of the wall.

**English Bond**  Alternating header and stretcher courses.

**Flemish Bond**  Headers and stretchers alternating in the same course. Often used in Philadelphia with glazed headers to create a distinctive pattern.

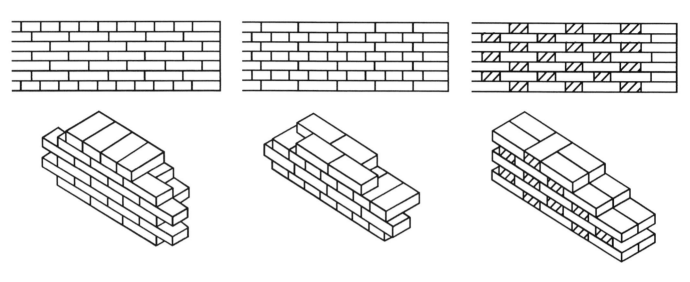

Figure 4. Above: Brickwork bonds used in the Delaware Valley.

Figure 5. Below: Classical column types (orders) commonly found in the Delaware Valley.

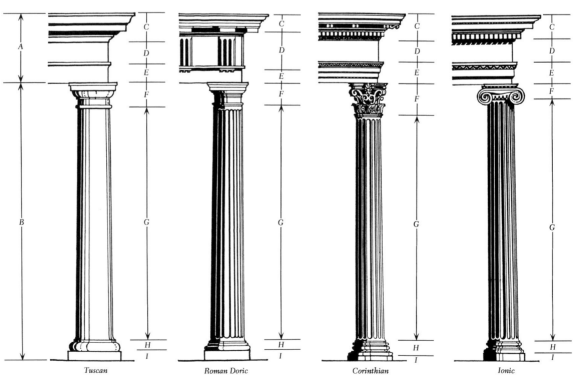

Tuscan          Roman Doric          Corinthian          Ionic

## PREFACE

1. These are the basic evaluation criteria for inclusion of a property in the National Register of Historic Places, United States Department of the Interior, National Park Service. The National Register is the official list of the Nation's cultural resources worthy of preservation. Virtually all the house museums discussed in this book are either on or eligible for the National Register.

## HISTORIC PRESERVATION IN PHILADELPHIA

1. Adolph B. Benson, ed., *The America of 1750: Peter Kalm's Travels in North America* (New York: Wilson-Erickson, 1937), 1: 33–34.

2. The standard histories of preservation in America are Charles B. Hosmer, Jr., *Presence of the Past: A History of the Preservation Movement in the United States Before Williamsburg* (New York: Putnam, 1965) and *Preservation Comes of Age: From Williamsburg to the National Trust, 1926–1949* (Charlottesville: University Press of Virginia, 1981). See also Constance M. Greiff, *Independence: The Creation of a National Park* (Philadelphia: University of Pennsylvania Press, 1987). Independence Hall remains the property of the City of Philadelphia under agreements with the National Park Service, which operates Independence National Historical Park.

3. *The Port Folio* (October 1818): 243–44. The Anthony Benezet House occupied a lot at the present 325 (old 115) Chestnut Street and was erected c. 1700 by David Brientnall. Benezet acquired the house in 1753 and occupied it until his death in 1784. N. Thomas Warner, "Anthony Benezet House, c. 1700–1818," paper, Historic Preservation Program, University of Pennsylvania, 1988. Copy on file at The Athenaeum of Philadelphia.

4. A similar desire motivated the founders of The Athenaeum of Philadelphia in 1814, who hoped "to call particularly upon the surviving characters of our revolutionary war to communicate such facts referring to the events of the war, or to the meritorious conduct of individuals engaged in it, as they may have in their power. The history of the war is lamentably deficient in many interesting particulars, which might have been supplied if this assistance had been afforded by those who have since the declaration of independence been dropping off the stage of existence." The Athenaeum of Philadelphia, Minute Book I, pp. 10–12 (February 23, 1814).

5. Edward M. Riley, "The Independence Hall Group," in *Historic Philadelphia: From the Founding until the Early Nineteenth Century*, Transactions of the American Philosophical Society 43 (Philadelphia: American Philosophical Society, 1953), pp. 33–42. Lee H. Nelson, "Independence Hall: Its Fabric Reinforced" and Penelope H. Batcheler, "Independence Hall: Its Appearance Restored," in Charles E. Peterson, ed., *Building Early America: Contributions Toward the History of a Great Industry* (Radnor, Pa.: Chilton, 1976), pp. 277–318.

6. Hosmer, *Presence of the Past*, pp. 35–62.

7. Roger W. Moss, "The Origins of The Carpenters' Company of Philadelphia," in Peterson, ed., *Building Early America*, pp. 35–53.

8. Charles E. Peterson, "Carpenters' Hall," in *Historic Philadelphia*, pp. 96–128.

9. See *Godey's Lady's Book* 51 (August 1855): 177–78; 55 (July 1857): 81–83. According to the recollections of a friend, Miss Ann Pamela Cunningham declared her intention to call for the preservation of Mount Vernon while in Philadelphia (Hosmer, *Presence of the Past*, p. 308 n17). She published her letter to the "Ladies of the South" In the *Charleston Mercury* (December 1853). Probably due to the support of her cause by Sarah Hale, "editress" of *Godey's*, the first northern committee of the Mount Vernon Ladies' Association was formed in Philadelphia.

10. Ellen Freedman, "The Slate Roof House: Historic Structure Report," paper, Historic Preservation Program, University of Pennsylvania, 1985; copy on file at The Athenaeum of Philadelphia.

11. *Memorial of the William Penn Parlor, in the Great Central Fair* (Philadelphia, 1864) contains a detailed catalogue of the objects exhibited, including a "model of William Penn's House, Second Street and Norris' Alley known as the Slate Roof House." In addition to the Philadelphia sanitary fair, similar charity bazaars were held in Brooklyn, Poughkeepsie, New York City, Saint Louis, and Indianapolis. See Rodris Roth, "The New England, or 'Olde Tyme,' Kitchen Exhibit at Nineteenth-Century Fairs," in Alan Axelrod, ed., *The Colonial Revival in America* (New York: Norton, 1985), pp. 159–83.

12. Hampton L. Carson, *A History of The Historical Society of Pennsylvania* (Philadelphia: Historical Society of Pennsylvania, 1940), 1: 334–36. The site of the Slate Roof House has been developed as a small park dedicated to William Penn; it is opposite the reconstructed City Tavern on Second Street above Walnut Street.

13. J. M. Read, Jr., "The Old Slate-Roof House," *Lippincott Magazine* 1 (Jan., Feb., March 1868): 29–39; 191–201; 298–305. R. Clipston Sturgis similarly recorded the John Hancock house in Boston a few years earlier, perhaps the earliest known instance in America of "preservation by graphic record." Fiske Kimball, "The Preservation Movement in America," *Journal of the Society of Architectural Historians* 1 (July–October, 1941): 15. For the archaeological report on the Slate Roof House site, see John L. Cotter, Daniel G. Roberts, and Michael Parrington, *The Buried Past: An Archaeological History of Philadelphia* (Philadelphia: University of Pennsylvania Press, 1992), pp. 1–85.

14. For a brief history of the park, see Theo B. White, *Fairmount, Philadelphia's Park: A History* (Philadelphia: Art Alliance Press, 1975), also George B. Tatum, "The Origins of Fairmount Park, *Antiques* 82 (November 1962): 502–7. The best short history of the waterworks is Jane Mork Gibson and Robert Wolterstorff, "The Fairmount Waterworks," *Philadelphia Museum of Art Bulletin* (Summer 1988).

15. *Report of the Committee on Plans and Improvements of the Commissioners of Fairmount Park, upon the Extension of the Park* (Philadelphia, 1868).

16. For Eaglesfield, see Kathleen A. Foster, *Captain Watson's Travels in America: The Sketchbooks and Diary of Joshua Rowley Watson, 1772–1818* (Philadelphia: University of Pennsylvania Press, 1997).

17. Original letter in Fairmount Park Commission Chamounix File, quoted in Jessica A. Sloop, "Chamounix Mansion Historic Structure Report," paper, Historic Preservation Program, University of Pennsylvania, 1994. Copy on file at The Athenaeum of Philadelphia.

18. Recent studies of the American Civil War suggest that the solders of the Union and Confederate armies—however different their conclusions might be—both appealed to the same ideals of liberty, republican government, and writings of revolutionary ancestors. See James M. McPherson, *What They Fought for, 1861–1865* (Baton Rouge: Louisiana State University Press, 1994).

19. Roth, "Kitchen Exhibit," pp. 173–78. For a general history of the Centennial, see John Maass, *The Glorious Enterprise: The Centennial Exposition of 1876* (Watkins Glen, N.Y.: American Life Foundation, 1973).

20. Deborah Dependahl Waters, "Philadelphia's Boswell: John Fanning Watson," *Pennsylvania Magazine of History and Biography* 98 (January 1974): 39–42. The location was, however, familiarly known as Letitia Court. The *Pennsylvania Gazette* (February 24, 1730) contains the reference, "At the house formerly Thomas Chalkley's, in Letitia Court, are taught Writing and Arithmetick . . . "

21. The Letitia Street House, moved to Fairmount Park in 1883, proved ultimately to have been built by Thomas Chalkley, c. 1713. The house, now something of an embarrassment, remains rather forlornly overlooked in the Park and is no longer open to the public. George B. Tatum, *Penn's Great Town: 250 Years of Philadelphia Architecture*, 2nd ed. (Philadelphia: University of Pennsylvania Press, 1961), p. 154.

22. The standard history of Germantown is Harry M. Tinkcom, Margaret B. Tinkcom, and Grant Miles Simon, *Historic Germantown, from the Founding to the Early Part of the Nineteenth Century* (Philadelphia: American Philosophical Society, 1955). This should be read together with a series of articles that appeared in the magazine *Antiques* (August 1983): 253–300, particularly the introductory "Germantown, 1683–1983," by Mark Frazier Lloyd, pp. 254–58.

23. George Roberts and Mary Roberts, *Triumph on Fairmount: Fiske Kimball and the Philadelphia Museum of Art* (Philadelphia: Lippincott, 1959), pp. 70–81. Letter from Fiske Kimball to Charles E. Peterson (November 24, 1954), Fairmount Park Office Archives, "Mount Pleasant" file. Fiske Kimball, "Philadelphia's 'Colonial Chain,'" *Art and Archaeology* 21 (April 1926): 198–99.

24. Sarah D. Lowrie and Mabel Stewart Ludlum, *The Sesqui-Centennial High Street* (Philadelphia, 1926).

25. Clarence Cook, *The House Beautiful* (New York, 1881), p. 187.

26. George T. B. Davis, "A Talk About Colonial Furniture," *House Beautiful* (June 1899): 19.

27. Letter from Fiske Kimball to Charles E. Peterson, November 24, 1954, Fairmount Park Office Archives, "Mount Pleasant" file.

28. *Proceedings of the 56th Convention, A.I.A., 1923*, quoted in Hosmer, *Presence of the Past*, p. 233.

29. For a brief history of the Old Philadelphia Survey of the 1920s and the role of the Historic American Buildings Survey, founded during the early days of the Roosevelt New Deal (1933), see Richard J. Webster, *Philadelphia Preserved: Catalog of the Historic American Buildings Survey* (Philadelphia: Temple University Press, 1976).

30. For a discussion of the Powel House and the founding of the Philadelphia Society for the Preservation of Landmarks, see George B. Tatum, *Philadelphia Georgian: The City House of Samuel Powel and Some of Its 18th-Century Neighbors* (Middletown, Conn.: Wesleyan University Press, 1976).

31. Margaret B. Tinkcom, "The Philadelphia Historical Commission: Organization and Procedures," *Law and Contemporary Problems* 36 (Summer 1971): 386–97. The *postponement of demolition* clause has subsequently been strengthened to create protections against owners who could run the clock and then demolish in total disregard of the greater public good.

## CENTER CITY AND NEARBY NEW JERSEY

1. Hannah B. Roach, "The Planting of Philadelphia: A Seventeenth-Century Real Estate Development," *Pennsylvania Magazine of History and Biography* 92 (January 1968): 3–47; (April 1968), 143–94. See also Gary B. Nash, "City Planning and Political Tension in the Seventeenth Century: The Case of Philadelphia," *Proceedings of the American Philosophical Society* 112 (February 15, 1968): 54–73.

2. Frances M. Trollope, *Domestic Manners of the Americans* (New York, 1832), p. 210.

3. Roger W. Moss, *Master Builders: A History of the Colonial Philadelphia Building Trades* (Ann Arbor, Mich.: University Microfilms, 1972).

4. "Instructions of William Penn to the Commissioners for settling the colony, 30 7th Mo. 1681," Mary Maples Dunn and Richard S. Dunn, eds., *The Papers of William Penn, 1680–1684* (Philadelphia: University of Pennsylvania Press, 1982), p. 121.

5. Albert Cook Myers, ed., *Narratives of Early Pennsylvania West New Jersey and Delaware, 1630–1707* (New York, 1912), pp. 262, 269–70. On the London plague of 1665 and fire of 1666, see John Bedford, *London's Burning* (London, 1966) and Leonard W. Cowie, *Plague and Fire, London, 1665–1666* (New York: Putnam 1970).

6. Myers, *Narratives*, pp. 269–70.

7. Sam Bass Warner, Jr., *The Private City: Philadelphia in Three Periods of Its Growth*, 2nd ed. (Philadelphia: University of Pennsylvania Press, 1987), pp. 3–21.

8. Bobbye Burke et al., *Historic Rittenhouse, a Philadelphia Neighborhood* (Philadelphia: University of Pennsylvania Press, 1985).

## SCHUYLKILL RIVER AND FAIRMOUNT PARK

1. The City of Philadelphia purchased both the John Bartram House and Bellair Manor as historic sites, and William Hamilton's The Woodlands became the headquarters of a rural cemetery company, thus saving it from almost certain demolition. Countless other houses, including the last great villa erected on the river, Samuel Sloan's Bartram Hall, erected in 1851 for Andrew M. Eastwick, disappeared as Philadelphia rapidly expanded in the late nineteenth century.

2. Quoted in *Pennsylvania Magazine of History and Biography* 12 (1888): 454.

3. Roger W. Moss, *The American Country House* (New York: Henry Holt, 1990), pp. 81–85. On Lansdowne see Marie G. Kimball, "The Furnishings of Lansdowne, Governor Penn's Country Estate, *Antiques* 19 (June 1931): 450–55; Margaret L. Brown, "Mr. and Mrs. William Bingham of Philadelphia," *Pennsylvania Magazine of History and Biography* 61 (July 1937): 286–324; and Robert C. Alberts, *The Golden Voyage: The Life and Times of William Bingham, 1752–1804* (Boston: Houghton Mifflin, 1969).

4. The entire quotation from John Adams's diary for September 25, 1775, reads: "Rode out of town, and dined with Mr. McPherson. He has the most elegant seat in Pennsylvania, a clever Scotch wife, and two pretty daughters. His seat is on the banks of the Schuylkill. He has been nine times wounded in battle; an old sea commander; made a fortune by privateering; an arm twice shot off, shot through the leg, &c. He renews his proposals of taking or burning ships." Quoted in Louis C. Madera, "Mount Pleasant," *Antiques* 82 (November 1962): 520.

5. Moss, *American Country House*, pp. 75–97. For a detailed discussion of the villa, see James S. Ackerman, *The Villa: Form and Ideology of Country Houses* (Princeton, N.J.: Princeton University Press, 1990). My thanks to Mark Bower for calling the Morris quotation to my attention.

6. Alison Hawver, "A Study of the Property Known as Rhoads' Place and Harmar's Retreat: A Lower Schuylkill River Country Villa," paper, Historic Preservation Program, University of Pennsylvania, 1993. Copy at The Athenaeum of Philadelphia. The house fell victim to late nineteenth-century railroad development.

7. Russell F. Weigley, ed., *Philadelphia: A 300-Year History* (New York: Norton, 1982), pp. 180–88.

8. William Breitkreutz, "Rockland, Fairmount Park, Philadelphia, PA," report, Historic Preservation Program, University of Pennsylvania, 1994. Copy at The Athenaeum of Philadelphia.

## GERMANTOWN

1. For a discussion of historic preservation in Germantown, see pages 12–14. In addition to the sources mentioned in the notes for that section, see Mark Frazier Lloyd and Sandra Mackenzie Lloyd, "Three Hundred Years of Germantown History: An Exhibition Celebrating the Tercentenary of This Community, *Germantown Crier* 35 (Winter 1982–83): 6–16.

2. Louise L. Strawbridge, "The 'Stylish Villas' of Victorian Germantown: West Tulpehocken Street and West Walnut Lane, *Germantown Crier* 34 (Winter 1982): 13–18.

3. Mark A. Bower, "Loudoun, Germantown, Philadelphia: Country House of the Armat Family in the Years 1801–1835, unpublished Master's thesis, Historic Preservation Program, University of Pennsylvania, 1984.

## DELAWARE RIVER

1. Journal of the Philadelphia Journey of Aaron and Nathan Stein, May 27–June 16, 1853. The Athenaeum of Philadelphia, gift of Willard R. Espy, 1994.

2. For a romantic history of the Delaware, see Harry Emerson Wildes, *The Delaware* (New York: Farrar and Rinehart, 1940), one of the Rivers of America series. For the scholarly history, see two books by C. A. Weslager, *Dutch Explorers, Traders and Settlers in the Delaware Valley, 1609–1664* (Philadelphia: University of Pennsylvania Press, 1961) and *The English on the Delaware, 1610–1682* (New Brunswick, N.J.: Rutgers University Press, 1967).

3. Helen Berkeley, "A Sketch of Joseph Bonaparte," *Godey's Lady's Book* 30 (April 1845): 184–87.

4. Today preservationists rank intervention at an historic site by level of authenticity. *Repair* of original material is favored over *restoration*, which may include replicas copied from an original element. *Restoration*, in turn, is favored over total *reconstruction*. *Reconstruction*, which may be based on highly detailed visual and documentary research, is favored over *recreation*, which usually relies on a range of period sources that may not be specific to the site. The Slate Roof House could probably have been reconstructed, but the Benjamin Franklin House—for which there were no images or measured drawings—would have been at best a recreation, as was Pennsbury. None of these projects could be called a "restoration."

This bibliography is divided into two distinct sections. The first section is arranged by house and lists in lieu of footnotes the sources specific to that site. Most of the research into original sources on which each entry is based dates from the last twenty years, a period of intense activity by many highly skilled researchers, which unfortunately has not been published and is often difficult to obtain. When many of the houses discussed in this book were acquired, restored, and opened to the public as museums, the standards of research differed greatly from those demanded today. No conscientious government agency, board of trustees, architect, or curator would now dare commence a restoration or develop an interpretive program without first preparing or commissioning an historic structures report —commonly abbreviated as "HSR." Such reports exhaustively compile what can be learned about the property. They are prepared by carefully and throughly sifting the public and private record to uncover the legal history of the site, its building history (architects, builders, and changes over time), the genealogical record of the owners and occupants, the iconography, written and oral history, archaeological record, and a physical description which may include decorative finishes. This material is then gathered into a single manuscript report, or a set of several reports broken out by topic. These reports contain reproductions of the key documents—especially the iconography—and cite their locations in public or private repositories so future researchers can find the originals should the need arise. This report is then reproduced in multiple copies, bound, and delivered to the commissioning agency. Reference copies are often placed in appropriate repositories against the likely possibility that the agency copy will be lost or filed and forgotten. (Reference copies of many Philadelphia-area HSRs have been deposited at The Athenaeum of Philadelphia, where they can be consulted by researchers.)

The second section of the bibliography lists published sources for the study of Philadelphia architecture which generally cover several sites or provide background material. Not included in this list are works on individual architects and builders, which can be accessed through directories such as Sandra L. Tatman and Roger W. Moss, *Biographical Dictionary of Philadelphia Architects*. Also omitted here are the general guidebooks to Philadelphia buildings such as John A. Gallery, *Philadelphia Architecture: A Guide to the City* sponsored by the Foundation for Architecture. Several of these books have been published in the past twenty years and are too general for research.

## SOURCES ARRANGED BY BUILDING

Entries for which short titles are given are listed in the general bibliography

### ANDALUSIA

Biddle, James. "Nicholas Biddle's Andalusia, a Nineteenth-Century Country Seat Today." *Antiques* 86 (September 1964): 286–90.

Govan, Thomas P. *Nicholas Biddle, Nationalist and Public Banker, 1786–1844.* Chicago: University of Chicago Press, 1959.

Moss, *American Country House*, pp. 104–25.

Wainwright, Nicholas. "Andalusia, Countryseat of the Craig Family and of Nicholas Biddle and His Descendants." *Pennsylvania Magazine of History and Biography* 101 (January 1977): 3–69.

### BARCLAY FARMSTEAD

Cocchiaraley, Pat. "Barclay Farmstead Restoration, Cherry Hill's Living Heritage."

Student paper, History of Landscape Architecture, University of Pennsylvania, 1980.

Dickey, John M. "Barclay Farmstead Research Files." Dickey Collection, The Athenaeum of Philadelphia. Includes research notes, restoration documents, specifications, 1975–80.

Halpern, Martha C. "Barclay Farmstead Preliminary Report." Report for Township of Cherry Hill, New Jersey, 1987.

Olejnik, Barbara and Robin Schulsinger. "The Barclay Farmstead Restoration." Student paper, History of Landscape Architecture, University of Pennsylvania.

### BARNS-BRINTON HOUSE

Chester County Historical Society. "Pennsbury Township Lands" file containing notes on the Ffew-Brinton House, deeds, inventories, court documents, etc.

Cotter et al., *Buried Past*, pp. 442–43.

Raymond, Eleanor. *Early Domestic Architecture of Pennsylvania.* Reprint of the 1931 edition with a new introduction by John Milner. Princeton, N.J.: Pyne Press, 1973.

Schiffer, *Survey of Chester County*.

### BELLAIR

Gurney, George. "Documents, Observations, and Stylistic Characteristics Related to the history and dating of the 'Bellair' House in Passyunk." Student report for Professor George B. Tatum, University of Delaware, 1971. Copy in Bellair file, The Athenaeum of Philadelphia.

Historic American Buildings Survey. Washington, D.C., Library of Congress. Set of thirty measured drawings c. 1932 and eight photographs c. 1936 document the house at time of first restoration. Copies at Art Department, Free Library, Philadelphia.

McIlhenny, John. "Historical Survey of Bellaire House." Report for Fairmount Park Commission, Philadelphia, 1973. Copy in Bellair file, The Athenaeum of Philadelphia.

Rambo, Ormand, Jr. "The House on Queen Christina's Land Grant." *Yearbook of the American Swedish Historical Museum*. Philadelphia, 1944.

Richardson, Herbert A. "A Study of Bellair, the Country Home of Samuel Preston, Mayor of Philadelphia and Provincial Treasurer of Pennsylvania." Student report, University of Pennsylvania, 1964. Copy in Bellair file, The Athenaeum of Philadelphia.

Rivinus, Marion W. *Bellaire Manor, 1714.* Philadelphia: Bicentennial Women '76, 1976.

## BETSY ROSS HOUSE

Canby, William J. "The History of the Flag of the United States." Paper read before the Historical Society of Pennsylvania, March 1870. Manuscript copy at the Historical Society of Pennsylvania.

Force, Debra Jean. "Betsy Ross, Upholsterer and Flag-Maker: A Proposal to Furnish Her Home." Report for the Betsy Ross Foundation, December 1976.

*Philadelphia: A Guide to the Nation's Birthplace.*

## BISHOP WHITE HOUSE

Greiff, Constance. *Independence: The Creation of a National Park.*

Hutchens, Carolyn. "When the House of Bishops First Met." *Living Church* 195 (October 1987): 8–9.

Johnson, Deirdre C. "What's New and What's Original in the Todd and Bishop White Houses." Independence National Historical Park, February 1990.

Judd, Henry A. et al. "Historic Structure Report, Part II, Supplement I, Restoration of the Bishop White House, Architectural Data Section." U.S. Department of the Interior, National Park Service, January 1961.

Stowe, Walter Herbert, ed. *The Life and Letters of Bishop William White.* New York: Morehouse, 1937.

Verplanck, Anne A. "Furnishings Plan for the Third Floor of the Bishop William White House." Report for Independence National Historic Park, May 1989.

Wallace, David et al. "Historic Building Report on Bishop White House." Report for Independence National Historic Park, April 1958.

## BRINTON 1704 HOUSE

Anderson, Bart. Historic American Buildings Survey Form for the Brinton House, 1958.

Brinton, John Hill. Diary for March, 1856. Chester County Historical Society.

Brinton Family Association. *Brinton 1704 House.* West Chester, Pa., 1959.

Brinton, Howard H. "The Brinton Country." *Friends Journal* (February 1956).

Gaster, Berthold. "A House to Be Reborn." *Sunday Star Magazine*, Wilmington, Delaware, 1952.

Schoonover, Janetta Wright, ed. *The Brinton Genealogy.* Baltimore: Gateway Press, 1992.

Schiffer, *Survey of Chester County.*

## BURHOLME

Day & Zimmerman Associates. "Burholme Mansion and Carriage House: An Evaluation of the Potential for Restoration and Renovation." Report for the City of Philadelphia, Fairmount Park Commission, 1977.

Hotchkin, *The York Road, Old and New.*

Philadelphia Historical Commission. Burholme File. Contains photocopies of deeds, wills, and insurance policies relating to the property. Copies also in Burholme file, The Athenaeum of Philadelphia.

Poor, Henry Vernon. *History of the Railroads and Canals of the United States of America.* New York: A. M. Kelley, 1860.

National Register of Historic Places. Inventory—Nomination Form, "Ryerss Mansion." 1972.

## CALEB PUSEY HOUSE

Albrecht, Josephine F. *A Visit to the Pusey House.* Upland, Pa.: Friends of Caleb Pusey House, Inc., n.d.

Albrecht, Josephine F. "Caleb Pusey House I: Penn's Mill and Its 'Keeper' at Landing Ford Plantation in Upland Pennsylvania." *Bulletin of the Archaeological Society of Delaware* (Fall 1969): 1–16.

Albrecht, Josephine F. "Caleb Pusey House III, History Hidden in the Earth." *Bulletin of the Archaeological Society of Delaware* (Spring 1972): 2–25.

Ashmead, Henry Graham. *History of Delaware County, Pennsylvania.* Philadelphia, 1884.

Cadbury, Henry J., ed. "Caleb Pusey's Account of Pennsylvania." *Quaker History* 64, 1–2 (1975).

Martin, John Hill. *Chester, Delaware County.* Philadelphia, 1877.

Patterson, Mary Sullivan. "Saving a Seventeenth Century Pennsylvania Home." *Germantown Crier* (September 1962): 75–76, 82–83.

Schiek, Allen G. "Caleb Pusey House, II: Chemical Analysis of Some Copper Coins from House Excavations." *Bulletin of the Archaeological Society of Delaware* (Fall 1969): 19–25.

Schiffer, *Survey of Chester County.*

## CEDAR GROVE

"Cedar Grove Inventory." Philadelphia Museum of Art Archives, 1993.

[Kimball, Fiske]. "Cedar Grove," *Pennsylvania Museum Bulletin* (February 1928): 5–14.

McElroy, Cathryn J. "Furniture in Philadelphia: The First Fifty Years." *Winterthur Portfolio* 13 (1979): 61–80.

Garvan, *Three Centuries of American Art*, pp. 25–27.

Solis-Cohen, Lita H. "Cedar Grove." *Antiques* 82 (November 1962): 511–14.

## CLIVEDEN

Anderson-Lawrence, Jennifer. "The Colonial Revival at Cliveden." Unpublished Master's thesis, University of Delaware, 1990.

Cloud, Dana. "An Examination of the Duche Mansion." Paper, Historic Preservation Program, University of Pennsylvania, 1996. Copy on file at The Athenaeum of Philadelphia.

Garvan, *Philadelphia: Three Centuries of American Art.*

Hendrickson, Hope C. "Cliveden." *Antiques* 124 (August 1983): 259–65.

Konkle, Burton A. *Benjamin Chew, 1722–1810.* Philadelphia: University of Pennsylvania Press, 1932.

Richards, Nancy. "Cliveden: The Chew Mansion in Germantown." Research report for Cliveden, Inc., 1993.

Rosenblum, Martin Jay and Associates. "Cliveden: Historic Structures Report." Report prepared for Cliveden, Inc., 1993.

Shepherd, Raymond V. "Cliveden." *Historic Preservation* (July–September 1972): 4–11.

Shepherd, Raymond V. "Cliveden and Its Philadelphia-Chippendale Furniture: A Documented History." *American Art Journal* 8 (November 1976): 2–16.

Tinkcom, Margaret B. "Cliveden: The Building of a Philadelphia Country Seat, 1763–1767." *Pennsylvania Magazine of History and Biography* 88 (January 1964): 3–36.

## DESHLER-MORRIS HOUSE

Alderson, Michael. "Historic Structural Report, Architectural Data Section, Deshler-Morris House." Report for Independence National Historical Park, March, 1982, revised.

Fanelli, Doris D. "The Deshler-Morris House." *Antiques* 124 (August 1983): 284–89.

Fanelli, Doris D. "Furnishings Plan: Deshler-Morris House." Report prepared for Independence National Historical Park, December 1976.

Toogood, Anna Coxe. "Historic Structure/Furnishings/Grounds Report: Deshler-Morris

House." Report prepared for Independence National Historical Park, 1976, 1980.

Wolf, Edwin II. "Why Not Call It the Deshler-Franks-Morris House?" *Germantown Crier* 33 (Fall 1981): 80–81.

## EBENEZER MAXWELL MANSION

Engle, Reed L. for John M. Dickey. "Historic Structure Report on the Original Kitchen, Ebenezer Maxwell Mansion." Report for Ebenezer Maxwell Mansion, Inc., September 1981.

Faust, Doreen. "Inventories of Furnishings in the Parlor and Dining Room of the Maxwell Mansion as of December, 1981." Student report, Historic Preservation Program, University of Pennsylvania, Fall 1981. Copy in Maxwell file, The Athenaeum of Philadelphia.

*Germantown Crier* (Spring 1979). Several articles on Maxwell by Mark Frazier Lloyd, William D. Hershey, Constance V. Hershey, and Charlotte C. Stokes—all of whom were involved with the restoration at that time.

Maass, John. *The Gingerbread Age: A View of Victorian Architecture.* New York: Bramhall House, 1957. The pioneering book making a case for Victorian architecture.

Magaziner, Henry J. "Every Well-Run Zoo Treats Its Animals That Well." *Germantown Crier* 44 (Winter 1991/92): 14–15.

Maxwell Mansion, Inc. *Restoration Made Practical: Experiences at the Maxwell Mansion.* Philadelphia: Ebenezer Maxwell Mansion, Inc., 1984.

Lloyd, Mark Frazier. "The Difficult Case of William Hunter, Jr." *Pennsylvania Genealogical Magazine* (Spring 1984).

Peterson, Karin E. "The Ebenezer Maxwell Mansion." *Antiques* 124 (August 1983): 290–95.

Tatman and Moss, *Biographical Dictionary*, pp. 396–97, 730–34.

Twiss-Garrity, Beth A. "The Factory in the Home: The Nineteenth-Century Kitchen Restoration at the Maxwell Mansion." *Germantown Crier* 37 (Winter 1984): 6–10.

Winkler, Gail Caskey and Roger W. Moss. *Victorian Interior Decoration.* New York: Henry Holt, 1986.

## ELFRETH'S ALLEY

Burnston, Sharon. "Urban Craftswomen: Mantuamakers Active in Philadelphia, 1785–1800." Report for Elfreth's Alley Association, n.d.

Roach, Hannah B. "An Account of Elfreth's Alley and Its People from the Earliest Times." Report for Elfreth's Alley Association, Inc., 1958.

Roach, Hannah B.. *Elfreth's Alley.* Philadelphia: Elfreth's Alley Association, 1962.

## FONTHILL

Dyke, Linda. "Henry Chapman Mercer: An

Annotated Chronology." *Mercer Mosaic* 6 (Spring/Summer 1989): 35–67.

Gemmill, Helen Hartman. *The Mercer Mile.* Doylestown, Pa.: Bucks County Historical Society, 1987.

Jackson, Donald D. "Henry Mercer Makes More Sense as Time Goes On." *Smithsonian* (October 1988): 111–20.

John Milner Associates. "Conservation Plan for *Fonthill*." Report for the Bucks County Historical Society, 1992.

Mercer, Henry C. "The Building of 'Fonthill,' at Doylestown Pennsylvania, in 1908, 1909, and 1910." *Bucks County Historical Society Papers*, vol. 6, pp. 321–31.

Reed, Cleota. *Henry Chapman Mercer and the Moravian Pottery and Tile Works.* Philadelphia: University of Pennsylvania Press, 1987.

## GLEN FOERD

Dalzell, Bonnie. "Glen Foerd: An Openness to All Things Lovely." *American Antiques* (April 1978).

Infield, Tom. "A Mansion, a Bequest, a Wealth of Problems." *Philadelphia Inquirer*, March 9, 1986.

John Milner Associates, Inc. "Building Materials Conservation Study for Glen Foerd on the Delaware." Report for Glen Foerd Conservation Corporation, August 1989.

McAuley & Company. "Specifications for Alterations and Additions to Residence of Hon. Robert H. Foerderer at Torresdale, Philadelphia, Pa." Philadelphia, 1902. Photocopy at The Athenaeum of Philadelphia.

Muhly, Frank, compiler. "Glen Foerd." National Register of Historic Places Inventory—Nomination Form. U.S. Department of the Interior, 1979.

Rivinus, Marion Willis Martin and Katharine Hansell Biddle. *Lights Along the Delaware.* Philadelphia: Dorrance, 1965.

Tatman and Moss, *Biographical Dictionary*, pp. 512–13.

## GRAEME PARK

Reinberger, Mark, for Martin Jay Rosenblum and Associates. "Graeme Park Historic Structures Report." Report prepared for the Pennsylvania Historic and Museum Commission, Philadelphia, 1987.

Wendel, Thomas H. "The Life and Writings of Sir William Keith." Unpublished Ph.D. dissertation, University of Washington, 1964.

Wosstroff, Nancy. "Graeme Park, an Eighteenth Century Country Estate in Horsham, Pennsylvania." Unpublished Master's thesis, University of Delaware, 1958.

## THE GRANGE

Dickey, John M. Collection, The Athenaeum of Philadelphia, Box 12, includes correspondence and copies of the following reports.

Downing, Andrew Jackson. *The Architecture of Country Houses.* New York, 1850; reprint New York: Dover, 1969.

Engle, Reed L. "The Grange Estate, Haverford Township." Report for the Office of John M. Dickey, 1981.

Engle, Reed L. "Historic Landscape Report: The Grange Estate." Report for the Office of John M. Dickey, 1986.

Garrison, Nancy L. "The Transformation of a Country House: The Grange Estate, 1700–1850." Upublished Master's thesis, University of Delaware, 1988.

Johnson, Margaret F. "The Grange." Pennsylvania Historical and Museum Commission Register Nomination Form, February, 1975.

O'Gorman et al., *Drawing Toward Building.*

Smith, George. *History of Delaware County.* Philadelphia, 1862.

Talbott, Page. "An Historical Report for Furnishing the Grange." Report for the Friends of the Grange, April 1991.

Tatman and Moss, *Biographical Dictionary*, pp. 133, 510–512.

## GREENFIELD HALL

Aiken, Joan L. *Haddonfield Historic Homes: Success Through Preservation.* Newtown Square, Pa.: Harrowood Books, 1991.

French, Howard B. *Genealogy of the Descendants of Thomas French.* 2 vols. Philadelphia, 1909.

Gill, John IV. Receipt book. John Gill Papers, Haddonfield Historical Society.

Historical Society of Haddonfield. *This Is Haddonfield.* Haddonfield, N.J.: Historical Society of Haddonfield, 1963.

## GRUMBLETHORPE

Eastwick, Suzanne Wister. "The 'Grumblethorpe' Garden." Reprinted from *The Herbarist.* The Herb Society of America, 1963.

Gill, Bruce Cooper. "Grumblethorpe." *Antiques* 124 (August 1983): 296–300.

Susanin, Jay Davison. "Grumblethorpe: An Historic Landscape Report." Unpublished Master's thesis, University of Pennsylvania, 1990.

Tinkcom and Tinkcom, *Historic Germantown.*

Wister, Charles Jones. *The Labor of a Long Life: A Memoir of Charles Jones Wister.* Germantown, 1866.

## HARRITON

Farrow, Barbara A. *The History of Bryn Mawr, 1683–1900.* Bryn Mawr, Pa.: Lower Merion Civic Association, 1962.

Gill, Bruce Cooper and Arthur P. Dudden. *Harriton of Bryn Mawr, Pennsylvania.* Bryn Mawr, Pa.: The Harriton Association, 1988.

Schlenther, Boyd Stanley. *Charles Thomson: A*

*Patriot's Pursuit.* Newark: University of Delaware Press, 1990.

Vaux, George. "Harriton Plantation and Family Cemetery." *Pennsylvania Magazine of History and Biography* 15 (1891): 212–17.

Vaux, George. "Settlers in Merion—the Harrison Family and Harriton Plantation." *Pennsylvania Magazine of History and Biography* 13 (1889): 447–59.

## HIGHLANDS

Dangremond, David W. "The Highlands: The Country Seat of Anthony Morris." Unpublished Master's thesis, University of Delaware, 1981.

Dickey, John M., FAIA and John R. Bowie, Sandra Mackenzie Lloyd, and Richard I. Ortega. "The Highlands Mansion, Fort Washington, Pennsylvania, an Historic Structure Report." Report prepared for the Highlands Historical Society and the Pennsylvania Historical and Museum Commission, 1990. Copy at The Athenaeum of Philadelphia.

Dickey, John M., FAIA and Sandra Mackenzie Lloyd. "Historic Structure Report, The Highlands Springhouse." Report prepared for the Highlands Historical Society and the Pennsylvania Historical and Museum Commission, 1988. Copy at The Athenaeum of Philadelphia.

McLean, Elizabeth. "History of the Gardens and Grounds at the Highlands." Report, 1990. Copy at The Athenaeum of Philadelphia.

## HISTORIC BARTRAM'S GARDEN

Engle, Reed L. for the Office of John Dickey. "Historic Structure Report on the Seedhouse, Bartram's Garden," Report for the John Bartram Association, April 1980.

Fry, Joel T. "The Barn at Bartram's Garden, An Historic Structures Report." Report for the John Bartram Association, July 1992.

Fry, Joel T. "Archaeological Survey of Bartram's Garden, Public Courtyard Project." Report for the John Bartram Association, March 1990.

Glenn, Marsha L. for the Office of John Dickey. "The John Bartram House, Historic Structures Report." Report for the John Bartram Association, 1978.

McCormick, Kathleen. "Grand Synthesis: Bartram's Garden Mingles History with Environmental Restoration." *Historic Preservation* (May/June 1994): 68–71.

Palmer, Carol R. "Research Report on John Bartram's Garden." Report for the John Bartram Association, June 1983.

[Pyle, Howard]. "Bartram and His Garden." *Harper's New Monthly Magazine* 60 (February 1880): 321–30.

Tatman and Moss, *Biographical Dictionary*, pp. 730–34.

Vieira, M. Laffitte. *West Philadelphia Illustrated.* Philadelphia, 1903.

## HOPE LODGE

"The Architectural Background of Old Philadelphia." *The Antiquarian* 17 (September 1931): 30–31. Includes photographs of Hope Lodge during Degn occupancy.

Copp, Andrew and Margaret Westfield, "Historic Structures Report: Recommendations for the Restoration and Maintenance: Hope Lodge, Whitemarsh, Pennsylvania." Report for Martin Jay Rosenblum and Associates, 1987.

Pennsylvania Historical and Museum Commission. "Interpretation Manual: Hope Lodge and Mather Mill." Unpublished report, 1983.

Tatman and Moss, *Biographical Dictionary*, pp. 881–82.

Talbott, Page and Martha C. Halpern "An Historic Report for Furnishing Hope Lodge, Flourtown, Pennsylvania." Unpublished report, 1992.

Templeton, Dorothy B. "Historical Narrative Research Report, Hope Lodge." Historic Structure Report, Martin J. Rosenblum and Associates, 1984.

Van Trump, James D. "History in Houses: Hope Lodge, Whitemarsh, Pennsylvania." *Antiques* 89 (April 1966): 542–45.

Wallace, Paul A. W. "Historic Hope Lodge." *Pennsylvania Magazine of History and Biography* 86 (April 1962): 115–42.

## JOHN CHADS HOUSE

Ashmead, Henry Graham. *History of Delaware County, Pennsylvania.* Philadelphia, 1884.

Hauser, Susan. "John Chads House." Pennsylvania Historic Resource Survey Form, Chadds Ford Historical Society, 1984.

Schiffer, *Survey of Chester County.*

## JOHNSON HOUSE

Lloyd, Mark Frazier. "The Johnson (Jansen) Family and Their Houses in 18th-Century Germantown." *Germantown Crier* 33 (Spring 1981): 36–43.

Rosenblum, Martin Jay and Associates. "The John Johnson, Jr., House: Historic Structure Report." Report prepared for the Germantown Mennonite Historic Trust, 1995.

## LAUREL HILL

Engle, Reed L. for the office of John M. Dickey. "Historic Structure Report. Laurel Hill Mansion." Report for Women for Greater Philadelphia, 1983.

Halpern, Martha C. "Laurel Hill: A Country Property Along the Banks of the Schuylkill." Report for Women for Greater Philadelphia, 1985.

Rawle, William B. "Laurel Hill and Some Colonial Dames Who Once Lived There." *Pennsylvania Magazine of History and Biography* 25 (1911): 384–414.

## LEMON HILL

Garvan, *Philadelphia: Three Centuries of American Art,* pp. 185–87.

Keyser, C. S. *Lemon Hill, in Its Connection with the Efforts of Our Citizens and Councils to Obtain a Public Park.* Philadelphia, 1856.

Moore, John Hebron, ed. "A View of Philadelphia in 1829: Selections from the Journal of B.L.C. Wailes of Natchez." *Pennsylvania Magazine of History and Biography* 78 (July 1954): 353–60.

Naude, Virginia Norton. "Lemon Hill." *Antiques* 82 (November 1962): 531–33.

Naude, Virginia Norton. "Lemon Hill Revisited." *Antiques* 89 (April 1966): 578–79.

Robbins, Owen Tasker. "Toward Preservation of the Grounds of Lemon Hill in Light of Their Past and Present Significance for Philadelphians." Unpublished Master's thesis, University of Pennsylvania, 1987.

## MOUNT PLEASANT

Dickey, John M. and Sandra Mackenzie Lloyd. "Mount Pleasant Historic Structures Report." Report for the Fairmount Park Council for Historic Sites, 1987.

Garvan, Beatrice B. "Mount Pleasant: A Scottish Anachronism in Philadelphia," *Journal of the Society of Architectural Historians* 34 (December 1975): 304.

Kimball, Fiske. "Mount Pleasant." *Pennsylvania Museum Bulletin* 22 (September 1926): 197–215.

Madeira, Louis C. "Mount Pleasant." *Antiques* 22 (November 1962): 520–24.

Nevell, Thomas. " Day Book, 1762–1773." Wetherill Papers, University of Pennsylvania, DB 1/1762; Case A, Shelf 4, Location 43.

Roach, Hannah B. "Thomas Nevell (1721–1797), Carpenter, Educator, Patriot," *Journal of the Society of Architectural Historians* 24 (May 1965): 153–64.

Tatman and Moss, *Biographical Dictionary*, pp. 568–69.

## PENNSBURY

Cavicchi, Clare Lise. "Pennsbury Manor Furnishing Plan." Research report, Pennsbury Society, 1988.

Cavicchi, Clare Lise. "The Recreated Pennsbury Manor." Research report, Pennsbury Society, October 1989.

Cotter et al., *Buried Past*, pp. 359–63.

Hosmer, *Preservation Comes of Age*, pp. 444–50.

Tidlow, Evelyn et al. "Historic Structures Report for Pennsbury Manor." Report for John Milner Associates, Inc., 1987.

Weaver, William W. and Nancy D. Kolb. "Okie Speaks for Pennsbury." *Pennsylvania Heritage* (Fall 1982): 22–26; (Winter 1983): 22–26.

Weener, Carol G. "Pennsbury Manor: A Study in Colonial Revival Preservation." Unpublished Master's thesis, University of Pennsylvania, 1986.

## PENNYPACKER MILLS

Dumas Malone, ed. "Samuel Whitaker Pennypacker." *Dictionary of American Biography.* New York, 1934. 14: 447–48.

Parrington, Michael and Robert Hoffman for John Milner Associates. "A Preliminary Archaeological Survey of Pennypacker Mills." Report for the Montgomery County Department of Parks and Historic Sites, 1984.

Pennypacker, Samuel Whitaker. "Pennypacker's Mills." *Bulletin of the Historical Society of Montgomery County* (Fall 1980): 188–224; (Spring,1981): 285–357.

Tatman and Moss, *Biographical Dictionary*, pp. 106–10.

## PETER WENTZ FARMSTEAD

Cotter et al., *Buried Past*, pp. 393–97.

Earnhart, Bertha. *Wentz: A Record of Some Descendants of Peter Wentz the Immigrant.* Kennett Square, Pa., 1939.

Gamon, Albert T. "The Peter Wentz Farmstead." *Antiques* (October 1982): 788–94.

National Heritage Corporation. "Master Plan, Peter Wentz Farmstead." Report for the Commissioners of Montgomery County, Pennsylvania, 1975.

Welsh, Frank S. "The Early American Palette: Colonial Paint Colors Revealed." In *Paint in America*, ed. Moss.

## PHYSICK HOUSE

Garfinkel, Susan. "Report on the Hill-Physick-Keith House." Report for the Philadelphia Society for the Preservation of Landmarks, September 1987.

Johnson, Curtis. "Documentation and Interpretation of the Hill-Physick House." Student report, Historic Preservation Program, University of Pennsylvania, May 1982.

Roberts, George B. "Dr. Physick and His House." *Pennsylvania Magazine of History and Biography* 92 (January 1968): 67–86.

Tatman and Moss, *Biographical Dictionary*, pp. 104, 250.

## POMONA HALL

Boyer, Charles S. "Pomona Hall, The Home of Joseph Cooper, Jr." *West Jersey Press*, May 2, 9, 16, 1935. Reprinted Camden, N.J.: Camden County Historical Society, 1968.

Milner, John D. "Pomona Hall, The Home of Joseph Cooper, Jr." Historic Structure Report prepared for the Camden County Historical Society, 1976.

Weatherly, Margaret. *Pomona Hall: A Quaker Plantation of the Eighteenth Century.* Camden, N.J.: Camden County Historical Society, 1986.

## POWEL HOUSE

Tatman and Moss, *Biographical Dictionary*, pp. 741–43.

Tatum, *Philadelphia Georgian.*

Wainwright, *Colonial Grandeur in Philadelphia.*

## RITTENHOUSETOWN

Green, James. *The Rittenhouse Mill and the Beginnings of Papermaking in America.* Philadelphia: Library Company of Philadelphia and Friends of Historic RittenhouseTown, 1990.

John Milner Associates, Inc. and Wallace, Roberts & Todd. "A Preliminary Master Plan Study for Historic RittenhouseTown." Report for the Friends of Historic RittenhouseTown, 1988.

Noble, Timothy et al. (Clio Group). "Historic Structures Report: The Abraham Rittenhouse Home in RittenhouseTown." Report for the Fairmount Park Commission and the Friends of Historic RittenhouseTown, 1989.

Watson, *Annals*, 2: 16–72.

## ROSENBACH MUSEUM

Curtis, Wayne. "A Library Where Rare Is Common." *New York Times*, April 23, 1989.

Driver, Clive E. "The Rosenbach Collection: Past, Present, and Future." *Grolier Club* 19 (December 1973)

Thomas, George and Jefferson M. Moak. "The Pennsylvania Historic Resource Form, Rosenbach Museum." Philadelphia: Clio Group, Inc., 1982.

Tatman and Moss, *Biographical Dictionary*, pp. 781–82, 842.

Wolf, Edwin II with John F. Fleming. *Rosenbach: A Biography.* Cleveland: World, 1960.

## STENTON

Cotter et al., *Buried Past*, pp. 332–37.

Engle, Reed L. "Historic Structure Report: Stenton." Report prepared for National Society of the Colonial Dames of America in the Commonwealth of Pennsylvania, November 1982.

Shepherd, Raymond V. "James Logan's Stenton: Grand Simplicity in Quaker Philadelphia." Unpublished Master's thesis, Early American Culture, University of Delaware, June 1968.

Stoddart, Mary G. and Reed L. Engle. "Stenton." *Antiques* 124 (August 1983): 266–71.

Tinkcom, Margaret B. "The Logans and Stenton." *Germantown Crier* (Fall 1985): 78–85.

Tolles, Frederick B. *James Logan and the Culture of Provincial America.* Boston: Little, Brown, 1957.

Tolles, Frederick B. "Town House and Country House." *Pennsylvania Magazine of History and Biography* 82 (October 1958): 397–410.

Wainwright, Nicholas B., ed. *A Philadelphia Perspective: The Diary of Sidney George Fisher, Covering the Years 1834–1871.* Philadelphia: Historical Society of Pennsylvania, 1967.

## STRAWBERRY MANSION

Lippincott, Beatrice B. "Strawberry Mansion." *Antiques* 82 (November 1962): 528–30.

Ludlum, Mabel Stewart. "The Story of Strawberry Mansion." *Pennsylvania Museum Bulletin* 26 (May 1931): 23–33.

Morrison, Craig. "A Historic Structure Report for Strawberry Mansion." January 1986. Copy in Philadelphia Museum of Art files.

Roberts, John C. "Strawberry Mansion—A Blend of Federal and Empire Styles." *American Antiques* 109 (April 1976): 17–23.

Warren, Jack D. "Strawberry Mansion, 1789–1989." Report, Fairmount Park Archives, March 1990.

## SWEETBRIER

Roberts, Joan Church. "Sweetbriar." *Antiques* 82 (November 1962): 525–27.

Levy, Herbert W. "Restoration of Sweetbriar Mansion, Architectural Research and Documentation." Report for Fairmount Park Commission, n.d.

Scudder, H. E., ed. *Recollections of Samuel Breck.* Philadelphia, 1877.

"Sweetbrier Inventory, 1991." (Furniture on display at time of photographs.) Philadelphia Museum of Art files.

## TODD HOUSE

Anderson, M. O. "The Todd House Grounds and Neighboring Properties: Fourth and Walnut Streets." Report for Independence National Historical Park, January 1963.

Campbell, William et al. "Historic Structures Report, Part II, Architectural Data Section." Report for Independence National Historical Park, December 1960.

Cohen, Shirley A. "The Todd House: A History, Description and Evaluation." Seminar report, Temple University, 1986. Copy at Independence National Historical Park.

DuPonceau, Peter Stephen. Letter of September 25, 1837, quoted in "Notes and Documents." *Pennsylvania Magazine of History and Biography* 63 (July 1939): 333–38.

"Historic Building Survey: Dilworth-Todd-Moylan House." Report for Independence National Historical Park, April 1958.

Johnson, Deirdre C. "What's New and What's Original in the Todd and Bishop White Houses." Report for Independence National Historical Park, February 1990.

Sifton, Paul G. " 'What a Dread Prospect . . . ': Dolly Madison's Plague Year." *Pennsylvania Magazine of History and Biography* 87 (April 1963): 182–88.

Tatman and Moss, *Biographical Dictionary*, p. 213.

## TRENT HOUSE

Cleary, Mickey. "William Trent and the Founding of Trent's Town." Unpublished paper, copy at Trent House.

Comstock, Helen. "The William Trent House in Trenton, New Jersey." *Antiques* 74 (October 1958): 318–21.

Johnston, Elma Lawson. "Civil Works Administration Is Giving Trenton History." *Trenton Sunday Times-Advocate*, February 4, 1934.

Tatman and Moss, *Biographical Dictionary*, p. 617.

Toothman, Stephanie Smith. "Trenton, New Jersey, 1719–1779: A Study of Community Growth and Organization." Unpublished Ph.D. dissertation, University of Pennsylvania, 1977.

Trenton Free Public Library. Vertical file of newspaper accounts of restoration, City Council resolutions, transcripts of 1929 deed of gift, etc.

Walker, Robert E. et al. *A History of Trenton, 1679–1929*. Princeton, N.J.: Princeton University Press, 1929.

## UPSALA

Beard, Donald S. "Upsala, a Monument to Gracious Living." *Germantown Crier* 27 (Fall 1975): 119–20.

Lloyd, Mark Frazier. "Upsala." *Antiques* 124 (August 1983): 272–75.

Ritter, Mrs. James Bradford. "Upsala, a Germantown Heritage." *Germantown Crier* 5 (May 1955): 12–13.

Tinkcom and Tinkcom, *Historic Germantown*, pp. 104–5.

United States Direct Tax of 1798. Lists for Philadelphia, Schedule "I" (p. 0234, microfilm reel #5). National Archives, Philadelphia Regional Office.

## WALT WHITMAN HOUSE

Keller, Elizabeth L. *Walt Whitman in Mickle Street*. New York: M. Kennerley, 1921.

Kocubinski Architects. "The Walt Whitman House: Historic Structures Report." Report prepared for the State of New Jersey, Department of Environmental Protection and Energy, Division of Parks and Forestry, Division of Building Construction, 1993.

Metzger, Charles R. "Whitman on Architecture."

*Journal of the Society of Architectural Histories* 16 (March 1957): 25–27.

"Walt Whitman House." National Register of Historic Places Inventory—Nomination Form. 1978.

Westcott, Ralph Wesley. *Walt Whitman in Camden*. Trenton, N.J.: Walt Whitman Foundation, 1952.

## WAYNESBOROUGH

Cotter et al., *Buried Past*, pp. 430–33.

Frens & Frens. "Historic Waynesborough, An Architectural History and Management Plan." Report for the Philadelphia Society for the Preservation of Landmarks, March 1988.

June, Orrin W. "History in Houses, Waynesborough, the Home of Anthony Wayne," *Antiques* 94 (October 1968): 578–82.

Mosca, Matthew J. "Paint Decoration at Mount Vernon." In *Paint in America*, ed Moss, pp. 105–27.

Tatman and Moss, *Biographical Dictionary*, pp. 670–71.

Tucker, Glenn. *Mad Anthony Wayne and the New Nation: The Story of Washington's Front-Line General*. Harrisburg, Pa.: Stackpole, 1973.

## WOODFORD

Philadelphia Museum of Art. "Woodford, Naomi Wood Collection Master Inventory." Philadelphia, 1990. Copy at Philadelphia Museum of Art.

Reinberger, Mark. "The Evolution of Woodford, an Eighteenth-Century 'Retirement.'" *Pennsylvania Magazine of History and Biography* 121 (January–April 1997): 27–51.

Sinkler, John P. B. *The Naomi Wood Collection, Woodford Mansion*. Philadelphia: Estate of Naomi Wood, 1947.

Snyder, June Avery and Martin P. Snyder. *The Story of the Naomi Wood Collection and Woodford Mansion*. Wayne, Pa.: Haverford House, 1981.

Snyder, Martin P. "Woodford," *Antiques* (November 1962): 515–19.

Tatman and Moss, *Biographical Dictionary*, pp. 727–29.

## WOODLANDS

"American Scenery—for the Portfolio. The Woodlands." *The Port Folio* 2 (December 1809): 504–7.

Betts, Richard J. "The Woodlands." *Winterthur Portfolio* 14 (August 1979): 213–34.

Brumbaugh, G. Edwin. "Preliminary Restoration Report No. 1, South Portico." April 28, 1965.

Dickey, John M. with Reed L. Engle. "The Saloon of the Woodlands, Woodlands Cemetery." Historic Structures Report, September 1981.

"For the Portfolio. The Woodlands." *The Port Folio* 1 (February 1809): 180–81.

Heintzelman, Patricia L. "Elysium on the Schuylkill, William Hamilton's Woodlands." Unpublished Master's thesis, University of Delaware, 1972.

John Milner Associates, Inc. "An Architectural/Historical Assessment and Space Planning Study of The Woodlands." Report for Friends of the Woodlands, 1992.

Long, Timothy Preston. "The Woodlands: A 'Matchless Place.'" Unpublished Master's thesis, Historic Preservation, University of Pennsylvania, 1991.

Pitcher, Donald Torrey. "Colonel James Swan and His French Furniture." *Antiques* 37 (February 1940): 69–71.

Stetson, Sarah P. "William Hamilton and His 'Woodlands.'" *Pennsylvania Magazine of History and Biography* 73 (January 1949): 26–33.

## WYCK

Claussen, W. Edmunds. *Wyck: The Story of an Historic House, 1690–1970*. Philadelphia: Privately printed, 1970.

Dickey, John M. "Architectural and Engineering Investigation of Wyck." Report for the Wyck Charitable Trust, 1974.

Dickey, John M. Collection. Wyck Files, Box 35. Architectural Archives, The Athenaeum of Philadelphia.

Doell, Christine and Gerald Doell. "Historic Landscape Report." Report for the Wyck Charitable Trust, 1992.

Lloyd, Sandra Mackenzie for John M. Dickey. "Historic Structures Report: Wyck House." Report for the Wyck Charitable Trust, 1986.

Lloyd, Sandra Mackenzie. "Wyck." *Antiques* 124 (August 1983): 276–83.

Pennell, Sarah M. "Exterior Documentation and Conditions Survey of Wyck House." Report, University of Pennsylvania Program in Historic Preservation, 1992.

Pennell, Sarah M. "The Quaker Domestic Interior, Philadelphia, 1780–1830: An Artifactual Investigation of the 'Quaker Esthetic' at Wyck House, Philadelphia and Collen Brook Farm, Upper Darby, Pennsylvania." Unpublished Master's thesis, University of Pennsylvania, 1992.

# GENERAL SOURCES

Ackerman, James S. *The Villa: Form and Ideology of Country Houses*. Princeton, N.J.: Princeton University Press, 1990.

Batcheler, Penelope H. "Independence Hall: Its Appearance Restored." In *Building Early America*, ed. Charles E. Peterson. Radnor, Pa.: Chilton, 1976, pp. 298–318.

Benson, Adolph B., ed. *Peter Kalm's Travels in North America: The English Version of 1770*. 2 vols. New York: Wilson-Erickson, 1937.

Brandt, Frances Burke and Henry Volkmer Gummere. *Byways and Boulevards in and About Historic Philadelphia*. Philadelphia: Corn Exchange National Bank, 1925.

Breitkreutz, William. "Rockland, Fairmount Park, Philadelphia." Report, Historic Preservation Program, University of Pennsylvania, 1994. Copy at The Athenaeum of Philadelphia.

Burke, Bobbye et al. *Historic Rittenhouse, a Philadelphia Neighborhood*. Philadelphia: University of Pennsylvania Press, 1985.

Carson, Hampton L. *A History of the Historical Society of Pennsylvania*. 2 vols. Philadelphia: Historical Society, 1940.

Cotter, John L., Daniel G. Roberts, and Michael Parrington. *The Buried Past: An Archaeological History of Philadelphia*. Philadelphia: University of Pennsylvania Press, 1992.

Cousins, Frank and Phil M. Riley. *The Colonial Architecture of Philadelphia*. Boston: Little, Brown, 1920.

Eberlein, Harold D. and Horace M. Lippincott. *The Colonial Homes of Philadelphia and Its Neighborhood*. Philadelphia: J. B. Lippincott, 1912.

Eisenhart, Luther P., ed. *Historic Philadelphia, from the Founding Until the Early Nineteenth Century*. Transactions of the American Philosophical Society 43, pt. 1. Philadelphia: American Philosophical Society, 1953.

Faris, John T. *Old Gardens in and About Philadelphia*. Indianapolis: Hackett, 1932.

——. *Old Roads Out of Philadelphia*. Philadelphia: J. B. Lippincott, 1917.

——. *The Romance of Old Philadelphia*. Philadelphia: J. B. Lippincott, 1918.

Foster, Kathleen A. *Captain Watson's Travels in America: The Sketchbooks and Diary of Joshua Rowley Watson, 1772–1818*. Commentaries on the Plates by Ken Finkel. Philadelphia: University of Pennsylvania Press, 1997.

Garvan, Beatrice B. *Philadelphia: Three Centuries of American Art*. Philadelphia: Philadelphia Museum of Art, 1976.

Gibson, Jane Mork and Robert Wolterstorff. "The Fairmount Waterworks." *Philadelphia Museum of Art Bulletin* (Summer 1988).

Greiff, Constance M. *Independence: The Creation of a National Park*. Philadelphia: University of Pennsylvania Press, 1987.

Hawver, Alison. "A Study of the Property Known as Rhoads' Place and Harmar's Retreat: A Lower Schuylkill River Country Villa." Paper, Historic Preservation Program, University of Pennsylvania, 1993. Copy on file at The Athenaeum of Philadelphia.

Hosmer, Charles B., Jr. *Presence of the Past: A History of the Preservation Movement in the United States Before Williamsburg*. New York: Putnam, 1965.

——. *Preservation Comes of Age: From Williamsburg to the National Trust, 1926–1949*. Charlottesville: University of Virginia Press, 1981.

Hotchkin, Samuel Fitch. *Ancient and Modern Germantown, Mount Airy, and Chestnut Hill*. Philadelphia, 1892.

——. *The York Road, Old and New*. Philadelphia, 1923.

Kimball, Fiske. *Domestic Architecture of the American Colonies and the Early Republic*. New York: Dover, 1922.

——. "Philadelphia's 'Colonial Chain.'" *Art and Archaeology* 21 (April 1926): 198–99.

——. "The Preservation Movement in America." *Journal of the Society of Architectural Historians* 1 (July–October 1941): 15.

Lloyd, Mark Frazier. "Germantown, 1683–1983." *Antiques* 124 (August 1983): 254–58.

Lowrie, Sarah D. and Mabel Stewart Ludlum. *The Sesqui-Centennial High Street*. Philadelphia: Lippincott, 1926.

Maass, John. *The Glorious Enterprise: The Centennial Exposition of 1876*. Watkins Glen, N.Y.: American Life Foundation, 1973.

McPherson, James M. *What They Fought For, 1861–1865*. Baton Rouge: Louisiana State University Press, 1994.

*Memorial of the William Penn Parlor, in the Great Central Fair*. Philadelphia, 1864.

Moss, Roger W. *The American Country House*. New York: Henry Holt, 1990.

——. *Master Builders: A History of the Colonial Philadelphia Building Trades*. Ann Arbor, Mich.: University Microfilms, 1972.

——. "The Origins of the Carpenters' Company of Philadelphia." In *Building Early America*, ed. Peterson, 35–53.

——, ed. *Paint in America: The Colors of Historic Buildings*. Washington, D.C.: Preservation Press, 1994.

Murtagh, William J. "The Philadelphia Row House." *Journal of the Society of Architectural Historians* 16 (December 1957): 8–13.

Myers, Alfred Cook, ed. *Narratives of Early Pennsylvania, West New Jersey, and Delaware, 1630–1707*. New York: Scribner's, 1912.

Nash, Gary B. "City Planning and Political Tension in the Seventeenth Century: The Case of Philadelphia." *Proceedings of the American Philosophical Society* 92 (February 15, 1968): 54–73.

Nelson, Lee H. "Independence Hall: Its Fabric Reinforced." In *Building Early America*, ed. Peterson.

O'Gorman, James F., Jeffrey A. Cohen, George E. Thomas, and G. Holmes Perkins. *Drawing Toward Building: Philadelphia Architectural Graphics, 1732–1986*. Philadelphia: University of Pennsylvania Press, 1986.

Peterson, Charles E., ed. *Building Early America: Contributions Toward the History of a Great Industry*. Radnor, Pa.: Chilton, 1976.

——, ed. *The Carpenters' Company of the City and County of Philadelphia 1786 Rule Book*. Princeton, N.J.: Pyne Press.

——. "Carpenters' Hall." In *Historic Philadelphia*, ed. Eisenhart, 96–108.

Raymond, Eleanor. *Early Domestic Architecture of Pennsylvania*. Intro. John Milner. Princeton, N.J.: Pyne Press, 1973. Originally published 1931.

Read, J. M., Jr. "The Old Slate-Roof House." *Lippincott Magazine* 1 (Jan.–Feb.–March 1868): 29–39; 191–201; 298–305.

*Report of the Committee on Plans and Improvements of the Commissioners of Fairmount Park, upon the Extension of the Park*. Philadelphia, 1868.

Riley, Edward M. "The Independence Hall Group." In *Historic Philadelphia*, ed. Eisenhart, 33–42.

Roach, Hannah B. "The Planting of Philadelphia: A Seventeenth-Century Real Estate Development." *Pennsylvania Magazine of History and Biography* 92 (January–April 1968): 3–47, 143–94.

Roberts, George and Mary Roberts. *Triumph on Fairmount: Fiske Kimball and the Philadelphia Museum of Art*. Philadelphia: Lippincott, 1959.

Roth, Rodris. "The New England, or 'Old Tyme,' Kitchen Exhibit at Nineteenth-Century Fairs." In *The Colonial Revival in America*, ed. Alan Axelrod, 159–83. New York: Norton, 1985.

Scharf, Thomas and Thompson Westcott. *History of Philadelphia, 1609–1884*. Philadelphia: L. H. Everts, 1884.

Schiffer, Margaret B. *Survey of Chester County: Pennsylvania Architecture, 17th, 18th, and 19th Centuries*. Exton, Pa.: Schiffer Publishing, 1976.

Seidensticker, Oswald. *Geschichte der Deutschen Gesellschaft von Pennsylvanien, 1764–1917*. Philadelphia, 1917.

Snyder, Martin P. *City of Independence: Views of Philadelphia Before 1800*. New York: Praeger, 1975.

Tatman, Sandra L. and Roger W. Moss. *Biographical Dictionary of Philadelphia Architects, 1700–1930*. Boston: G. K. Hall, 1985.

Tatum, George B. "The Origins of Fairmount Park." *Antiques* 82 (November 1962): 502–7.

——. *Penn's Great Town: 250 Years of Philadelphia Architecture*. Philadelphia: University of Pennsylvania Press, 1961.

——. *Philadelphia Georgian: The City House of Samuel Powel and Some of Its 18th-Century Neighbors*. Middletown, Conn.: Wesleyan University Press, 1976.

Tinkcom, Harry M., Margaret B. Tinkcom, and Grant Miles Simon. *Historic Germantown, from the Founding to the Early Part of the Nineteenth Century*. Philadelphia: American Philosophical Society, 1955.

Tinkcom, Margaret B. "The Philadelphia Historical Commission: Organization and Procedures." *Law and Contemporary Problems* 37 (Summer 1971): 386–97.

Trollope, Frances M. *Domestic Manners of the Americans*. London: Whittaker, Treacher, 1832.

Wainwright, Nicholas B. *Colonial Grandeur in Philadelphia: The House and Furniture of General John Cadwalader*. Philadelphia: Historical Society of Pennsylvania, 1964.

——, ed. *A Philadelphia Perspective: The Diary of Sidney George Fisher Covering the Years, 1834–1871*. Philadelphia: Historical Society of Pennsylvania, 1967.

Wallace, Philip B. *Colonial Houses, Philadelphia, Pre-Revolutionary Period*. New York: Bonanza Books, 1931.

Warner, N. Thomas. "Anthony Benezet House, c. 1818." Paper, Historic Preservation Program, University of Pennsylvania, 1988. Copy on file at The Athenaeum of Philadelphia.

Warner, Sam Bass, Jr. *The Private City: Philadelphia in Three Periods of Its Growth*. Second edition. Philadelphia: University of Pennsylvania Press, 1987. Originally published 1968.

Waters, Deborah Dependahl. "Philadelphia's Boswell: John Fanning Watson." *Pennsylvania Magazine of History and Biography* 98 (January 1974): 39–42.

Watson, John Fanning. *Annals of Philadelphia and Pennsylvania in the Olden Time: being a collection of earliest settlement of the inland part of Pennsylvania from the days of the founders*. Vols. 1, 2. Philadelphia: published for the author, 1830, 1850. Vol. 3 added by Willis P. Hazard. Philadelphia: E. S. Stuart, 1877.

Webster, Richard J. *Philadelphia Preserved: Catalog of the Historic American Buildings Survey*. Philadelphia: Temple University Press, 1976.

Weigley, Russell, ed. *Philadelphia: A 300-Year History*. New York: Norton, 1982.

Westcott, Thompson. *The Historic Mansions and Buildings of Philadelphia*. Philadelphia, 1877.

White, Theo B. *Fairmount, Philadelphia's Park: A History*. Philadelphia: Art Alliance Press, 1975.

——, ed. *Philadelphia Architecture in the Nineteenth Century*. Philadelphia: University of Pennsylvania Press, 1953.

*The WPA Guide to Philadelphia*. Federal Writers' Project of the Works Progress Administration for the Commonwealth of Pennsylvania. Preface by E. Digby Baltzell. Philadelphia: University of Pennsylvania Press with the Pennsylvania Historical and Museum Commission, 1988. Originally published 1937 as *Philadelphia, a Guide to the Nation's Birthplace*.